YACHTING
MONTHLY

EAST COAST RIVERS

CRUISING COMPANION

A yachtsman's pilot and cruising guide to the

waters from Lowestoft to the Swale

JANET HARBER

Cruising Companion series editor:
LUCINDA ROCH

© Janet Harber 2003
© Nautical Data Limited 2003
Published by Nautical Data Ltd, The Book Barn
Westbourne, Hampshire, PO10 8RS
ISBN I-904358-24-1

NAUTICAL DATA LIMITED

Cover picture: The venerable East Coast smack, *Boadicea* (built 1808), taking part in
West Mersea Town Regatta 2003

Photographs by Janet Harber
Aerial photograph on page 11 by Charles Hodge Photography
Aerial photograph on page 86 by Patrick Roach

Art direction: Chris Stevens
Charts: Chris Stevens & Scott Stacey

Published by Nautical Data Ltd
The Book Barn, Westbourne, Hampshire, PO10 8RS
Second edition of this Cruising Companion volume 2003,
revised from the sixteenth edition of *East Coast Rivers*,
originally published 1956 by *Yachting Monthly*

OTHER CRUISING COMPANIONS

This Cruising Companion is one of a series. Other titles include:

Solent Cruising Companion
Channel Cruising Companion
West Country Cruising Companion
North France & Belgium Cruising Companion
North Brittany & The Channel Islands Cruising Companion
West France Cruising Companion
North West Spain Cruising Companion
South West Spain & Portugal Cruising Companion

Also published by Nautical Data: *Reeds Nautical Almanac, Reeds Eastern Almanac*

IMPORTANT NOTE

This Companion is intended as an aid to navigation only. The information contained within should not be relied on for navigational use, rather it must be used in conjunction with official hydrographic data. Whilst every care has been taken in compiling the information contained in this Companion, the publishers, author, editors and their agents accept no responsibility for any errors or omissions, or for any accidents or mishaps which may arise from its use.

Readers are advised at all times to refer to official charts, publications and notices. The charts contained in this book are sketch plans and are not to be used for navigation. Some details are omitted for the sake of clarity and the scales have been chosen to allow best coverage in relation to page size.

Neither the publisher nor the author can accept responsibility for errors, omissions or alterations in this book. They will be grateful for any information from readers to assist in the update and accuracy of the publication: any information should be e-mailed to editorial@nauticaldata.com. As they become available, updates will be posted on the www.nauticaldata.com website.

Printed in Italy

CONTENTS

Low Water on the River Stour near Manningtree

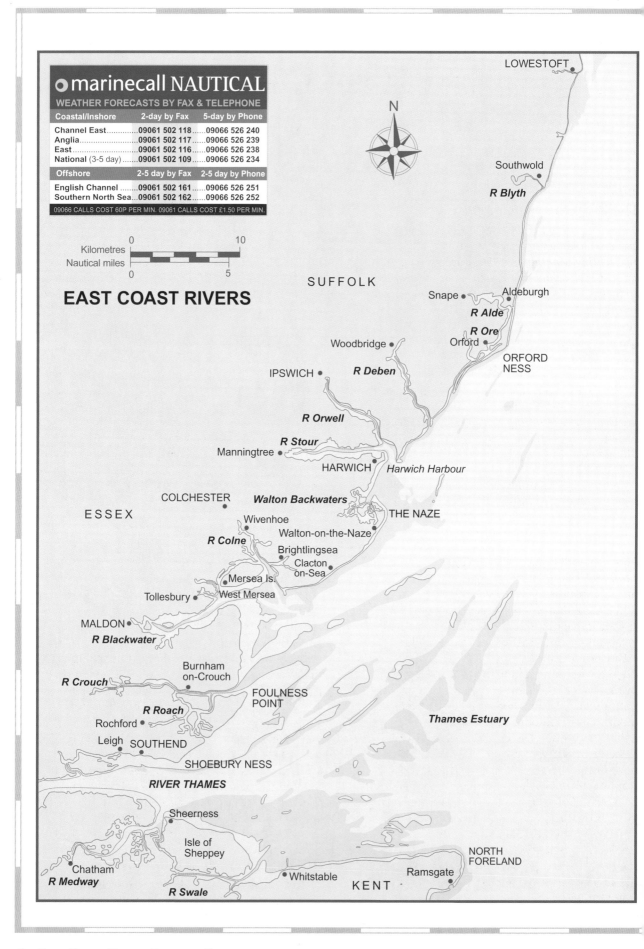

INTRODUCTION

HISTORY OF EAST COAST RIVERS

A pilot book called East Coast Rivers, produced by SCSV Messum RN, was published in 1903 by JD Potter. It is thought by some that this 100 year old publication, long since out of print, could have been the 'drab little book' referred to by Erskine Childers in The Riddle of the Sands.

The first edition of the current East Coast Rivers was produced by my father, Jack Coote, and published by Yachting Monthly in 1956, price 9s. 6d. A cloth-covered book containing hand-drawn charts and black and white photographs, it was based on a series of articles that had appeared in YM, at that time edited by Maurice Griffiths. Like my father, Maurice had a lifelong fascination with the rivers and creeks along the Thames Estuary, and was later to describe the book as 'the East Coast yachtsman's bible'.

In those days, weather and tide permitting, every weekend and summer holiday were spent by the Coote family sailing first, the old and leaky 11 ton Iwunda, and later, another centreboarder Blue Shoal, in the myriad of rivers and creeks of the East Coast.

Revised editions of East Coast Rivers were regularly produced in the ensuing years. In 1977 soundings were changed from feet to metres, which involved a major revision of both charts and text. Marinas began to appear and glassfibre boats were being built to fill them. The IALA buoyage system was introduced. As a result, there was a great deal of new information to be incorporated. Much midnight oil was burned by Jack as he painstakingly altered the red cans and green conicals on his original charts to cardinal symbols. In 1983 entirely new charts were produced. Jack died, aged 80, in 1993, just after he had completed the 14th edition of the book.

Since then my sister, Judy, and I have produced four further editions of East Coast Rivers, including this one – keeping up the family tradition of shoal-draught cruising and combining with it the pleasurable task of updating the book – battered and heavily-annotated copies of East Coast Rivers are always to be found in the cockpit.

THE 18TH EDITION

This, the 18th edition of *East Coast Rivers*, includes even more shoreside information and a greater number of photographs. We hope that this will ensure that the book continues to be an authoritative guide to the East Coast both for local sailors and visiting yachtsmen alike.

Developments since the publication of the previous edition include the new Associated British Ports Lowestoft Haven Marina on Lake Lothing and the finished conversion from pile moorings to pontoons at Brightlingsea.

At Woodbridge Haven, the entrance to the Deben underwent a radical change in 2003 and, interestingly, the new buoyage through the Knolls looks remarkably similar to that shown in Messum's *East Coast Rivers* published 100 years previously.

In the Thames Estuary, the North Edinburgh Channel has silted and is no longer buoyed, while the well-marked Fisherman's Gat is now the designated commercial channel. An alternative route for leisure craft across the Long Sand exists through Foulger's Gat, slightly further north, and this is marked at either end.

Construction of the Gunfleet Sands Offshore Wind Farm will start in 2004. There will be six rows of five wind turbines athwart the south west end of the sands, near the meterological mast established in 2002. It could be that the completed wind farm will make it easier to locate the Swin Spitway in future. A similar wind farm is to be established on the Kentish Flats off Whitstable.

It is hard now to remember how the London River looked before high rise buildings totally altered the face of the Docklands. On a lesser scale, during the past few years re-development has changed the character of several rivers and creeks. The St Mary's Island bank of the Medway, opposite the lovely Cockham Woods, is now covered with wall to wall modern houses. Former creekside quays and wharves at little ports such as Faversham, Conyer, Wivenhoe and Colchester are being lined with residential buildings, and public access to the waterside is often restricted as a consequence. At Standard Quay, Faversham, a campaign to stop further development, such as has already been built on the other side of the creek, has been successful so far. On the Burnham-on-Crouch waterfront and at the old Whisstocks yard, Woodbridge, there is stiff local opposition to planning applications for similar schemes.

Much of the buoyage on the East Coast rivers is the responsibility of the local authority, the fairways committee or, in some cases, the local club or marina. The members of Walton & Frinton YC, for example, do a great job in maintaining and improving the buoyage into Walton Backwaters, while at Conyer Creek on the Swale the new owners of Swale Marina are re-instating buoys and beacons and have produced a helpful chartlet.

Withies, whether in tree-like or broomhead form, are a familiar sight on East Coast creeks, but I have always been puzzled by the 'nun' buoys which occur at Conyer and Rainham. Medway Ports Harbour Master, Captain PR White, kindly enlightened me – it seems they are round buoys tapering at the top and bottom and, according to the OED, nun is an obsolete term for 'a child's spinning top'. Nice to think that not every navigation mark comes in standard IALA form!

The directions and charts in this edition were as up to date as possible at the time of going to press, but the reader should be aware that changes are constantly taking place, particularly in the case of the Ore and Deben entrances, which are capable of altering in a matter of months. Because of such changes, neither the author nor the publisher can accept responsibility for any errors or omissions which may exist initially or come about after publication.

ACKNOWLEDGEMENTS

In his original preface Jack wrote: 'any success the book may have will be largely due to the enthusiastic help that I have received from many kindred spirits who sail the rivers of the Thames Estuary.' I doubt if he envisaged then that the input from countless friends and fellow sailors, some of whom are sadly no longer with us, would still be helping us to keep *East Coast Rivers* up to date nearly fifty years later.

For this edition I am particularly indebted to Nick Ardley (Smallgains, Canvey, Medway and Swale); Ian Bell (Crouch Harbour Authority); James Hancox (Foulgers Gat); Bernard Hetherington (Brightlingsea and the Colne); John Langridge (Roach, Havengore and Benfleet); Maxine Owles (Southwold Harbour Master); Vicky Platt (Deben, Alde and Southwold); Mike, Sue, Toby and Holly Ramsay (W Mersea, Tollesbury and the Blackwater); Tony Ward (Pin Mill); John White and the late Duncan Read

(Woodbridge Haven pilotage); and The Ore and the Alde Association.

I must thank Judy and Graham Jones (my sister and brother-in-law), as well as my nephews Timothy and Nicholas, for their information-gathering, photography (Lowestoft and Southwold) and proof reading for this and previous editions. With special thanks to Graham for piloting me over the Ore and Deben entrances and beyond on our successful aerial photography missions.

Finally, I am most grateful to Chris, Lucy, Scott and the team at Nautical Data for being patient and supportive, right up to the deadline!

Janet Harber
Sudbourne, November 2003

ABBREVIATIONS & SYMBOLS

The following abbreviations and symbols may be encountered in this book; many others will be found which are deemed to be self-explanatory

	Boatyard		Fuel berth		Launderette	✕	Restaurant
	Boathoist		Fish Harbour/Quay	✦	Lifeboat	⇌	Railway station
	Chandlery		Holding tank pumpout	Ldg	Leading		Slip
┼	Church	⊕	Hospital	L.Fl	Long-flashing light		Stores/Supermarket
	Fuel by cans		Harbour Master	Oc	Occulting light	Ⓥ	Visitors berth/buoy
F	Fixed Light	*i*	Information Bureau	✉	Post Office	VQ	Very quick flashing light
Fl	Flashing light	Iso	Isophase light	Q	Quick flashing light	⊕	Waypoint

NOTES

Chart datums

Lowest Astronomical Tide (LAT)
Although it has the effect of indicating that some creeks, swatchways and anchorages sometimes dry out, when many of us have never seen them without water, adoption of (LAT) as the datum for this book is necessary in order to be in accord with Admiralty charts. Horizontal datum of waypoints is WGS 84.

Bearings

The bearings given throughout the book are magnetic and the variation in the area of the Thames Estuary is approximately 3 degrees W, decreasing by about 10 minutes annually.

Tides

Although there are times when tides, as Para Handy said, 'is chust a mystery', they do tend to follow patterns that are useful to know. Spring tides occur a day or so after both new and full moons – hence the term High Water Full and Change (HWFC).

Neap tides occur midway between each spring tide.

Remember there is always more water at low water neaps than at low water springs.

The time of High Water at any given place is roughly 50 minutes later each day.

All tidal information is approximate, so allow a safety margin whenever possible. Watch the barometric pressure – a change of one inch in pressure can make a difference of a foot in the level of water.

The level of water does not rise and fall at a constant rate during the flood or ebb tide. The amount by which a tide will rise or fall in a given time from Low or High Water can be estimated approximately by the 'Twelfths' rule, which is simply indicated as follows:

Rise or fall during	1st hour	$^1/_{12}$	of range
" " " "	2nd hour	$^2/_{12}$	" "
" " " "	3rd hour	$^3/_{12}$	" "
" " " "	4th hour	$^3/_{12}$	" "
" " " "	5th hour	$^2/_{12}$	" "
" " " "	6th hour	$^1/_{12}$	" "

NAVIGABLE DISTANCES

RIVER THAMES	M
Sea Reach No 1 Buoy to	
Southend Pier	6
Sheerness	5
Holehaven	11
Gravesend	19
Erith	25
Greenwich	35
London Bridge	41
Southend Pier to	
Sheerness	6
Havengore entrance	9½
Leigh (Bell Wharf)	3
Benfleet	6½
RIVER MEDWAY	
Sheerness (Garrison Pt) to	
Queenborough	1½
Gillingham	8
Upnor	10½
Rochester Bridge	12½
RIVER SWALE	
Queenborough to	
Kingsferry Bridge	2
Harty Ferry	9
Columbine Buoy	15
RIVER CROUCH	
Whitaker Beacon to	
Foulness	7
Roach Entrance	9½
Burnham	12
Burnham to	
Fambridge	5
Hullbridge	7
Battlesbridge	9

Foulness to	M
Bench Head Buoy (via Ray Sand)	8
Bench Head Buoy (via Spitway)	18
RIVER ROACH Entrance to	
Paglesham	4
Havengore Bridge	5
RIVER BLACKWATER	
Bench Head Buoy to	
Sales Point	4
Nass Beacon (West Mersea)	5
Bradwell Quay	6
Osea Island	10
Heybridge Basin	13
Maldon (Hythe)	14½
RIVER COLNE	
Colne Bar Buoy to	
Brightlingsea	4½
Wivenhoe	8
Colchester (Hythe)	11
THE WALLET	
Knoll Lightbuoy to	
Clacton Pier	4
Walton-on-the-Naze (Pier)	9
Stone Banks Buoy	12½
Harwich Entrance	15
HARWICH Harbour Entrance to	
Burnham (via Wallet and Spitway)	30
West Mersea (via Wallet)	23
Brightlingsea (via Wallet)	22
Woodbridge Haven (Deben Entrance)	6
Orford Haven (Ore Entrance)	10

RIVER STOUR	M
Harwich Harbour Entrance to	
Wrabness	6½
Mistley	9½
Manningtree	11
RIVER ORWELL	
Harwich Harbour Entrance to	
Pin Mill	6½
Ipswich	11
RIVER DEBEN	
Felixstowe Ferry to	
Ramsholt	3
Waldringfield	5½
Woodbridge	9
RIVER ORE	
Shingle Street to	
Havergate Island	3
Orford Quay	5
RIVER ALDE	
Orford Quay to	
Slaughden Quay (Aldeburgh)	6
Iken Cliff	11
Snape Bridge	12½
Southwold to	
Orford Haven	20
Harwich Harbour	30
LOWESTOFT Harbour Entrance to	
Southwold	10
Orford Haven	30
Woodbridge Haven (Deben entrance)	33
Harwich	40

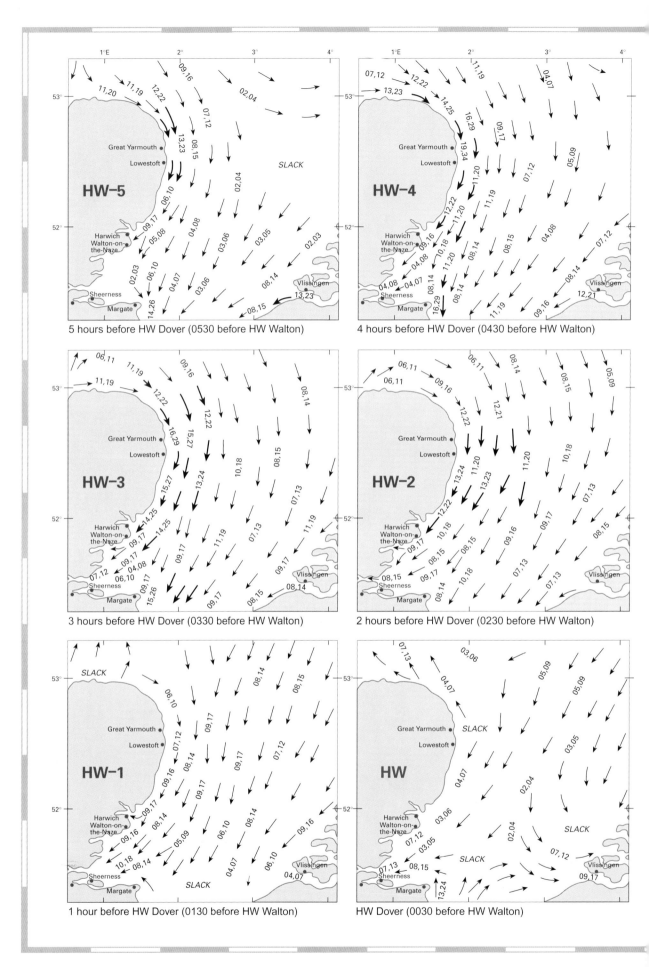

5 hours before HW Dover (0530 before HW Walton)

4 hours before HW Dover (0430 before HW Walton)

3 hours before HW Dover (0330 before HW Walton)

2 hours before HW Dover (0230 before HW Walton)

1 hour before HW Dover (0130 before HW Walton)

HW Dover (0030 before HW Walton)

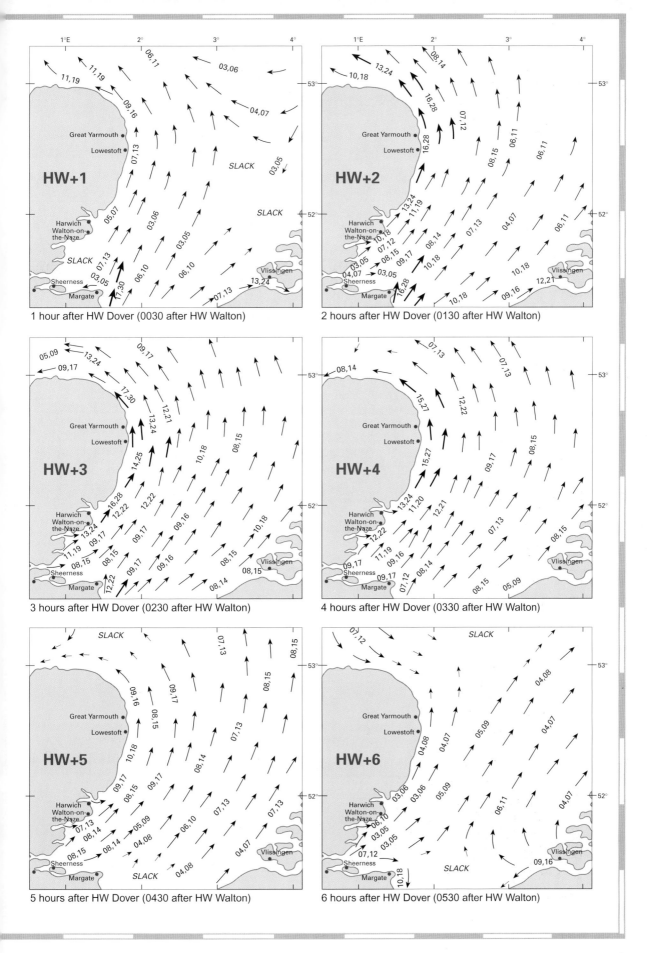

1 hour after HW Dover (0030 after HW Walton)

2 hours after HW Dover (0130 after HW Walton)

3 hours after HW Dover (0230 after HW Walton)

4 hours after HW Dover (0330 after HW Walton)

5 hours after HW Dover (0430 after HW Walton)

6 hours after HW Dover (0530 after HW Walton)

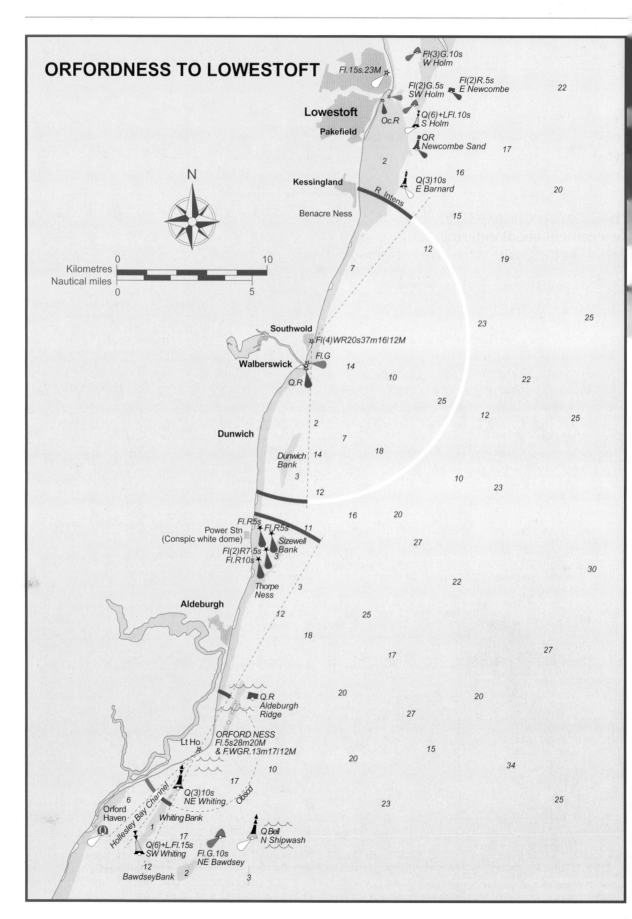

ORFORDNESS TO LOWESTOFT

Fl(3)G.10s
W Holm

Fl.15s.23M

Lowestoft

Fl(2)G.5s
SW Holm

Fl(2)R.5s
E Newcombe

22

Pakefield

Oc.R

Q(6)+LFl.10s
S Holm

QR
Newcombe Sand

17

2

16

Kessingland

Q(3)10s
E Barnard

20

R Intens

Benacre Ness

15

12

N

19

7

Kilometres 0 — 10
Nautical miles 0 — 5

25

23

Southwold

Fl(4)WR20s37m16/12M

25

Fl.G

Walberswick

14

10

22

Q.R

25

Dunwich

2

12

25

7

**Dunwich
Bank**

14

18

10

3

23

12

16

20

Fl.R5s

Fl.R5s

11

Power Stn
(Conspic white dome)

**Sizewell
Bank**

27

Fl(2)R7.5s

3

Fl.R10s

30

**Thorpe
Ness**

3

22

Aldeburgh

12

25

18

17

27

Q.R
Aldeburgh
Ridge

20

20

27

ORFORD NESS
Fl.5s28m20M
& F.WGR.13m17/12M

Lt Ho

15

34

10

20

17

Obscd

Q(3)10s
NE Whiting

10

6

**Orford
Haven**

23

25

Whiting Bank

1

Q(6)+L.Fl.15s
SW Whiting

17

Q Bell
N Shipwash

12

Fl.G.10s
NE Bawdsey

2

BawdseyBank

3

LOWESTOFT

Tides	HW Dover −1.33 Range: Springs 1.9m Neaps 1.1m
Charts	Admiralty 1536, 1543, Stanford 3; Imray C28; OS 156/134
Waypoints	E Barnard 52°25'.14N 01°46'.38E, Corton 52°31'.14N 01°51'.37E, N Pierhead 52°28'.32N 01°45'.39E
Hazards	Shoals and drying areas, sands continually shift and buoyage moved. Tides set strongly across entrance

In *Coastwise Cruising* (1929) Francis B Cooke describes 'the element of pleasurable excitement about entering a strange port in one's own vessel, for one never knows quite what one will find inside the pierheads.' He wrote this on his approach to Lowestoft from the

south and, having passed Kessingland, home of the novelist Sir Rider Haggard, they looked through the glasses and saw '...smack after smack emerge from the pierheads, bound for the Dogger Bank in quest of the nation's breakfast.'

Once inside the harbour they found it to be '...a jolly nice place. The band is discoursing music for us on the pier, and pretty girls in white frocks gaze at us as we get tea ready in the well. We have not been berthed very long ere a boat comes alongside with a cordial invitation from the Royal Norfolk and Suffolk Yacht Club to make use of their club-house during our stay.'

The nation no longer eats herring for breakfast

Lowestoft Harbour looking south-west. Waveney Dock is in the lower half of the picture, with the Outer Harbour, Trawl Basin and Yacht Harbour beyond. The lifting road bridge and Inner Harbour leading to Lake Lothing are in the top right

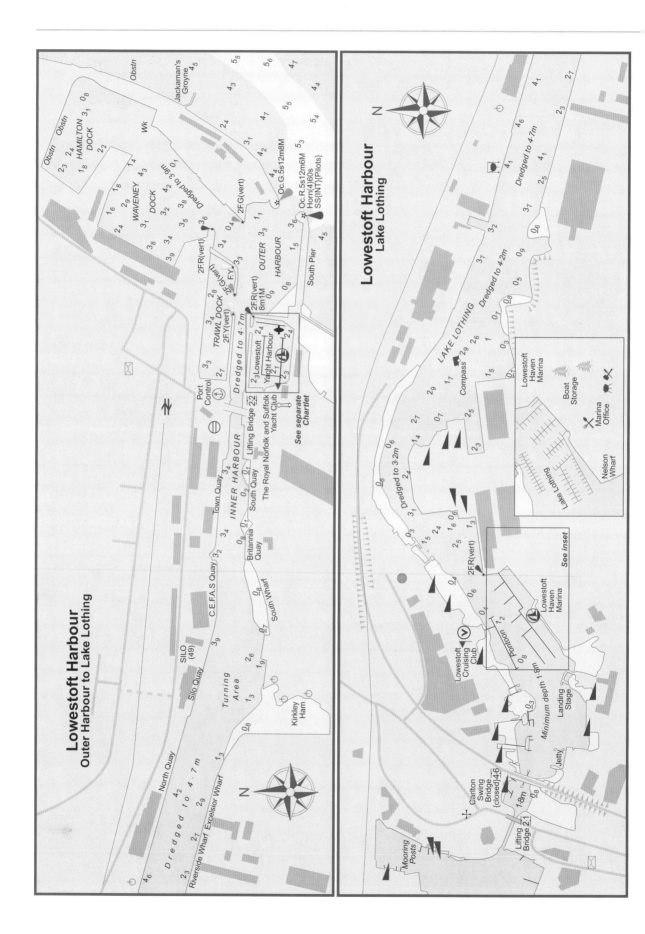

Lowestoft Harbour
Outer Harbour to Lake Lothing

Obstn
Obstn Obstn
HAMILTON 0.8
2.3 2.4 DOCK 3.1
1.8
Obstn 2.2
Wk

1.6 1.8
WAVENEY 4.3
2.4 3.1 DOCK 3.2 0.1
3.8 3.4 3.5 3.4 3.6
3.9
2FR(vert) 3.4 3.3

Dredged to 3.9m

2FG(vert)
2.8 F.Y. 3.3
2FY(vert)

TRAWL DOCK 3.4
2FY(vert) 2FR(vert) 8m1M

Dredged to 4.7m

3.3 2.3 Lowestoft 2.4 2.4
2.7 Yacht Harbour 2.4
2.3

The Royal Norfolk and Suffolk Yacht Club 2.2
Lifting Bridge 2.2

See separate Chartlet

Port Control

INNER HARBOUR 3.4
Town Quay 3.4
South Quay 0.1
0.8 0.1
Britannia 0.1
Quay
C.E.F.A.S Quay 3.2
0.8
0.7

South Wharf

SILO
(49) 3.9

Silo Quay

Turning Area
2.6
1.9 1.3
2.4

Kirkley Ham

North Quay
0.8

Dredged to 4.7m 4.2

Riverside Wharf Excelsior Wharf 2.9
2.3 1.3

4.6

N

2FG(vert)
0.4
OUTER 3.3
0.9
HARBOUR 1.5 3.6
0.8 South Pier 4.5

Oc.G.5s12m8M
Oc.R.5s12m6M 5.3
Horn(4)60s
SS{INT}{Pilots}

Jackaman's Groyne 4.5
5.5
5.6
4.3 4.7
2.4 4.7
5.5
3.1
4.4 5.4
4.4
1.1

Lowestoft Harbour
Lake Lothing

N

LAKE LOTHING Dredged to 4.2m

Dredged to 4.7m
4.1
4.6
4.1 4.1 2.3 2.7
3.7 2.5 2.4
3.2
0.6 0.9

Dredged to 3.2m

3.1 Compass 2.9 2.6 1
2.5 1 0.3
0.6 0.5 0.3
1.5

Lowestoft Haven Marina
Boat Storage
Marina Office
Nelson Wharf
Lake Lothing

See inset

2.7 1.7 1.5
0.6 2.9
0.6 2.5
2.7 1.4 2.3
2.1

3.1 1.6 0.6
0.3 2.4 1.3
0.3 1.5 2.4 2.5
0.4 2FR(vert)

Lowestoft Haven Marina
Lowestoft Cruising Club
Pontoon 1.2
0.8

Minimum depth 1.8m Landing Stage
0.3
Jetty

Carlton Swing Bridge (closed) 4.6
1.8m 0.8
Lifting Bridge 2.1

Mooring Posts

and the fishing fleet is not what it was, but visiting yachtsmen continue to appreciate the unique mixture of seaside resort and commercial port to be found at Lowestoft.

In the late 1990s the Royal Norfolk and Suffolk YC, together with the RNLI, Associated British Ports and Waveney District Council, instigated a major civil engineering project to close off the existing entrance to the yacht basin, which faced east and opened directly to the Outer Harbour. A new entrance was built at the end of the Inner South Pier, opposite the Trawl Basin on the north bank, and a new lifeboat station was constructed on the Heritage Pier which bridges the filled-in gap of the old entrance. With the completion of this ambitious project, a wave-free marina has been created with serviced pontoons replacing the sometimes uncomfortable and not very convenient moorings. Since the opening of this new facility many more yachtsmen are calling at Lowestoft which, as the most easterly point in Britain, serves as a useful departure or arrival point for Holland and the Continent, as well as being a gateway to the southern Broads.

APPROACHES

The strong appeal of Lowestoft to the visiting yachtsman is that the harbour can be entered at any state of tide, 24 hours a day, although conditions just outside the narrow entrance are sometimes extremely lively in wind-against-tide conditions. The fairway is dredged to a least depth of 4.7m but the sands shift and the buoys are moved accordingly.

The tide can set strongly across the entrance between the piers. About one mile east of the harbour entrance the south-going stream begins at HW Dover −0600, and the north-going at HW Dover.

Lowestoft Lt Hse (Fl 15s) is one mile north of the harbour entrance. The prominent white-

LOWESTOFT PORT GUIDE

Lowestoft Harbour and Bridge Control	Tel 01502 572286; VHF Ch 14
Royal Norfolk & Suffolk YC, Lowestoft Yacht Harbour	Tel 01502 566726; Fax 517981; VHF Ch 80
Facilities	Toilets, showers, laundry, pump out
Water and Electricity	On pontoons
Lowestoft Haven Marina	Tel 01502 580300; Fax 581851; VHF Ch 80
Fuel	Diesel at Yacht Harbour and Haven Marina, petrol from garages in town
Stores	Supermarkets and shops across road bridge in town
Repairs	Small crane at Yacht Harbour; 70 ton hoist at Haven Marina; Lowestoft Yacht Services (Lake Lothing) Tel 01502 585535; Mobile 07887616846; F Newson (Lake Lothing) Tel 01502 574902. Other yards and chandlery on Oulton Broad beyond Mutford Bridge
Chandlery	Lowestoft Yacht Services Tel 01502 585535
Marine Engineers	Small & Co, Commercial Road Tel 01502 513538
Marine Electronics	Charity & Taylor, Battery Green Road Tel 01502 581529
Chart Agents	Charity & Taylor
Food and drink	Bar and restaurant at Royal Norfolk & Suffolk YC, restaurants, pubs nearby
Transport	Railway station across road bridge; bus station town centre

Opening Times for Inner Harbour Bridge
Mon−Fri 0700, 0930, 1100, 1600, 1900, 2100
Sat/Sun/Bank Hols 0745, 0930, 1100, 1400, 1730, 1900, 2100

Lowestoft can be entered at any state of the tide, although conditions just outside are sometimes lively when the tide sets strongly across the narrow entrance between the piers

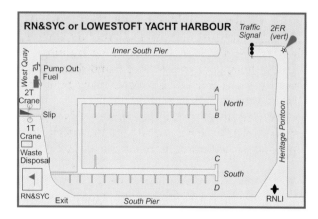

painted light towers on the Outer Harbour piers are very easy to distinguish: the North Pier shows Oc G 5s and the South Pier Oc R 5s.

Approaching from the south or east, it is necessary to pick up the Newcome Sand and South Holm buoys, which mark the entrance to the Stanford Channel. This channel provides a safe, well-lit, deep water approach to the port between the two sandbanks. From the north (for example, coming from Great Yarmouth) it is normal to use the Corton Road channel, inside the Holm Sand, which is also lit.

In daylight and reasonable conditions, yachts approaching from the south are able to save time by using the unlit Pakefield Road channel, inside the Newcome Sand. Using this route, the Barnard shoal off Benacre Ness can be avoided by passing the Ness about a mile offshore, just inside the E Barnard (E Card) buoy.

Approaching the entrance, it is essential to observe the traffic signals on the south pier (green, white, green ENTER; red, white, red DO NOT ENTER). Some of the ships that use the harbour only just fit through the entrance so it would be disastrous to meet one coming the other way. A call to Lowestoft Harbour on VHF Channel 14 is always advisable. Once inside the entrance there is shelter from all quarters, but bear in mind that the outer harbour is fairly small so sails need to be dropped and stowed promptly before entering the yacht basin.

Once in the Outer Harbour, the entrances to

the commercial Waveney Dock and then to the Trawl Basin open up to starboard on the north side. The Yacht Harbour is in the south-west corner, with its entrance to port off the main channel to the lifting road bridge, the Inner Harbour and Lake Lothing. Beyond the road bridge on the north bank is a conspicuous silo.

Before entering the yacht harbour, you should contact the Royal Norfolk & Suffolk YC (on Marina Control Ch 80), which will give directions to a suitable berth. There are traffic control signals on the eastern side of the yacht harbour entrance (only visible from inside) and, as it is relatively narrow and visibility is restricted, it is important to observe these signals on leaving – 3FR vertical no exit; GWG vertical proceed on instruction.

LOWESTOFT YACHT HARBOUR

The Royal Norfolk & Suffolk YC administers the Yacht Harbour and has excellent amenities available around the clock at its imposing, Grade 2 listed clubhouse – when the club was founded in 1857 it was originally housed in an old railway carriage. Visiting yachtsmen are given a friendly welcome by manager David Schonhut and his staff. Among the facilities are an attractive sun lounge overlooking the marina as well as a bar and restaurant. Bar meals are available from the sun lounge (fish and chips highly recommended) or there is an *à la carte menu* in the more formal dining room; breakfast is served daily, but needs to be booked in advance.

Various class championships are hosted by the club, the waters off Lowestoft being well suited to racing, and there are home fleets of Dragons,

Lowestoft Yacht Harbour looking east from the roof of the Royal Norfolk and Suffolk YC. The outer harbour and entrance between the piers can be seen in the top of the picture. The entrance to the yacht basin is in the top left

Squibs, Flying Fifteens, 707s and dinghies. During Lowestoft Sea Week regatta, usually in August, all the local classes are raced including the venerable Broads One-Designs, designed by Linton Hope for the Royal Norfolk & Suffolk YC in 1900. These elegant 24ft gaff-rig keelboats were originally varnished, which is why they became known as Brown Boats, although in recent years white glassfibre hulls have been built and the class has undergone a tremendous revival.

Historic vessels such as sailing trawlers are berthed on the Heritage Pontoon at the eastern end of the yacht harbour. The beach at Lowestoft is a stone's throw from the club and regularly wins best beach awards. Supermarkets, shops and restaurants are not far away in the town centre, just across the road bridge.

BRIDGE TO INNER HARBOUR

The road bridge to the Inner Harbour lifts at six appointed times a day during the week, slightly more often at weekends, and at other times when commercial ships are entering or leaving. Lowestoft Harbour Control manages the bridge and requires 20 minutes notice. In 2003 there were plans for a waiting pontoon in the Trawl Basin.

LAKE LOTHING

Lake Lothing is mainly commercial, particularly on the south side where there are docks and shipyards. In October 2003 a new 140-berth marina, Lowestoft Haven, was opened on the south bank, one and a quarter miles upriver from the bridge. Established by Associated British Ports, facilities include power and water to all pontoons (with 24-hour supervision), diesel, gas, 70-ton boat hoist, toilets, showers, a launderette, bar and restaurant. A repair workshop, chandlery and provisions shop are planned. Lowestoft town can be reached on foot via School Road. For further information contact John Baldry on Tel 01502 580300 or Fax 581851.

Opposite Lowestoft Haven marina, on the north side of Lake Lothing, is the Lowestoft Cruising Club, incorporating a small but attractive purpose-built new clubhouse, hard standing and a secure car park. Members' yachts are berthed on either side of an extensive and secure pontoon along the bank in front of the club. Next door to the club, Lowestoft Yacht Services has a modest shed, slip and crane, with a small chandlery alongside.

Various wrecks and hulks lying along the Lake Lothing shore give the place an air of dereliction, but at the International Boatbuilding Training Centre things look more hopeful and there are usually interesting wooden boats being built or undergoing restorations.

The yard near the railway bridge is F Newson which has a slip for up to 80 tons and specializes in wooden boat restoration and mast making.

THE BROADS

To reach Oulton Broad from Lake Lothing, a rail bridge, a road bridge and then a lock must be negotiated. The openings are co-ordinated and available seven days a week during working hours by arrangement with the Mutford Bridge/Lock keeper who will also advise you if your craft draws more than 1.7m.

Oulton Dyke links the western end of Oulton Broad with the River Waveney, which can be cruised upstream to just below Beccles. For craft with an air draught of less than 7.3m, the Yare can be reached from the Waveney by using New Cut to avoid the low A143 bridge at St Olaves. The Yare and the Waveney flow into Breydon Water to reach the sea at Yarmouth. The other tidal river, the Bure, also meets the sea at Yarmouth, but cruising on this river is restricted by fixed bridges which in addition prohibit access to the North Broads unless the mast can be lowered.

Licences are compulsory on The Broads – a temporary licence can be obtained from the Broads Authority in Norwich, www.tolls@broads-authority.gov.uk, or from Mutford Lock.

Mutford Bridge and Lock

Fee £6 – Operates in response to bookings
0800–1100 and 1300–1600 daily
Tel 01502 531778, or VHF Ch 09 or 14 (occas).

Due to commercial shipping, it is essential to observe the traffic signals and call harbour control before entering or leaving Lowestoft Harbour

SOUTHWOLD

Tides	HW Dover −1.05 Range: Springs 1.9m Neaps 1.2m
Charts	Admiralty 1543, SC2695 Entrance only, Stanford No 3, Imray C28, OS 156
Waypoints	Aldeburgh Ridge 52°06'.73N 01°36'.92E, Southwold N Pier 52°18'.80N 01°40'.53E
Hazards	Entrance. Not to be attempted in strong onshore winds

Rowland Parker, in his book *Men of Dunwich*, tells how – 'On the Night after New Year's Day' in 1286, 'through the Vehemence of the Winds and Violence of the Sea' the river Blyth found its way directly out to sea between Walberswick and Southwold rather than through the port of Dunwich.

The men of Dunwich did in fact manage to stop up the gap for a few years after, but on the afternoon of 14 January 1328, a NE'ly gale again coincided with the high tides of the month and the town of Dunwich was devastated; this time beyond any hope of recovery. From that time Southwold has been a port; at first for trading and fishing, but in recent years simply as a pleasant haven for cruising yachts from both sides of the North Sea.

Southwold harbour is about as far north of Orfordness as Landguard Point is south of it – roughly 15 miles. There are several shoals lying a

mile or so offshore between Orford Haven and Southwold. The largest of them, the Whiting Bank, is guarded at its northern end by an E Cardinal buoy and at its southern end by a S Cardinal buoy, while the red can, Whiting Hook buoy, marks the western edge of the shoal. All three buoys are unlit.

A solitary unlit red can buoy identifies the eastern side of the Aldeburgh Ridge, which lies about a mile offshore but has six to eight metres on its western side, very close to the shingle shore of the Ness itself. The only snag when taking this inshore course round

The River Blyth at Southwold, looking east towards the harbour entrance and the North Sea. The Bailey Bridge can be seen in the foreground with the wooden stagings on either bank while, in the top right, is the village of Walberswick

The harbour entrance at Southwold is constantly subject to change owing to the shifting offlying sand and shingle shoals

Orfordness is that overfalls occur on the ebb.

There is one other shallow patch, the Sizewell Bank, about a mile offshore opposite the conspicuous atomic power station, but this unmarked patch has some three metres over it at LWS.

It should be noted that the direction of buoyage changes to the N of Orfordness; and N of Dunwich you leave the Thames Coastguard area and enter the Yarmouth Coastguard area.

A lighthouse – Fl (4) WR – is situated in the town of Southwold about a mile to the north of the harbour.

Since entry to Southwold harbour should be made on the flood (the ebb runs out at anything up to 6 knots), it will often pay, when coming from the south, to use the north-going ebb and then wait off the harbour entrance for a while, either by heaving-to or lying to an anchor about a quarter of a mile S of the pierheads if the wind is light and offshore.

The best time to go in is during the second half of the flood, but whenever there is a strong wind from any direction between the NE and SE, the entrance can be dangerous and certainly must not be attempted if two red flags or three vertical flashing red lights are shown on the N pier.

A flashing green light is shown from the N pier and a flashing red from the S pier.

The harbour entrance is constantly subject to change on account of the shifting off-lying sand and shingle shoals. For this reason it is imperative for both first time visitors (and those who may have been into Southwold in previous years) to consult the Harbour Master, Maxine Owles, beforehand to get the latest instructions. Maxine can provide up-to-date information by telephone or fax on 01502 724712, and she will give verbal pilotage via VHF Ch 9, after initial contact on VHF Ch 12.

In the height of the summer Southwold harbour

SOUTHWOLD PORT GUIDE	
Harbour Master	Maxine Owles Tel 01502 724712; VHF Ch 12 (also pilotage)
Water	Near visitors' berth
Stores	Basic requirements from chandlery at boatyard, otherwise from Southwold (approx one mile)
Boatyard	Harbour Marine Services Tel 01502 724721; Fax 722060; email j.buckley@netcom.co.uk; www.southwoldharbour.co.uk
Repairs	Services, slip (up to 30 tons) and three hoists up to 30 tons, boatyard, marine engineering
Chandlery	At boatyard
Transport	Railway stations at Darsham and Halesworth, bus to Lowestoft
Telephones	At chandlers, near N pier and at pub
Club	Southwold Sailing Club
Food and Drink	Harbour Inn (on quayside) Tel 01502 722381 Many good hotels, pubs, restaurants, tea rooms in town

can be very crowded and it is important to telephone before your visit to ascertain the availability of moorings. You should be prepared to raft up, and have plenty of rope ready for the necessary shorelines and springs. Bear in mind that the tidal flow up and down the narrow river is strong, up to six knots on a spring ebb.

Once inside the pierheads, steer for a pile structure at the inshore end of the north pier. This staging, known as the Knuckle, is marked by a beacon bearing two vertical green lights. When abreast the Knuckle, cut tight around and follow the line of the dock wall. There is deep water for about 10 metres off the wall with room for two

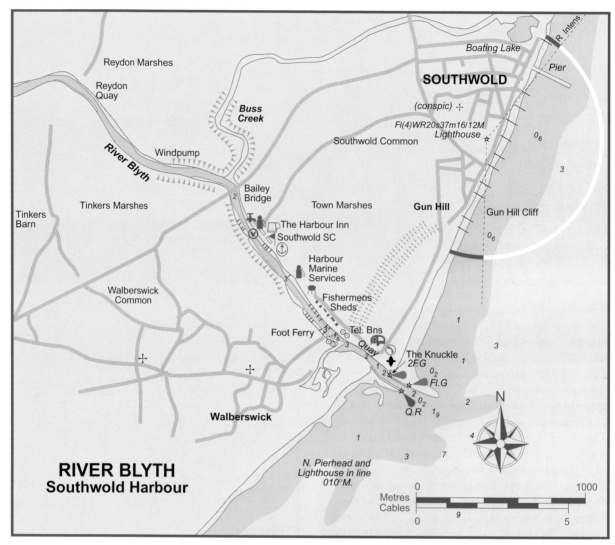

RIVER BLYTH
Southwold Harbour

boats to pass, so it is as well to remember that collision regulations apply. At the end of the wall at the starboard-hand mark, alter course to port, heading towards the power cable warning sign until you are in mid-river. Continue upriver midway between the stagings on either side.

There are permanent moorings on these wooden stagings, while the staging reserved for visiting yachtsmen is about a quarter of a mile beyond the ferry, on the north bank, just by the Harbour Inn.

Waveney District Council administers the harbour, and the harbour master's office is in the old Lifeboat shed near the visitors' pontoons.

John and Adele Buckley at Harbour Marine Services run a thriving boatyard and

chandlery on the north bank at Blackshore, near the fishermen's sheds, where they specialize in work on traditional wooden boats. An annual rally of smacks and classic boats has become established in recent years (usually in June) at Southwold, the event being sponsored by Adnams, the local brewery.

The seaside resort of Southwold, with its good shops and hotels, is about one mile away. The road from the harbour crosses the town marshes and leads to one of several attractive greens at Gun Cliff where there are six eighteen-pounder Tudor guns said to have been captured by the Duke of Cumberland at Culloden. The Sailors' Reading Room is well worth a visit. Situated close to the lighthouse, it is home to a collection of maritime paintings, prints,

Southwold Harbour looking across from the Walberswick shore towards the visitors' berths, the Harbour Inn and the Southwold SC

photographs and models, including some of the local beach yawls, the lines of which were later used for pulling and sailing Norfolk and Suffolk class lifeboats. The church is one of Suffolk's finest, filled with good wood carving and a rare 15th century, brightly painted pulpit.

Southwold overlooks Sole Bay where, in 1672, the townspeople watched from the cliff tops as the British and Dutch fleets fought a bloody naval battle in which both sides suffered heavy losses. The British were eventually deemed to have won a narrow victory.

At the north end of the town is Southwold Pier. Originally constructed in 1900 but later swept away by storms, it has been completely rebuilt by private owners Chris and Helen Iredale. Opened in 2001, the new pier extends to 623ft and boasts a bar restaurant, family amusements and a landing stage for visiting ships such as PS *Waverley* and MV *Balmoral*.

WALBERSWICK

Although most yachtsmen land on the N side of the harbour and visit Southwold, Walberswick too is a charming little place that has attracted artists ever since the days of Charles Keene and Wilson Steer at the end of the last century. There is a pub, a craft centre and teashop, and close by is an attractive little beach with good walks southward across the marshes to Dunwich or westward to the heathlands of the Suffolk Sandlings.

Walberswick has also long been the holiday haunt of theatrical folk, and the Scottish architect, designer and water-colourist, Charles Rennie Mackintosh, lived here for a time. The village

can be reached by crossing the Bailey bridge upstream of the Harbour Inn and walking back down the south bank of the River Blyth. Alternatively you can cross to the Walberswick side by getting the ferryman to row you over from near the fishermen's sheds.

Alongside at Southwold looking downriver across to Walberswick

ORFORD RIVER

Tides (at entrance)	HW Dover +0.15 Range: Springs 2.0m Neaps 1.7m
Charts	Admiralty SC2695, 2693, Stanford No 6, Imray C28, OS Map No 156
Waypoints	Orford Haven Buoy (liable to be moved) 52°01'.85N 01°28'.28E
	For latest position contact Thames Coastguard – Frinton-on-Sea (01255) 675518
Hazards	Shoals and strong tides in entrance (Seek up-to-date information from Aldeburgh YC)

Orford Haven lies at the southern end of Hollesley Bay, some four or five miles N of the entrance to the Deben, but it is not easy to locate the actual entrance. The only helpful landmarks are a Martello Tower about a mile SW of the entrance proper and a few houses in two small rows just N of the tower.

The offing buoy ('Orford Haven' Sph RWVS Bell LFl.10s) is in about 6m of water at LWS and situated just under a mile E of the cottages at Shingle Street. The port and starboard-hand buoys, Oxley and Weir, are laid during the season to indicate the passage into the river between the shingle islet and the shingle bank extending south of North Weir Point.

As with the River Deben, the Ore reaches the sea through a narrow shingle banked outlet and as a result there is a shingle bar and several drying and shifting shingle banks or 'knolls' in the entrance. The bar and the knolls, and the fact that the tides run in and out of the river very strongly indeed, combine to make Orford Haven rather more difficult to enter than the Deben, together with the fact that there is no pilot on hand.

Shingle Street and Orford Haven looking north up the River Ore with Orfordness in the top right. This picture was taken in early 2003 – by October 2003 the lagoon in the foreground had disappeared, demonstrating that this is indeed an area of frequent change

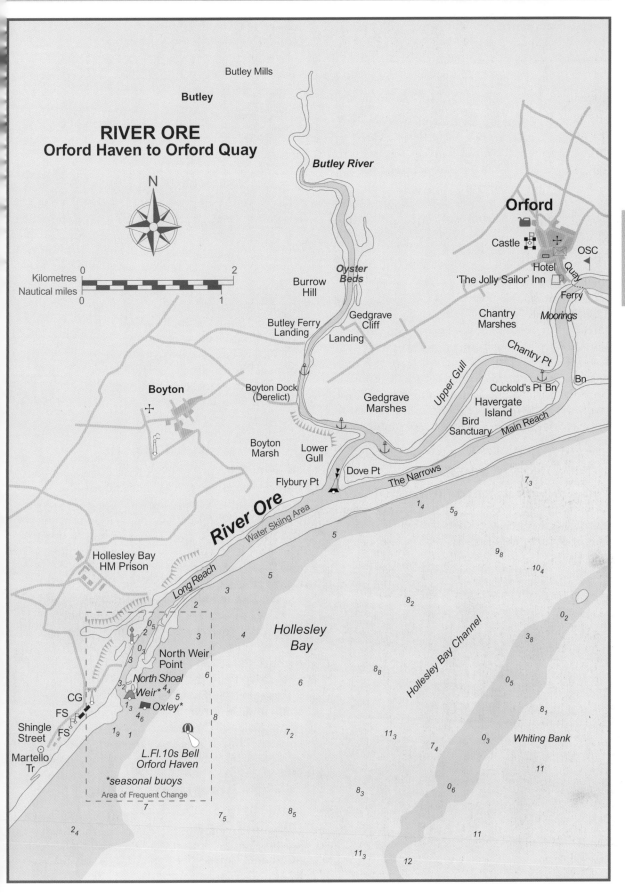

A beacon (orange and white post with orange diamond shaped topmark) was erected by Trinity House in 1975 on the mainland shore just inside North Weir Point and has not been moved since. It is no longer possible to follow a direct course between the offing buoy and the beacon. Responsibility for the maintenance of the beacon has been taken over by the Alde and Ore Association.

As the directions change from year to year, yachtsmen are fortunate that a survey of the entrance is carried out at the beginning of each season. The findings are incorporated in the annual *Information and Guidelines* leaflet published by the Alde and Ore Association. This invaluable publication is available from the chart agents Small Craft Deliveries, 12 Quay Street, Woodbridge IP12 1BX Telephone 01394 382655.

Although given the dual names, the Ore and the Alde are merely different parts of a single river; the Ore being that part between the entrance (Orford Haven) and Randalls Point (between Orford and Slaughden Quay, while the Alde is the river thereon up to its navigable limit at Snape Bridge, a distance of about 16 miles.

THE RIVER ORE

Within the entrance the tidal streams run very strongly indeed; probably up to 4 knots on the flood and as much as 5 knots during the latter half of a spring ebb. Because of this, entry against the ebb is virtually impossible, while departure on the ebb is certainly inadvisable.

Probably the time to enter or leave the river is from about one hour after LW, depending on draught, when there should be sufficient water over the bar and the worst of the shingle banks will still be uncovered.

While waiting for the flood a safe anchorage may be found inshore just S of the Martello Tower at Shingle Street, provided the wind is somewhere between SW and N.

Given sufficient power (not less than 5 knots), it is safest to leave the river on the early flood when the tide outside will assist any boat bound south.

Both the flood stream and the ebb continue to run into and out of the river for an hour after the change in Hollesley Bay.

The Entrance
When entering on the flood, a boat will tend to be carried into the river on the tidal stream. At the narrows at North Weir Point the streams are strongest and there is considerable turbulence caused by the streams from and to seaward round N Weir Point meeting the main north/south streams in the river.

LONG REACH

From the entrance to Dove Point, two miles to the NE, the river is little more than 100m wide and runs between a featureless steep-to shingle bank to the SE and a somewhat shallow shingle and mud shore backed by a sea wall to the NW. This part of the Ore is known as Long Reach and there is an average of 6m all along it, although because the tides are so fierce and the holding in shingly mud is not very good, it is not advisable, except in an emergency, to bring up below Dove Point. There is a water ski area in the upper part of Long Reach, below Flybury Point.

At Dove Point the river divides around Havergate Island, one part running along the south and the other along the north side of this narrow island. There is a fairly extensive mud spit extending from Dove Point, which is marked by a black buoy bearing a N Cardinal topmark.

HAVERGATE ISLAND

Havergate is now an important and well-known bird sanctuary under the control of the Royal Society for the Protection of Birds and landing is prohibited unless permission has been obtained from the Society.

The Orford Haven safe water mark (L Fl 10s Bell) needs to be located before entering the Alde

Peace and quiet in the Butley River near the old Boyton Dock

MAIN REACH

The most direct route up river to Orford Quay is Main Reach, which passes between the E side of Havergate Island and the attenuated shingle bank that stretches from Orfordness down to North Weir Point. The southern half of Main Reach is known as the Narrows. Here the river is hardly more than half a cable wide and the tides, particularly the ebb, still run very strongly. At the top of Main Reach the river turns northerly towards Orford, about a mile away, and it is then possible to find good holding ground out of the main tidal stream.

A red spherical buoy is sometimes located in Main Reach at the point where the other arm of the river emerges from the W side of Havergate Island. This other arm first of all turns northerly round Flybury Point, and for about half a mile the reach is known as the Lower Gull; one of the best anchorages for a boat waiting to leave the river. The tides still run strongly in Lower Gull, but the holding is better than anywhere in Long Reach. Another good anchorage is in Abraham's Bosom, off the north side of Havergate Island abreast its narrowest part.

At the top of Lower Gull a fairly large creek known as the Butley River branches off in a north-westerly direction. The main stream at this point turns south-easterly for about half a mile and then again turns to the NE into Upper Gull. At the northern end of the Upper Gull the channel turns easterly once more and continues for nearly a mile before uniting with Main Reach between Chantry and Cuckold Points.

On average there is a greater depth of water through Lower Gull and Upper Gull than through Main Reach.

THE BUTLEY RIVER

This river or large creek leaves Lower Gull and at first follows a westerly direction for a quarter of a mile before turning north past Boyton Dock and Butley Ferry. The entrance to the creek is marked by a port-hand withy, and there is good anchorage just inside with about 2m at LWS. Shallow draught boats can sometimes lie afloat as far up as Gedgrave Cliff amid pleasant surroundings.

The Butley Oysterage is active in the upper reaches of the river near the Cliff. The beds or

Orford Sailing Club is just up river of the quay at Orford. Orford Castle in the background is a conspicuous landmark

trays may not be marked by withies, but there are courteous notice-boards indicating the extent of the layings (beds), so visiting yachtsmen should respond by taking care not to anchor above Gedgrave.

Landing is possible at most states of the tide, either at the semi-derelict Boyton Dock or at the Ferry hards, half a mile further north. In 2002 the ferry service between the Boyton and Orford shores was discontinued due to prohibitive costs of insurance and health and safety cover. From Gedgrave beach on the E bank there is a pleasant walk of about two miles to Orford – the nearest source of supplies.

ORFORD QUAY

Above Chantry Point the river widens and deepens a little, having between 8 and 10m of water up to Orford Quay. Extending from the E bank just below the moorings at Orford there is a mud bank that diverts the channel towards the opposite shore for a short distance. The drying edge of the mud is marked by a perch.

The keep of Orford Castle (90ft) is a conspicuous landmark from anywhere in the river S of Orford, and will have been clearly visible from Lower Gull or Main Reach.

In 1165 Henry II decided to build a castle at Orford, which was when the original quays were constructed for unloading the building materials. The castle was completed in 1173, just in time to be used in Henry's conflict with his Barons. Orford became a flourishing port, sending wool to the Continent at first and later handling coastal trade in coal and grain until 1939.

The view from the top of the keep well repays the climb, as does the equally impressive panorama from the tower of St Bartholomew's church, which was built around the same time as the castle and where there are some excellent brasses and a pair of stocks.

Moorings are laid on both sides of the channel for half a mile above and below Orford Quay; for temporary use of a mooring apply to the Harbour Master, Ralph Brinkley. A few moorings (with pink pick-up buoys) are made available by the Orford Town Trust for visitors and these can usually be found halfway along the trot of moorings below the Quay on the Orfordness shore. In common with other popular destinations in the area, in the summer holiday period the demand for visitors' moorings often exceeds the supply. The Town Trust has a warden's office on the quay and a workboat operates on the river between Orford and the entrance.

Landing at the quay itself or at the shingle beach north of it is possible at all states of the tide. The MFV *Lady Florence*, a familiar sight on the river, operates mini cruises from the quay, and the RSPB ferry also runs from the quay to the society's reserve on Havergate Island. There is a public slipway beside the quay, which should not be obstructed.

Landing on the opposite shore, that is on the Orfordness side, is prohibited by the National Trust, which owns Orfordness. A secret military site from 1913 to the mid-80s, the Ness is the largest vegetated shingle spit in Europe and is well worth a visit for its fascinating natural, local and military history. The NT ferry runs from the quay in July, August and September

Formerly a secret military site, Orfordness is steeped in natural, local and weapon-testing history

Chapter 3

During summer months a National Trust passenger ferry runs from Orford Quay to the Ness

between 10am and 2pm (Tuesday to Saturday); from Easter to the end of June and in October visits are on Saturdays only. Buy your tickets and an informative guidebook from the NT office on the Quay.

Upstream of the quay, on the seawall, is the Orford SC clubhouse; the club has its own launching ramp and pontoon and welcomes visiting yachtsmen.

Orford's market square boasts the Butley-Orford Oysterage seafood restaurant and shop, plus The Kings Head pub,

The Jolly Sailor is a short walk from the quay

the Crown and Castle hotel with its Trinity Restaurant and, down Bakers Lane beside the Town Hall, Richardson's Smokehouse (follow your nose to the source of the enticing oak smoke). Nearest the quay is The Old Warehouse teashop, while a little further up Quay Street is the Jolly Sailor, steeped in local history and serving locally-caught fish and chips (does not take bookings). Legend has it that the body of the infamous eighteenth century smuggler, Will Laud, was brought to this inn after he had been shot by the Preventative men on the beach near Orfordness.

ORFORD PORT GUIDE	
Harbour Master	Ralph Brinkley Tel 01394 450481
Orford Town Trust	Office on the Quay Tel 01394 459950
Water	Stand-pipe on the quay
Stores	General store (off licence and PO) off square. Butcher, fish shop and smokehouse near square
Chandlery	Limited stock from Marine Services Tel 01394 450844 VHF Ch 8
Petrol	Garage in town (0.75 mile, cans)
Diesel	From Marine Services or garage (cans)
Crane	On quay; contact the harbour master
Scrubbing	Near quay
Transport	Buses from market square to Ipswich and Woodbridge (infrequent)
Club	Orford Sailing Club
Telephone	In car park
PO	In general store
Food and Drink	Butley Orford Oysterage restaurant Tel 01394 450277; Crown & Castle hotel Tel 01394 450205; Jolly Sailor Tel 01394 450243; King's Head Tel 01394 450205; Old Warehouse Teashop at Quay. Fish & Chip van by the Castle Wed evenings 4.30 to 7.30pm

The Butley Orford Oysterage restaurant also has a fish shop

THE RIVER ALDE

Tides	HW Slaughden Quay approx 1hr 15mins after HW at entrance. HW Snape Bridge approx 1hr after Slaughden. Range: Slaughden Quay Springs 2.5m Neaps 1.1m
Charts	Admiralty 2693, Stanford No 6, Imray C28, OS Map 156.
Hazards	Because of winding gutway, make passage between Slaughden and Snape only on rising tide

Above Orford the river turns easterly for a short way and then, abreast Raydon Point, the direction becomes north-easterly along Pigpail Reach. At Raydon Point a water pipe crosses the river to connect with the lighthouse at Orfordness, and the position of the pipe is marked by notice boards.

About one and a quarter miles above Orford, the river becomes the Alde and turns more northerly with deeper water towards the W bank, although all through Blackstakes Reach and Home Reach up to Slaughden Quay the best water will be found roughly midway between the banks. Several racing marks (spar buoys) are located in midstream along these upper reaches of the Alde; fleets of Dragons, Squibs, other keelboats and the local Lapwing clinker-built dinghies are raced from Aldeburgh YC. Between Orford and Slaughden the depths vary between 5 and 7m at LW, and the width of the LW channel remains about 200m.

SLAUGHDEN QUAY

Abreast the conspicuous Martello Tower, about a quarter of a mile below Slaughden, the river narrows and shallows for a short distance before deepening again and changing direction abruptly off the quay itself. At this point, the river Alde is separated from the sea only by the sea wall and shingle beach – not much more than 100m in all.

In the 16th century Slaughden Quay was the port area of Aldeburgh – busy with fishing, shipbuilding and coastal trade in salt, fish and coal. Nowadays trade is in pleasure craft – boatyards, two sailing clubs and many moorings. The moorings are administered by the Aldeburgh Yacht Club and are laid athwart the stream on both sides of the channel at Slaughden Quay – boats are moored fore and aft and are closely packed. If you require a mooring, consult the yacht club or Upson's Boatyard, where Russell Upson is the local CA Boatman.

The best place to bring up is between the Martello Tower and the clubhouse on the E side of the river; this particular Tower, known

Looking across the Aldeburgh YC pontoon into Westrow Reach. The ketch is being towed towards Upson's boatyard at Slaughden Quay on the right of the picture

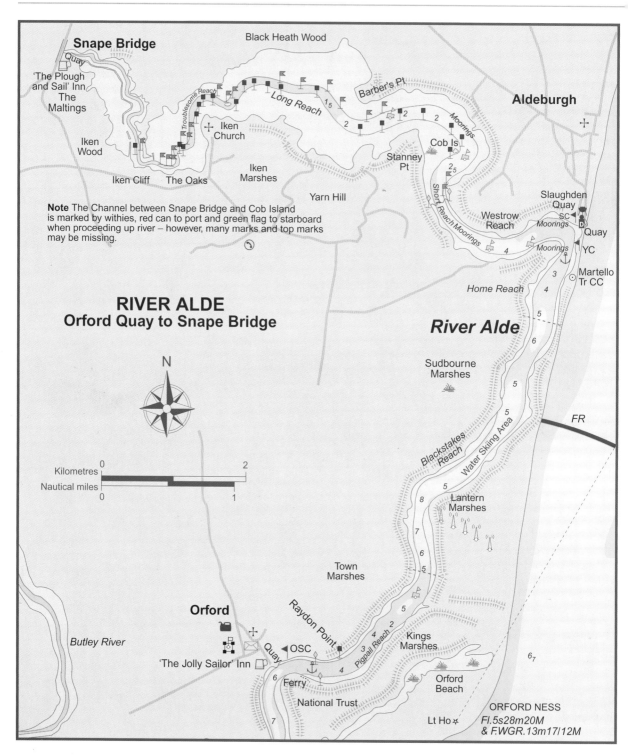

Snape Bridge

Black Heath Wood

Quay

'The Plough and Sail' Inn
The Maltings

Iken Wood

Iken Cliff   The Oaks

Troublesome Reach

Iken Church

Iken Marshes

Long Reach

Barber's Pt

Moorings

Aldeburgh

Cob Is

Stanney Pt

Yarn Hill

Short Reach Moorings

Westrow Reach

Moorings

Slaughden Quay

SC

Quay

YC

Moorings

Martello Tr CC

Home Reach

Note The Channel between Snape Bridge and Cob Island is marked by withies, red can to port and green flag to starboard when proceeding up river – however, many marks and top marks may be missing.

RIVER ALDE
Orford Quay to Snape Bridge

N

River Alde

Sudbourne Marshes

FR

Blackstakes Reach

Water Skiing Area

Lantern Marshes

| Kilometres | 0 | | 2 |
| Nautical miles | 0 | | 1 |

Town Marshes

Raydon Point

Orford

'The Jolly Sailor' Inn

Quay

OSC

Ferry

National Trust

Butley River

Pigtail Reach

Kings Marshes

Orford Beach

ORFORD NESS
Lt Ho
Fl.5s28m20M
& F.WGR.13m17/12M

as 'CC', was the northernmost of the chain that stretched round from the south coast and it is completely different from all the others, being quadrafoil in shape.

When you have either anchored or moored, there is clean landing at the quay near Upson's, on the shingle next to it, or at the fine pontoons in front of Aldeburgh Yacht Club, which welcomes visiting yachtsmen. Peter Wilson's Aldeburgh Boatyard, about a quarter of a mile from the quay, offers laying-up facilities and chandlery, and specializes in wooden boat restoration. The major boatyard, with slipway and boathoist, is RF Upson at Slaughden Quay, where it builds wood and glassfibre fishing and work boats as well as offering repair facilities.

Fishermen still work open boats off the shingle beach at Aldeburgh

The old Customs House at the top of the High Street in Aldeburgh

ALDEBURGH

Aldeburgh has long been held in high regard by visiting yachtsmen. Frank Cowper wrote in his *Sailing Tours* that it was '...a capital place for boating;' he went ashore to try out an Aldeburgh bathing machine and declared his dip to be '...very salt and pick-me-uppish.' The fine town, with its Tudor moot hall, has many cultural connections starting with George Crabbe, the 19th century poet, who was born in The Borough. His poem *Peter Grimes* became the inspiration for Benjamin Britten to write the opera of that name. Britten, who lived in Crabbe Street, founded the now world famous Aldeburgh Festival in 1948.

The High Street is a good place to provision – there is a Co-op, several shops offering fresh seafood and other local produce. For eating ashore there is a choice of hotels, restaurants, bistros, bars, pubs and the justly popular Aldeburgh Fish and Chip Shop.

ABOVE SLAUGHDEN

Above Slaughden the river changes direction and turns inland in a general westerly direction for the five or six miles to Snape Bridge. The character of the river now begins to change and, while the banks become further apart, the LW channel becomes narrower.

Hazelwood Marshes and the Inner Alde Mudflats are Suffolk Wildlife Reserves. A footpath, known as the Sailors' Walk, runs from Aldeburgh to Snape on the north bank – it offers an alternative route on foot to Snape (at any state of the tide).

From Westrow Reach, the river is frequently marked by withies (some of which have been replaced by posts), with red can topmarks to port and green or with twiggy branches to starboard.

These marks are necessarily very numerous – Aldeburgh YC moorings committee members do their best to maintain them – and we owe them thanks for undertaking this formidable task. However, in early 2003 many of the marks were in a poor state having lost or broken topmarks and some were missing altogether. Recent silting has caused changes, particularly in the Little Japan area of Long Reach and around Iken church. For this reason a small boat able to take the ground safely, a lifting keeler or a dinghy is perhaps the best bet for exploring the upper reaches. *The Ore and Alde Association Guidelines* contains a sketch chart showing the marks, but this is no

SLAUGHDEN QUAY, ALDEBURGH PORT GUIDE

Moorings	Aldeburgh YC Tel 01728 452562 or Russell Upson Tel 453047
Water	At yacht club or stand-pipe on quay
Stores	Shops in Aldeburgh (1 mile). Co-op Foodstore 0830–2000 Mon to Sat 1000–1600 Sun. EC Wed
Fuel	Diesel from Upson's. Petrol in town
Gas	From chandlery
Repairs	Upson's Boatyard. Derrick on quay
Chandlery	At Aldeburgh Boatyard nearby
Transport	Buses from Aldeburgh to Saxmundham (8 miles). Trains from Saxmundham to Ipswich and London
Clubs	Aldeburgh Yacht Club Tel 452562 Slaughden Sailing Club
Food & Drink	Many hotels, pubs and restaurants in town

The upper reaches of the Alde above St Botolph's Church at Iken looking towards the head of the river at Snape Bridge. The LW gutway can be seen winding its tortuous way past The Oaks and Iken Cliff to the left of the picture

guarantee of their position or their existence. The OS Explorer Map 212 Woodbridge and Saxmundham is also useful.

The marks are not very conspicuous in certain conditions of light, so a very careful look-out must be kept to see that none is missed. It is advisable to commence a trip to Iken Cliff or Snape Bridge early on the tide so that the tortuous channel can be seen and the marks understood.

Through Westrow Reach and Short Reach there is about 4m in the channel at LW, and a starboard-hand beacon marks the edge of mud extending from the N bank. In Short Reach a power cable crosses the river and is pinpointed by the usual triangular topped beacons. At the top of Short Reach the channel turns north-easterly past two starboard-hand beacons and a port-hand beacon to Stanny Point. A racing buoy is usually located off Stanny Point, but in any case a metal beacon marking the site of the now eroded Cob Island will serve to identify this point in the river. A derelict brick dock and some moorings will be seen over on the E shore and here the channel turns back to the NW, round a series of three port-hand beacons into Colliers Reach. Three beacons to

starboard and three beacons to port mark the channel round Barber's Point and into Long Reach. By this time, the LW channel is but a cable wide, with depths of about 1.5m.

Past Barber's Point, the river widens towards HW to nearly a mile between its banks and, while marshland lies to the south, Black Heath Woods reach down to a sandy beach on the north shore at a spot known locally as 'Little Japan'. At the western end of Long Reach a series of four port-hand beacons follow the course of the channel to where it turns sharply to the south towards Sandy Point. Then the channel turns north-westerly into Short Reach and south-westerly again into Church Reach – the ancient thatched church of St Botolph's stands on a wooded promontory less than a quarter of a mile away. After this the channel turns westerly into Lower Troublesome Reach and south again into Upper Troublesome Reach.

Beyond the two Troublesome Reaches, the channel closely approaches the shore near a sandy beach, above which a group of oak trees grows. This spot, known as 'The Oaks', is very pleasant and offers good landing near HW. Then comes Cliff Reach, leading up to Iken Cliff itself, where the LW channel again comes to within 20 yards of the shore.

SNAPE BRIDGE PORT GUIDE

Maltings Quay Office	Tel 01728 688303
Water	On quayside
Stores	Shop in Snape village
Food and Drink	Plough and Sail Tel 688413; The Crown Tel 688324; Golden Key Tel 688510; Concert Hall restaurant, teashop at Maltings
Snape Maltings Concert Hall	Box Office Tel 453543

IKEN CLIFF

There is only a metre or so of water at best in the channel abreast Iken Cliff, but the bottom is mud and the spot provides one of the most attractive anchorages on the Alde. There are one or two small boat moorings here and a few dinghies on the foreshore.

SNAPE BRIDGE

From Iken Cliff to Snape Bridge is just over a mile, and the channel, which becomes little more than a gutway, winds between mudbanks and virtually dries out at LW. However, it is possible for craft drawing up to 2m to reach the quay alongside the Maltings at Snape Bridge, where they must take the mud if staying for more than an hour or so. The last mile or two are irregularly marked by some port hand cans and starboard perches.

The virginia creeper-clad maltings were built in the mid-19th century by Newson Garrett, father of the pioneering woman doctor, Elizabeth Garrett Anderson. The malt was taken to London in two steam barges which brought back barley. The maltings closed in 1965 and soon afterwards the concert hall was built as a centre for the Aldeburgh Festival, but now it is used throughout the year for many other performances.

The original maltings buildings have been developed into the Snape Riverside Centre comprising craft shops, exhibitions, galleries and restaurants. As a result they have become a popular tourist attraction, so the quayside can be crowded on bank holidays and fine summer days.

There is a nominal charge for overnight mooring alongside the Maltings Quay. The Plough and Sail, the Concert Hall restaurant and the Granary Tea Shop offer a variety of meals. There is water on the quayside, but the nearest supplies, plus two more pubs, the Crown and the Golden Key, are at Snape village, about half a mile away.

Chapter 4

A flotilla of four visiting shoal-draught yachts have taken the ground during their stay alongside the quay at Snape Maltings. Snape Bridge can be seen in the background

THE RIVER DEBEN

Tides	At entrance. HW Dover +0.25 Range: Springs 3.2m Neaps 1.9m (HW Woodbridge approx 45mins after HW in entrance)
Charts	Admiralty 2693, Stanford No 6, Imray Y16, OS Map No 169
Waypoint	Woodbridge Haven Buoy 51°58'.55N 01°24'.26E (liable to be moved – for latest position contact Thames Coastguard Frinton-on-Sea 01255 675518)
Hazards	Strong tide and shoals in entrance (Seek up-to-date information from Felixstowe Ferry Harbour Master). Shoal near W bank between Felixstowe Ferry SC and Bawdsey Manor. 'Horse' shoal just upstream of Felixstowe Ferry

Inviting a friend to stay with him aboard his schooner *Scandal*, Edward FitzGerald, translator of *The Rubaiyat of Omar Khahyyam*, wrote: 'I think you would like this Bawdsey, only about a dozen Fishermen's Houses, built where our River runs into the Sea over a foaming Bar,

on one side of which is a goodsand to Felixstowe and on the other an orange coloured crag Cliff towards Orford Haven; not a single respectable House or Inhabitants or Lodger; no white Cravats, an Inn with scarce a table and chair and only Bread and Cheese to eat, I often lie here with my Boat: I wish you would come and do so.'

That was a hundred and twenty years ago, but the Ferry Boat Inn remains, although you may now have more than bread and cheese to eat should you wish.

For today's yachtsman who keeps his boat in the Medway, the Crouch or the Blackwater, a visit to the Deben must usually be made during the summer holiday cruise. The Woodbridge river, as the Deben is sometimes called, is only about nine miles long, but it is very attractive and nowadays entirely free from commercial traffic.

Woodbridge Haven – entrance to the River Deben – photographed in Spring 2003 when the channel between the Knolls on the Bawdsey side had just been buoyed. The extremely narrow channel on the Felixstowe shore, used in previous years, can be seen centre left

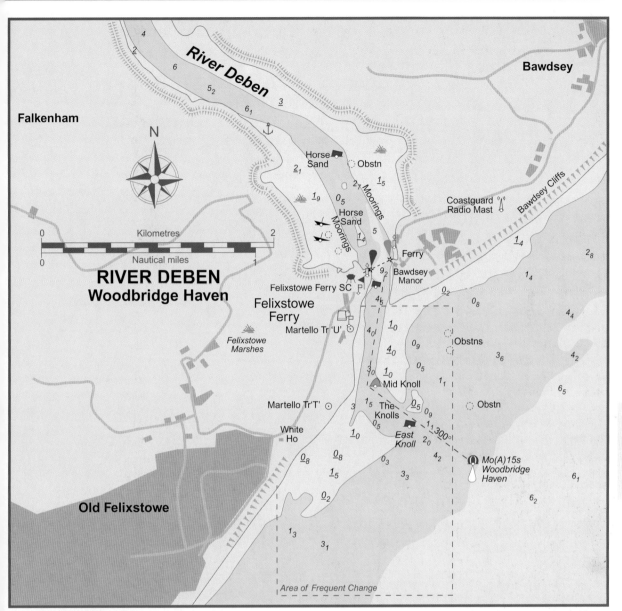

Perhaps the thing that comes first to the East Coast yachtsman's mind when he thinks of the Deben is that there is a shifting shingle bar at the entrance to Woodbridge Haven. This bar ought not to worry anyone unduly because there is a pilot on hand at almost all times during the summer months.

Many more yachts enter and leave the river now than ever before and since most of them hail from Woodbridge, Waldringfield, Ramsholt or Felixstowe Ferry, their skippers usually have the benefit of local knowledge and so can often act as guide for the newcomer. Nevertheless, when there are no other yachts about and particularly for the first time 'over the bar', it is still a sound idea to consult the Harbour Master, John White, who will usually hear a call on VHF Channel 8, or come off

by prior arrangement. His telephone number is Felixstowe (01394) 270106; mobile 0780 3476621.

Before visiting the Deben you are strongly advised to obtain the sketch chart produced each year by the Harbour Master. This is available from Small Craft Deliveries in Woodbridge (Tel 01394 382655) and can also be found at marinas and chandleries.

APPROACHES

Most yachts will approach Woodbridge Haven from the south – often from Harwich harbour, which is only 6 or 7 miles away. A good time to enter the river is about two hours after low water, when there will be a least depth of about 2m over the bar. At LWS in 2003 there was 0.9 metres on the bar. With so little water to spare, an entrance

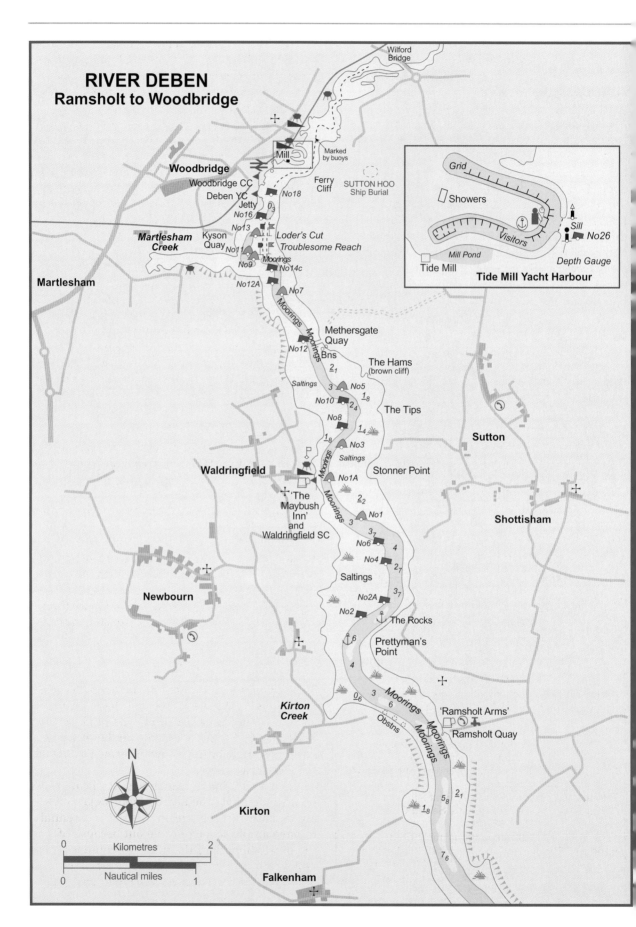

RIVER DEBEN
Ramsholt to Woodbridge

Wilford Bridge

Mill

Marked by buoys

Woodbridge

Woodbridge CC

Deben YC

Jetty

No18

Ferry Cliff

SUTTON HOO
Ship Burial

Tide Mill Yacht Harbour

Grid

Showers

Visitors

Sill

No26

Mill Pond

Tide Mill

Depth Gauge

No16

0 3

No13

Martlesham Creek

Kyson Quay

Loder's Cut

Troublesome Reach

No11

Moorings

No9

No14c

No12A

No7

Martlesham

Methersgate Quay

Moorings

No12

Bns

2 1

The Hams
(brown cliff)

Saltings

3

No5

1 8

No10

2 4

The Tips

No8

1 4

Moorings

1 8

No3

Waldringfield

Saltings

No1A

Stonner Point

'The Maybush Inn' and
Waldringfield SC

2 2

No1

3 7

No6

4

No4

2 7

Saltings

Sutton

Shottisham

Newbourn

No2A

3 7

No2

The Rocks

6

Prettyman's Point

4

Kirton Creek

0 6

3

6

Moorings

'Ramsholt Arms'

Ramsholt Quay

Obstns

Moorings

Moorings

N

1 8

5 8

2 1

Kirton

7 6

0 ——— Kilometres ——— 2

0 —— Nautical miles —— 1

Falkenham

should never be attempted when there is a bad sea running. But the appearance of the surrounding shoal-water would presumably be enough to scare anyone away on such occasions. A spring ebb can run out of the entrance at 6 knots and any attempt to enter at such times is certainly not recommended.

When the approach is from Harwich or from the Wallet, a course should be shaped to pass about half a mile off Felixstowe Pier. When approaching the Deben entrance, most of the details along the low lying shore will be distinguishable – in particular the two Martello Towers (Tower 'T' and Tower 'U'); the conspicuous and historic radar pylon just to the north of the entrance to Woodbridge Haven has been replaced by a new Coastguard Radio Mast.

Woodbridge Haven lit Mo (A) 15s buoy is maintained by Trinity House and is spherical with red and white vertical stripes.

Over the past decade the Deben bar has extended further and further south and the entrance has become so narrow and shallow that in 2002 even local boats were having difficulty finding the best water.

In 2003, following a survey, Trinity House moved the Woodbridge Haven buoy some half a mile to the north east and repositioned the green conical (previously Bar) and the red can (previously Martello Spit) buoys to mark a 'new' entrance channel through The Knolls. The latter two buoys have been re-named Mid Knoll and East Knoll respectively.

FELIXTOWE FERRY PORT GUIDE

Harbour Master	John White Tel 01394 270106; Mobile 0780 3476621; or call Odd Times on VHF Ch 8
Water	At yard
Stores	Limited supplies from café. Fish stall behind SC
Chandler	Near slipway
Repairs	Felixstowe Ferry Boatyard Tel 282173
Fuel	Diesel from fuel berth nr ferry jetty, petrol from garage in Felixstowe approx three miles
Transport	Infrequent bus service to Felixstowe (three miles)
Telephone	Box near Ferry Boat Inn
Clubs	Felixstowe Ferry Sailing Club Tel 283705 Bawdsey Haven Yacht Club
Food and Drink	Ferry Boat Inn Tel 284203 and the Victoria Inn Tel 271636; Ferry Cafe Tel 276305 fish and chips and all-day breakfasts

In 2003 the course to steer from the Haven Buoy was approximately 300 degrees T to take you through this passage. Leave East Knoll red can buoy to port and turn to starboard into the river once the Mid Knoll green conical buoy comes abeam – about a quarter of a mile north of Martello Tower 'T'.

Going in on the flood, the tide will now be pushing you really hard and, once abeam of Martello Tower 'U', it is necessary to cross towards the Bawdsey shore in order to leave to port the red can buoy marking a shoal near the Felixstowe Ferry Sailing Club. The only obstacle then remaining is the Horse Shoal, which occupies the centre of the river immediately above the Felixstowe-Bawdsey Ferry. The Horse Shoal is extensive and dries out in parts to a height of about 1m. The main channel is to eastward of the shoal, the channel to port being full of moored craft. It is safer therefore for a stranger to take the main or starboard channel, where there is plenty of water, until the Horse buoy (red can) is reached at the N end of the shoal.

DEPARTURE

While it is easier to leave Woodbridge Haven on the ebb tide, this results in any south-bound yacht having to face the remainder of the ebb after leaving the river. It is usually more convenient therefore to set off from the Haven at about half-flood, depending upon auxiliary power to push a boat over the fast running tidal stream near Felixstowe Ferry. The force of this stream should never be underestimated and, if an exit is to be made during springs, an engine capable of driving the boat at 5 knots will be no more than sufficient unless some help can also be obtained from the sails.

MOORINGS

The boatyard will usually find a buoy for visiting yachts among the many moorings between the shoal and the Felixstowe bank. One can land from a dinghy at all states of the tide on the convenient steep-to shingle beach by the fishermen's huts on the Felixstowe shore.

When anchoring hereabouts, special care must be taken to avoid the nearby moorings, which are laid athwart the stream. Also, it is essential to have ample scope of cable out because of the great strength of the tide – sometimes amounting to 5 knots. Whether you pick up a mooring or anchor, take care when using a dinghy to get ashore.

BAWDSEY

At Bawdsey, on the north shore opposite Felixstowe Ferry, the former RAF sailing association clubhouse and slipway is used as a watersports centre by the International Community School at Bawdsey Manor.
The Manor was built in 1886 by the wealthy stockbroker Sir Cuthbert Quilter. Following its purchase by the Air Defence Committee in 1935, Sir Robert Watson-Watt and his team began their historic work on the development of radar at Bawdsey which, during the Second World War, became part of a chain of RAF radar stations and later a training base.

There has been a ferry between the Felixstowe and Bawdsey shores for hundreds of years. At one time horses used to swim across while passengers used a rowing boat, after which a chain ferry ran from 1894 to 1931. Nowadays a foot passenger ferry service operates on demand at weekends and during school holidays from Easter to September.

For a mile or two above Felixstowe Ferry the Deben looks very much like a river in Essex rather than Suffolk – with low-lying mudbanks and saltings bordered by a sea wall. The channel, which in its centre has no less than 6m at low water, runs rather closer to the west bank up as far as Ramsholt Reach, where a somewhat abrupt change of scenery occurs.

RAMSHOLT

On the east bank the land rises sharply to form a modest cliff topped by a pleasant group of pine trees. Nestling under the cliff, close to the old barge quay, is an inn, the Ramsholt Arms, and there are few places more attractive than this on any East Coast river.

In recent years the moorings at Ramsholt, like everywhere else, have multiplied. There may be room to anchor in mid-channel if there is no vacant buoy, or the harbour master, George Collins, usually to be found near the quay or on his yacht *Brio*, will advise on the availability of moorings. His mobile telephone number is 0775 1034959, his home number is 01394 384318 and he keeps a listening watch on VHF Ch 77.

From the sandy landing place near the old quay a delightful walk leads along the shore and across a meadow up to Ramsholt Church – in fact the whole Bawdsey peninsula is criss-crossed with footpaths and byways. The Ramsholt Arms (Tel 01394 411229) serves meals and has a metered water tap outside (for which you need to purchase a token), but the only other facilities at Ramsholt are refuse bins, a public telephone and a post box.

Continuing up-river from Kirton Creek, the channel closely approaches the west bank for a while and then crosses to the east side abreast Ramsholt Woods. There is a very pleasant landing

High Water at Ramsholt. There is a sandy landing place just upstream of the quay and then a very short stroll to the nearby Ramsholt Arms

A mooring may be available from the Waldringfield Boatyard, just upstream of the Maybush Inn

Club, so that a limited number of visiting yachts can anchor. But when this space is taken up and the fairway opposite the beach is likely to become congested, or racing is in progress, it is better to move either up or down river to anchor with more space, preferably on the west side of the channel. If you require a mooring, Waldringfield Boatyard will be able to advise whether one is available.

Clean landing from a dinghy is possible along the shingle foreshore at almost any time and the Maybush Inn offers splendid views up and down the river.

Continuing up-river from Waldringfield the channel becomes narrower and the mud flats proportionately wider, so that special care must be taken between half-flood and half-ebb when the mud is only just covered.

No 3 buoy, conical green, marks the northern end of the tidal island and, having left this mark to starboard after passing Waldringfield, the next two red can buoys (Nos 8 and 10) identify an extensive spit off the W bank.

Under Ham Woods there is a low cliff and sandy beach which just invites a picnic – but beware! At high water the beach is hard and sandy, although this hard bottom only extends for a limited distance, after which it abruptly changes to soft mud about a metre deep. If a landing is to be made at 'The Tips',

here beneath the trees on a sandy beach known locally as 'The Rocks', so called because of a layer of sandstone rock on the river bed. There are no roads nearby, but on a fine day there is sometimes a 'traffic jam' of yachts! Yachtsmen are asked to refrain from cutting wood to make fires on the beach – otherwise there would soon be no trees left.

At the top of the Rocks Reach, opposite Shottisham Creek, is the first of the up-river marks, which continue as buoys or beacons all the way up to Woodbridge. The first two can buoys, 2 and 2a, and all subsequent port hand buoys are numbered evenly, while those on the starboard hand are odd-numbered.

The next two red cans (4 and 6) mark the mud that stretches out from the west bank at this bend of the river. Just above these buoys there is a patch of shallow water over a horse (shoal), carrying as little as 1m at LWS. Above No 6 buoy the channel turns NW.

A conical green buoy (No 1) is the first to be left to starboard and it marks the downstream end of an extensive tidal island lying between Waldringfield and Stonner Point. At or near high water there is about 1.5m of water between the east bank and the island, but any boat using this route should proceed cautiously and take frequent soundings past Stonner Point.

WALDRINGFIELD

The main channel runs to the west of the island, between two lines of moorings and past green conical buoy No 1A. A gap is left in the moorings opposite the beach, off the Waldringfield Sailing

A Squib getting under way from a mooring just off Waldringfield SC

one should return to the dinghy before the mud is uncovered; which happens quickly, for the shore is quite flat hereabouts.

The sandy shore at 'The Tips' resulted from an attempt at the end of the last century by Robert Cobbold to reclaim 150 acres of land from the river. The attempt was stopped by Trinity House, who felt that the scheme would alter the course of the river and interfere with its navigation.

After leaving No 8 and No 10 buoys to port, a green buoy (No 5) is left to starboard below Methersgate Quay, then follows No 12, a red buoy to be left to port opposite the quay.

There are moorings pretty well all the way up from Methersgate Quay to Woodbridge and for the most part they indicate the direction of best water, but additionally there is a closely spaced sequence of channel buoys to guide newcomers through the twists and turns of the Troublesome Reaches. Here even local knowledge is not always enough, as a native of Waldringfield confided to H Alker Tripp (in his book *Suffolk Sea Borders*, 1926), 'Lots of 'em gets stuck wot's used to it, let alone strangers.'

All the navigational and mooring buoys between Methersgate and Woodbridge are under the control of the Kyson Fairways Committee, who decided to name the channel buoys according to the reaches in which they are located. So we now have buoys with names such as Upper Troublesome, Lower Troublesome, Granary Reach and Crummy Moore.

There are drying moorings and pontoons with water and power at the boatyard on the S side of Martlesham Creek.

One more spherical green (No 13) and one

WALDRINGFIELD PORT GUIDE	
Water	On quay and at sailing club
Fuel	Diesel at boatyard, petrol from garage on Woodbridge Road (one mile)
Repairs and Chandlery	Waldringfield Boatyard Tel 01473 736260; slip and 40-ton crane
Scrubbing Posts	Near sailing club
Transport	Buses to Ipswich
Telephone	Box near pub
Club	Waldringfield SC
Food and Drink	The Maybush Inn Tel 736215

more red (No 16) Granary buoy mark the way to the line of moorings extending down-river from Woodbridge.

Four more port hand (red can) buoys (Nos 18 to 24) mark the channel between Everson's shed and the entrance to the Tide Mill Yacht Harbour, and are helpful because deeper water changes from side to side of the river hereabouts.

LODERS' CUT

Towards the end of the last century a channel was cut to avoid the bend past Kyson Quay. The purpose of Loders' Cut, as the channel is called, was to revive Woodbridge's failing maritime trade. The plan was not very successful, although the cut remains and can be safely used by light draught boats for about $1\frac{1}{2}$ to 2 hours either side of high water. There are port and starboard hand marks at both ends of the cut, which now has the same water as in the main channel.

WOODBRIDGE

Seafaring connections at Woodbridge began with the Anglo Saxons, who arrived by sea and settled in the area. From Tudor times the town was a thriving commercial port and centre for shipbuilding – merchant ships and Royal Naval vessels as large as 600 tons were launched. As well as timber, Suffolk butter was exported and the Deben was busy with vessels engaged in all sorts of trade, including smuggling. After the coming of the railways shipping diminished and the quays silted up.

There are moorings on both sides of the channel at Woodbridge, but

Approaching Woodbridge where there are moorings on both sides of the channel and most boats take the ground at LW. The tide mill buildings can be seen in the distance

A yacht entering the Woodbridge Tide Mill Yacht Harbour, passing the tide gauge and crossing the sill near the top of the tide

most of the boats take the ground at low water. A few deeper draught craft are located in 'holes' where there is more water; one of these being in midstream abreast of Everson's old building shed, quite close to the re-built bandstand on the river wall promenade. The clubhouse of the Deben Yacht Club, established in 1838, lies at the southern end of the River Wall and about halfway between here and the railway station is the Woodbridge Cruising Club whose clubhouse was extended in 2002. The old ferry dock, near the station, is fitted out as a yacht harbour which dries out at LW. However there are stagings to lie to and the mud is soft.

Generally, a visiting yacht must expect to come and go on a tide – high water at Woodbridge varies between 30 and 50 minutes later than at Felixstowe Ferry. If you want to stay longer and remain afloat, you will need a berth in the Tide Mill Yacht Harbour further upstream. The old tide mill pool was excavated in the 1960s to form a horseshoe-shaped yacht basin, where yachts can lie afloat at all states of the tide. The Yacht Harbour has a sill over which there is 1.6m at MHWN and 2.5m at MHWS. Craft drawing more than 1.5m (5ft) should not attempt entry after HW on a neap tide. Moorings for waiting yachts, fitted with pick-up buoys and ropes, are placed just outside the entrance where there is an accurate tide gauge.

There has been a tide mill where the present Woodbridge Mill stands since 1170. Thanks to an energetic Preservation Society, this last remaining tide mill on the East Coast can be seen in operation, subject to tides, from May to September – details of times are on the notice-board.

Just across the railway line from the yacht harbour is a cinema/theatre and a swimming pool; art galleries and antique shops abound in

the town; and the Shire Hall on Market Hill is home to the Suffolk Horse Museum.

There are three yards above the mill; the first is Roberton's with a slipway and a travel lift. The Granary Yacht Harbour at Dock Lane, Melton, is about a mile above the mill and staff there will send you a sketch chart showing the buoyed channel up to their pontoon berths. Larkman's yard at Melton wharf mainly uses its 9 ton crane for lifting boats out for their winter lay-up.

A public footpath from Ferry Cliff, opposite the Tide Mill, leads to the site of the Saxon burial ship at Sutton Hoo on the east bank of the river. The burial ground of the Anglo Saxon pagan kings of East Anglia has been called 'page one of English history.' The visitor centre, opened by the National Trust (NT) in 2002, includes an exhibition displaying some of the original treasure on loan from the British Museum. For opening hours telephone the NT on 01394 389700.

WOODBRIDGE PORT GUIDE

Tide Mill Yacht Harbour	Tel 01394 385745; Fax 380735; VHF Ch 80; email info@tidemillyachtharbour.co.uk
Harbour Master	Mike Ellis VHF Ch 80
Water	Yacht Harbour; stand pipe on Ferry Quay
Stores	Many shops in town. EC Wed. Budgens in Turban shopping centre 0800–2000 Mon–Sat, 1000–1600 Sun. Good Food Shop (deli) and Loaves and Fishes (natural foods and fresh fish) both in The Thoroughfare.
Fuel	Diesel and gas from Yacht Harbour and all yards. Petrol from garage across town
Chandlers	At Lime Kiln Quay and Dock Lane, Melton
Chart Agents	SCD Ltd, 12 Quay Street Tel 01394 382655
Repairs	Engineering services, shipwright, cranage to 12 tons at Yacht Harbour
Sailmaker	Near Yacht Harbour
Telephone	Box in station yard
Transport	Train service to Ipswich, then to London. Buses to Ipswich
Clubs	Deben Yacht Club Tel 01394 386504. Woodbridge Cruising Club Tel 01394 382028
Food and Drink	Riverside Restaurant (Tel 382587) next to cinema has dinner and film menu; The Captain's Table (Tel 383145) in Quay Street specializes in fish; many hotels, pubs and traditional tea rooms

Chapter 5

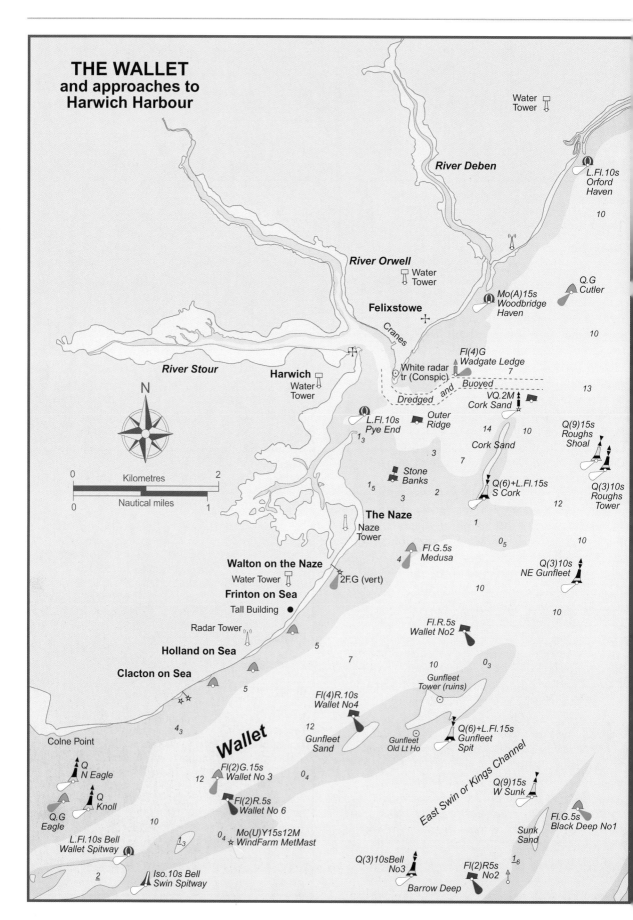

THE WALLET
and approaches to Harwich Harbour

Water Tower

River Deben

L.Fl.10s
Orford Haven

10

Q.G
Cutler

10

Mo(A)15s
Woodbridge Haven

River Orwell

Water Tower

Felixstowe

Cranes

Fl(4)G
Wadgate Ledge

7

Dredged and Buoyed

VQ.2M
Cork Sand

13

White radar tr (Conspic)

Outer Ridge

14   10

Q(9)15s
Roughs Shoal

River Stour

Harwich

Water Tower

L.Fl.10s
Pye End

1₃

Cork Sand

7

Q(6)+L.Fl.15s
S Cork

Q(3)10s
Roughs Tower

12

N

Stone Banks

3

1₅   2

1

0₅

10

Q(3)10s
NE Gunfleet

0	Kilometres	2

| 0 | Nautical miles | 1 |

3

The Naze

Naze Tower

Fl.G.5s
Medusa

4

10

10

Walton on the Naze

Water Tower

2F.G (vert)

Fl.R.5s
Wallet No2

Frinton on Sea

Tall Building ●

Radar Tower

5

7

10

0₃

Holland on Sea

Gunfleet Tower (ruins)

Clacton on Sea

☆☆

5

Fl(4)R.10s
Wallet No4

Gunfleet Old Lt Ho

Q(6)+L.Fl.15s
Gunfleet Spit

Colne Point

4₃

Wallet

12
Gunfleet Sand

Q
N Eagle

Q
Knoll

Fl(2)G.15s
Wallet No 3

12

0₄

East Swin or Kings Channel

Q(9)15s
W Sunk

Q.G
Eagle

Fl(2)R.5s
Wallet No 6

Fl.G.5s
Black Deep No1

L.Fl.10s Bell
Wallet Spitway

10

0₄   Mo(U)Y15s12M
☆ WindFarm MetMast

Sunk Sand

1₃

1₆

2

Iso.10s Bell
Swin Spitway

Q(3)10sBell
No3

Fl(2)R5s
No2

Barrow Deep

HARWICH HARBOUR

Tides	HW Dover +00.50 Range: Springs 3.6m Neaps 2.3m
Charts	Admiralty 1491, Stanford No 6, Imray Y16
Waypoints	Pitching Ground Buoy 51°55'.44N 01°21'.05E Landguard Buoy 51°55'.45N 01°18'.84E
	Cliff Foot Buoy 51°55'.71N 01°18'.54E S Shelf Buoy 51°56'.20N 01°18'.56E
	Guard Buoy 51°57'.08N 01°17'.86E Shotley Spit Buoy 51°57'.21N 01°17'.69E
Hazards	Shipping entering and leaving (Keep clear of dredged channel)

The earliest indirect reference to a harbour at Harwich is to be found in the *Anglo-Saxon Chronicle* for the year 885: 'The same year sent King Alfred a fleet from Kent into East Anglia. As soon as they came to Stourmouth there met them sixteen ships of the pirates and they fought with them, took all ships and slew the men.

As they returned homeward with their booty they met a large fleet of pirates and fought with them the same day, but the Danes had the victory.'

Some people believe that Bloody Point off Shotley owes its name to the first of these two battles, fought more than a thousand years ago.

Nowhere else on the East Coast is there an expanse of protected deep water as extensive as that formed at the junction of the rivers Orwell and Stour, which emerge to the sea as one between Beacon Cliff and Landguard Point.

The Haven Ports, comprising Felixstowe, Harwich and Ipswich, between them now handle so much traffic that there are approximately 35,000 commercial movements annually, day and night. With the deeper dredged channel now open, some of the world's largest container ships use it and small boat sailors must therefore stay well clear of the channel.

The Stena ferry arrives at Parkeston around 1000 and 1900hrs daily and departs about 50 minutes later. These High Speed Craft can create long period wash waves especially near low tide, which cause large, steep-fronted breaking seas on offshore banks such as Cork Sand, Shipwash Bank, Cutler Bank and the Deben Bar Knolls. On their outward passage

Harwich town and the circular Redoubt Fort, looking north up the River Orwell with the River Stour and Shotley Point in the top left and a huge Trinity container terminal at Felixstowe in the top right of the picture

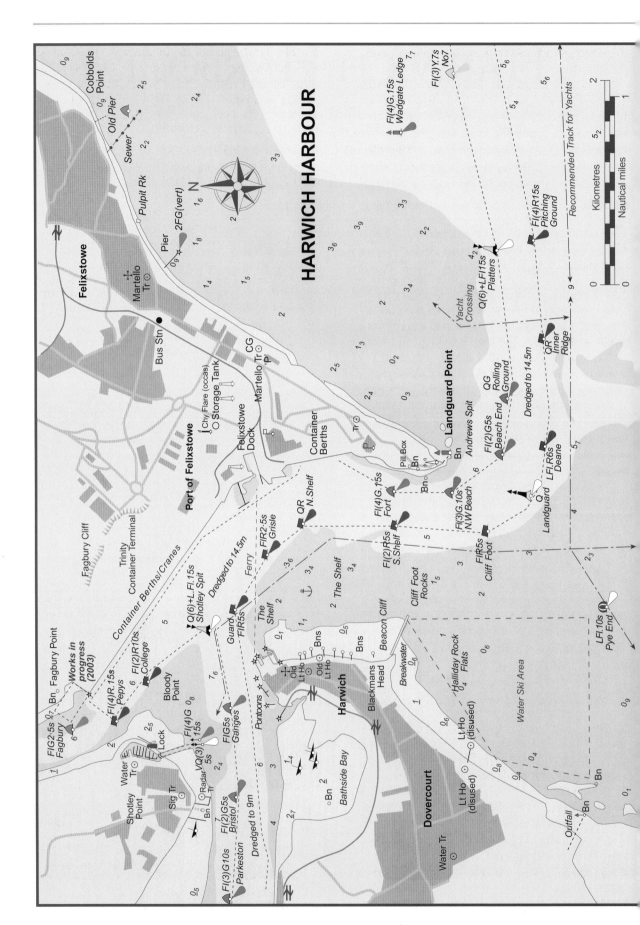

HARWICH HARBOUR

Felixstowe

Cobbolds Point

Old Pier

Sewer

Pulpit Rk

Pier

2FG(vert)

N

Martello Tr ⊙

Bus Stn

Chy Flare (occas)

Storage Tank

Martello Tr ⊙ CG ⊙

Port of Felixstowe

Felixstowe Dock

Container Berths

Tr ⊙

Pill Box

Landguard Point

Bn

Andrews Spit

Fl(4)G.15s
Wadgate Ledge

Fl(3)Y.7s
No7

Fl(4)R.15s
Pitching Ground

Q(6)+LFl.15s
Platters

QR Inner Ridge

QG Rolling Ground

Fl(2)G.5s Beach End

Q LFl.R.6s Deane

Fl(4)G.15s Fort

Fl(3)G.10s N.W.Beach

Bn

Landguard

Fl.R.5s Cliff Foot

Fl(2)R.5s S.Shelf

Cliff Foot Rocks

Beacon Cliff

Recommended Track for Yachts

Yacht Crossing

Dredged to 14.5m

Kilometres
Nautical miles

QR N.Shelf

Fl.R.2.5s Grisle

Ferry

The Shelf

Fagbury Cliff

Trinity Container Terminal

Container Berths/Cranes

Works in progress (2003)

Fl.G.2.5s Fagbury

Bn. Fagbury Point

Q(6)+L.Fl.15s Shotley Spit

Dredged to 14.5m

Fl(2)R.10s College

Fl(4)R.15s Pepys

Guard. Fl.R.5s

Bloody Point

Fl(4)G Ganges

Fl.G.5s

Pontoons

Old Lt Ho
Old Lt Ho

Bns

Bns

Harwich

Blackmans Head

Halliday Rock Flats

Breakwater

Water Ski Area

LFl.10s Pye End

Lt Ho (disused)

Lt Ho (disused)

Shotley Point

Water Tr ⊙

Radar Tr

Sig Tr

Bn VQ(3).5s

Fl(2)G.5s Bristol

Fl(3)G.10s Parkeston

Dredged to 9m

Bathside Bay

Bn

Dovercourt

Water Tr ⊙

Lt Ho ⊙

Outfall

Bn

Bn

Lock

Fl(4)G.15s

The Shelf

these ferries increase rapidly to full speed after passing the Cork Sand Beacon.

The buoyage and marking of Harwich Harbour and the River Stour are the responsibility of the Harwich Haven Authority. In 2003 a number of yellow special marks (Group Fl Y 20s) with yellow cross topmarks may be established within the harbour approaches, the rivers Stour and Orwell and approaches to Walton Backwaters. They are to measure turbidity.

APPROACHES

From the S or SE the harbour can be approached in small craft by two routes, both avoiding the many shoals and banks that lie off the entrance. The course from the S, through the Medusa Channel, is described in a later chapter under Approaches to Walton Backwaters, and the same directions will serve until the Landguard Buoy (BY N Card Q) is in sight.

Another way into Harwich Harbour from the SE is through a channel known as the Gullet, passing about midway between the Medusa (Con G Fl G 5s) and the S Cork (S Card) and leaving the unlit Stonebanks (Can R) to port.

From the E the main deep water channel is exceptionally well marked by pairs of buoys, starting with the Shipway (S Card) and Cross (Y Pillar) buoys out beyond the Cork Sand.

Because of the big ship traffic, a yacht needs to keep to a track south of the well marked dredged channel.

When approaching Harwich Harbour from the Deben or the Alde, the deep water channel must be crossed as quickly as possible to keep away from the berths at the Port of Felixstowe. The recommended crossing point is from between the Platters (S Card) buoy and the Rolling Ground (G) buoy, to a point between the Pitching Ground (R) buoy and the Inner Ridge (R) buoy.

When approaching from the E it is best for yachts to keep to the S of the dredged channel, past the Cork Sand, Pitching Ground and Inner Ridge buoys, before turning to the N, leaving the Landguard and Cliff Foot buoys to starboard.

The old disused leading light towers on the Harwich shore, built in the time of Charles II and still standing, no longer serve as aids to navigation, but the lower one now houses a maritime museum.

The harbour is entered between Beacon Cliff breakwater to the W and Landguard Point, with its conspicuous radar tower, to the E. The width of the entrance is rather less than a mile including the water over the Cliff Foot Rocks, located 1.5 to

3 cables off the end of the breakwater. These rocks have as little as 2m over them at LWS and, when entering the harbour from Dovercourt Bay, they can be avoided by passing within a cable of the beacon on the end of the breakwater. Whenever the latter course is taken it is important to continue in a north-easterly direction over towards the Felixstowe shore after clearing the breakwater. Any temptation to turn to the N across the Guard shoal must be resisted until a position has been reached about midway between the Harwich and Felixstowe shores, near the N Shelf red can buoy. The Guard shoal has no

HARWICH PORT GUIDE	
Harbour Master	Tel 01255 243030 or 243000
Harbour Operation Harbour Patrol Launch	Listen on VHF Ch 71 (summer weekends 0800 to 1800) provides assistance and advice VHF Ch 11
Moorings	Pontoon berths at Halfpenny Pier (free 0900 to 1600, pay piermaster other times)
Water	Halfpenny Pier
Toilets, showers, waste disposal	Halfpenny Pier
Stores	Shops in town inc Co-op. EC Wed
Fuel	Nearest garage in Dovercourt
Repairs	Chandlery in town
Transport	Good train service to London. Buses from quayside to Colchester, Manningtree, Walton-on-the-Naze. Coach service to London Passenger Ferry service Baines Boats – Parkeston, Felixstowe, Shotley and the Orwell (weekends Easter to September, daily in summer months) Tel 07970 115382 (mobile) or VHF Ch M (ex-37)
Clubs	Harwich and Dovercourt Sailing Club Harwich Town Sailing Club
Food and Drink	Harwich Pier Hotel (two restaurants), Halfpenny Pier Cafe, pubs in town. Fresh fish from Pier Seafoods

Harwich Haven Authority's annual Guide to Harwich Harbour and its Rivers is available free from Navigation House, Angel Gate, Harwich CO12 3EJ

Chapter 6

Yachts can lie alongside both sides of the Haven Authority pontoons at Halfpenny Pier, a convenient way to go ashore for a meal or a walk around the historic town of Harwich

more than a metre over it in patches at LWS.

The E or Felixstowe shore is entirely given over to container docks that are in constant use: ferries, including the twice-daily HSS (High Speed Craft), operate frequently from Parkeston Quay. It is therefore prudent to keep a very sharp lookout for movement of ships or ferries berthing or leaving the port and to keep to the recommended yacht track on the Harwich side.

Harbour Operations frequency, VHF Ch 71, is extremely busy at all times and yachtsmen are asked not to use it. However, it is useful to monitor that frequency in order to anticipate the movements of shipping. On weekends during the summer months the Harbour Patrol Launch will provide assistance and advice to yachtsmen and maintains a listening watch on VHF Ch 11.

ANCHORAGES

There are several areas within which anchoring is always prohibited because of the necessity to maintain a clear passage for the heavy traffic to and from Ipswich, Parkeston Quay, Harwich and Felixstowe. The principal areas prohibited are:

(1) Anywhere in the fairway or within 200ft thereof between Parkeston Quay and the Rolling Ground buoy.

(2) Between the western edge of the dredged channel and a line joining the Guard and Shelf buoys.

HARWICH QUAY

The UK lighthouse authority, Trinity House, has a long tradition in Harwich – Trinity Pier, the waterfront buildings and buoy store have been its main operations base for 190 years.

Harwich Haven Authority pontoon mooring berths, which can be used overnight, are located at Harwich Quay between Halfpenny (Town) and Trinity Piers. Mooring is on a first come first served basis and is free between 0900 and 1600; there is a fee for staying outside these hours which is collected by the Pier Master. In good weather it may be possible for yachts to double or triple berth on both sides of the outer pontoon. Fishing vessels moor inside the pontoon and alongside the quay. Water, showers and toilets are nearby.

Halfpenny Pier, overlooked by the Pier Hotel,

Harwich is steeped in maritime history

has been redeveloped with the opening of the Cafe on the Pier (open daily serving all day breakfasts among other food) and Pier Seafoods, selling fresh fish. A seasonal passenger ferry service runs from the Pier to Felixstowe, Parkeston and Shotley.

Harwich town offers historic attractions, most of them nautical, around every corner. Among the many museums open during summer months are the Maritime Museum in the Low Lighthouse, the Lifeboat Museum, the Redoubt fort, the Wireless and TV Museum in the High Lighthouse and the RNLI Boathouse museum. The ancient treadmill crane is on the green near the lighthouses, and town tours are organised from the Ha'Penny Pier visitor centre.

Much of the large expanse of drying mud known as Bathside Bay, to the W of Harwich and N of Dovercourt, is due to be filled in as a new container port is constructed to double existing cargo facilities at Harwich.

SHOTLEY

On the north shore at Shotley there is good anchorage except in strong southerly or westerly winds. Probably the best spot to choose is inside the trot of moorings situated about two cables SE of Shotley Pier. Three or four metres with a mud bottom is easy to find here, within a short distance from both the hard and the pier.

The Ganges training base is no more. Only the flagstaff remains to remind us that once a year some brave cadet would stand proudly atop its cap.

The Electric Palace cinema in King's Quay Street, Harwich, is a 1911 picture palace with a beautifully-restored auditorium

SHOTLEY POINT MARINA

To reach the marina from Shotley Spit S Cardinal buoy, a yacht should proceed parallel to the deep water channel into the River Stour, passing close N of the conical green Ganges buoy to the posts marking the outer end of the dredged channel leading to the marina lock-gates. The port-hand post is yellow and black Q (3) 5s and the starboard-hand post is green Fl (4) G 15s.

A special form of indicating signal operates at the Shotley marina to facilitate keeping to the dredged channel leading to the lock (which is manned 24 hours a day). The INOGON system, as it is called, depends upon the 'passive interaction between the helmsman's line of vision and a mosaic pattern produced by the leading mark.' The practical result is that when a yacht is

A yacht aground on Shotley Spit at LW, looking across from the Orwell to the Stour and Parkeston beyond. Shotley Point Marina is on the right of the picture

on the correct bearing, a vertical black line will be seen down the middle of the screen, while any deviation from the correct course will cause the moire pattern to form arrows indicating whether course should be changed to port or to starboard. The density of the arrow pattern will indicate how great the correction should be.

There are waiting pontoons on the port-hand just outside the lock. A passenger ferry service links Shotley with Harwich and Felixstowe, calling at the marina Easter to mid September at weekends and daily during summer months.

FELIXSTOWE DOCK

When, in 1886, Colonel Tomline dug out a dock at the end of his private railway, he could never have dreamed of the port of Felixstowe as it is today.

The container terminal at Felixstowe now extends up river almost as far as Fagbury Point and the original dock is no longer suitable for yachts, even as a temporary berth. Anchoring in the vicinity is strictly prohibited.

Gone are the days of *Goblin* anchored here while Jim rowed ashore for petrol in *We Didn't Mean to Go to Sea*.

SHOTLEY POINT MARINA PORT GUIDE	
Telephone	01473 788982 VHF Ch 80, M (ex-37) www.shotleymarina.co.uk
Berths	350
Water	On pontoons
Fuel	Diesel just inside marina, petrol from garage in Shotley
Gas	Calor and camping gaz from lock control tower (collect at lock gates)
Stores	During summer months, plus off-licence
Repairs	Full range of services, 30 ton travel-lift, 10 ton crane
Chandler	On site
Transport	Bus service from Shotley to Ipswich Passenger Ferry Service Baines Boats – Felixstowe, Harwich, Parkeston (seasonal Easter to September) Tel 07970 115382 or VHF Ch M (ex-37)
Telephones	In shower block and in Shipwreck lobby
Food and Drink	Restaurant and Shipwreck pub with two bars at marina (breakfast available in summer months), Bristol Arms pub in Shotley village

Shotley Point Marina can be entered via a lock at all states of the tide – in this picture a yacht is passing the waiting pontoons on her way out. The water tower in the trees above the marina is a conspicuous landmark

THE RIVER ORWELL

Tides	HW Dover +0100 Range: Springs 3.7m Neaps 2.3m. HW Ipswich approx 15mins after Pin Mill
Charts	Admiralty 2693, Stanford No 6, Imray Y16, OS Map No 169
Waypoints	Pepys 51°57'.74N 01°16'.90E, College Buoy 51°57'.55N 01°17'.33E
	Orwell No 1 Buoy 51°58'.28N 01°16'.66E
Hazard	Large ships in narrow dredged channel

In his book *Orwell Estuary*, WG Arnott commented on the unchanging nature of much of the river: 'One wonders that the river and its surroundings remain so unspoilt and have suffered so little from the overspill of Ipswich. For this we have largely to thank the much maligned landowners of the estates along its banks. These estates represented a system for which some will say there is little moral justification, but…in the case of the Orwell (it) has saved its banks from spoilation.'

In the year 2000, nearly 50 years later, the river from Collimer Point to the Orwell Bridge is still lined with delightful wooded banks and sandy foreshores, just as Arnott described it in 1954.

The Orwell extends for about nine miles in a general north-westerly direction from the northern side of Harwich Harbour to the docks at Ipswich.

Commercial traffic uses the river, some of which is surprisingly large. For the benefit of these ships, up to 20 a week, a dredged and well-buoyed channel is provided by the Ipswich Port Authority.

On leaving Harwich Harbour, the entrance to the Orwell lies between Shotley Point to the W and the northern extension of Felixstowe's deep-water quays to the E. The two channel marks indicating the entrance are Shotley Spit Buoy (S Card YB Q (6)+L Fl 15s) and the red can College buoy (Fl(2)10s) on the west bank opposite the Trinity container terminal. This terminal, the UK's

Looking north up the River Orwell from Harwich. The Trinity container terminal at Felixstowe, on the right, now extends to Fagbury Point and is constantly in use by very large ships

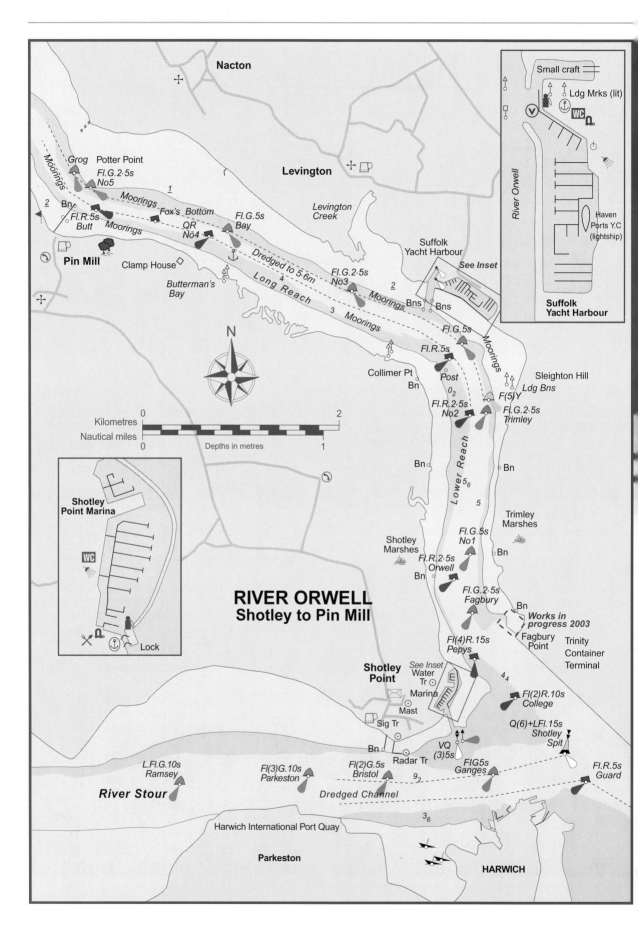

Nacton

Levington

Grog Potter Point
Fl.G.2·5s
No5

Moorings
Moorings
Fox's Bottom
Bn
Fl.R.5s
Butt
Moorings
QR
No4
Fl.G.5s
Bay
Levington
Creek

Pin Mill
Clamp House
Butterman's
Bay
Dredged to 5·6m
Long Reach
Fl.G.2·5s
No3
Moorings

Suffolk
Yacht Harbour

See Inset

Bns
Bns

Fl.G.5s

Fl.R.5s

Collimer Pt
Bn
Post
Fl.R.2·5s
No2

Moorings

Sleighton Hill
Ldg Bns

F(5)Y
Fl.G.2·5s
Trimley

Bn
Bn

Lower Reach

Trimley
Marshes

Bn

Fl.G.5s
No1

N

Kilometres
Nautical miles
0   2
Depths in metres
0   1

Shotley
Point Marina

WC

Lock

Shotley
Marshes
Fl.R.2·5s
Orwell
Bn

Fl.G.2·5s
Fagbury

Bn
*Works in
progress 2003*
Fagbury
Point
Trinity
Container
Terminal

RIVER ORWELL
Shotley to Pin Mill

Fl(4)R.15s
Pepys

**Shotley
Point**
See Inset
Water
Tr
Marina

Mast

Sig Tr

Bn

Radar Tr

Fl(2)R.10s
College

Q(6)+LFl.15s
Shotley
Spit

VQ
(3)5s

Fl.R.5s
Guard

L.Fl.G.10s
Ramsey

Fl(3)G.10s
Parkeston

Fl(2)G.5s
Bristol

FIG5s
Ganges

Dredged Channel

River Stour

Harwich International Port Quay

Parkeston

HARWICH

Small craft
Ldg Mrks (lit)
WC

River Orwell

Haven
Ports Y.C
(lightship)

**Suffolk
Yacht Harbour**

The sailing barge, Lady Jean, *on the Sail Barge Association mooring at Buttermans Bay, with the National Trust woods and Clamp House in the background*

SUFFOLK YACHT HARBOUR PORT GUIDE	
Yacht Hbr office	Tel 01473 659465 VHF Ch 80 and M (ex-37) (Daylight hours)
Berths	500
Water	Near entrance. All pontoons
Fuel	Petrol and diesel from pumps near entrance, gas from chandler
Stores	Provisions and off-licence on site
Repairs	Shipwrights, sailmaker Quantum Parker & Kay 01473 659878, and engineers on site. Travelhoist, slipway and scrubbing posts
Chandler	Store on site 01473 659240
Telephone	Available
Transport	Buses Felixstowe and Ipswich (1 mile walk). Local taxi service
Club	Haven Ports YC aboard LV87 Tel 01473 659658 during opening hours
Food and Drink	Bar and restaurant at YC, The Ship Inn, Levington Tel 01473 659573

longest continuous quay (2,084m), was being extended in 2003 so that it can handle two of the largest container ships at the same time, increasing container throughput to 415,000 per year. Some ships are unable to turn off the berths and have to manoeuvre stern first to or from the swinging area E of Shotley Spit and Guard buoys.

There is an average depth of 7.5m in the main channel, for a width of about two cables, although at HW, with the mud all covered, the width from bank to bank is almost a mile.

When entering the Orwell from the Stour it is not necessary to round Shotley Spit buoy, which can be safely left a cable or so to starboard.

EAST SHOTLEY

Barges used to be seen lying at anchor just inside the river on the W shore, roughly NE of E Shotley Martello Tower (now topped by a large green water tank). However, the proximity of the extended Trinity container terminal on the opposite bank makes the Stone Heaps anchorage less desirable these days.

The red can lit buoys, Pepys and College, up

Chapter 7

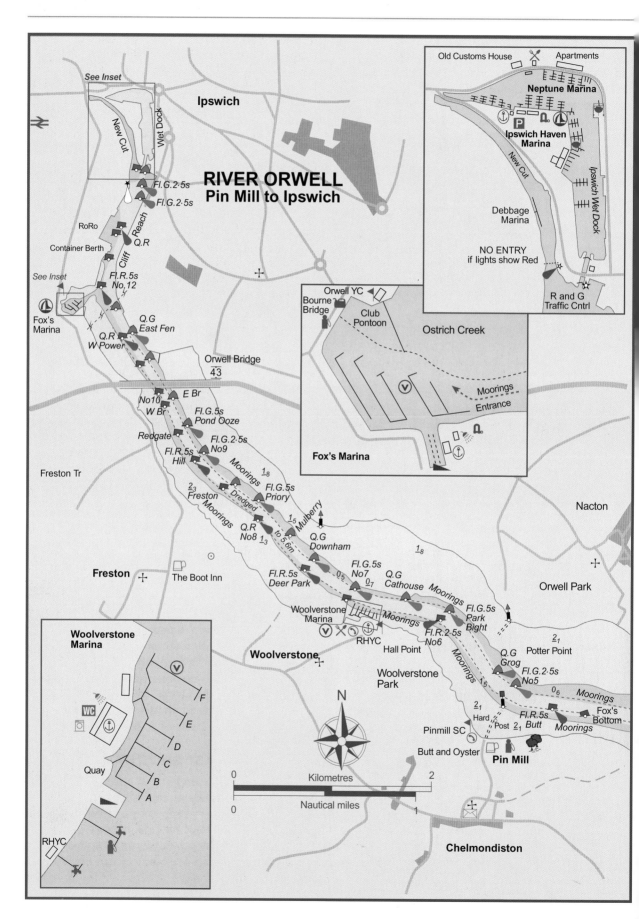

RIVER ORWELL
Pin Mill to Ipswich

Ipswich

See Inset

New Cut

Wet Dock

Fl.G.2·5s

Fl.G.2·5s

RoRo

Cliff Reach

Q.R

Container Berth

See Inset

Fl.R.5s
No.12

Fox's Marina

Q.R
W Power

Q.G
East Fen

Orwell Bridge
4·3

No10
E Br
W Br

Redgate

Fl.G.5s
Pond Ooze

Freston Tr

Fl.R.5s
Hill

Fl.G.2·5s
No9

Moorings

1·8

Dredged

2·3
Freston

Q.R
No8 1·3

Fl.G.5s
Priory

1·5

Mulberry

to 5·6m

Moorings

Q.G
Downham

1·8

Freston

The Boot Inn

Fl.R.5s
Deer Park

0·5

Fl.G.5s
No7

0·7

Q.G
Cathouse

Moorings

Q.G
Grog

Nacton

Orwell Park

Fl.G.5s
Park Bight

2·1

Woolverstone Marina

Moorings

RHYC

Hall Point

Fl.R.2·5s
No6

Potter Point

Fl.G.2·5s
No5

0·6
Moorings

Woolverstone

Woolverstone Park

Moorings

1·5

Fox's Bottom

Moorings

2·1

Hard
Post 2·1

Fl.R.5s
Butt

Pinmill SC

Butt and Oyster

Pin Mill

N

Chelmondiston

Bourne Bridge inset
Orwell YC

Club Pontoon

Ostrich Creek

Moorings

Entrance

Fox's Marina

Ipswich inset
Old Customs House

Apartments

Neptune Marina

P

Ipswich Haven Marina

Debbage Marina

Ipswich Wet Dock

New Cut

NO ENTRY
if lights show Red

R and G
Traffic Cntrl

Woolverstone Marina inset
Woolverstone Marina

V

WC

F

E

D

C

B

A

Quay

RHYC

Scale bar
0 Kilometres 2
0 Nautical miles 1

river of Shotley Point Marina, and the green conical buoy (Fl G 2.5s) off Fagbury Point are maintained by the Harwich Harbour Authority, but all of the other buoys in the Orwell are the responsibility of the Ipswich Port Authority. The first pair of their buoys are the Orwell (red can F1R 2.5s) and No 1 (Con G F1G 5s). A telegraph cable crosses the river between Fagbury Point and the Shotley shore, its precise position being indicated by red and white beacons with diamond-shaped topmarks. Other cables cross the river further up and are all marked in the same way, with a beacon on each shore.

Above Fagbury Point the river follows a northerly direction through Lower Reach to Collimer Point. There is low, marshy ground on either side of Lower Reach, but behind the marshes are hills which close in on the river abreast Collimer Point. A little below the point is a pair of buoys marking the width of the channel that is dredged to 6m all the way up to Ipswich. The starboard-hand green conical buoy of the pair is marked Trimley and it flashes green every 2.5 seconds. Abreast of Collimer Point itself is a second pair of buoys – both of which are lit. There is also a tide gauge on the Point, and inshore of that are the remains of another of the hards that once were in regular use along both banks of the river. On the opposite shore it is also possible to land fairly conveniently just S of a small area of saltings below Sleighton Hill. There are a few small boat moorings nearby.

After rounding Collimer Point and entering Long Reach, the direction of the river becomes north-westerly and the true character of the Orwell is revealed.

Just above Collimer Point, on the N side of the river, is the Suffolk Yacht Harbour at Stratton Hall, near Levington Creek. The entrance to the harbour is a dredged channel about 30m wide, holding some 1.5m of water at LW neaps.

The entrance channel is marked at its outer end by a spherical orange buoy and then by port and starboard poles with topmarks. There are leading lights at night. (Outer Iso Y 1s and Inner Oc Y 3s + 1s).

Visitors can, if there is space, temporarily leave their yachts at a pontoon just inside and opposite the entrance, while reporting to the harbour master for instructions. The harbour has been extended over the years and now provides 500 permanent berths plus visitors. The focal point of the pontoons is the Haven Ports Yacht Club HQ on the old Cromer light vessel No 87. From the yacht harbour a pleasant walk of just over a mile

Suffolk Yacht Harbour photographed from the air in 2003. In the lower right corner of the picture, a new deep water harbour is being constructed for completion in 2004

Chapter 7

The wide upper hard and scrubbing posts at Pin Mill, with a Harwich One-Design being fitted out in the foreground

will bring you to the village of Levington and the Ship Inn.

Deep draught boats, unsure of the entrance, can sometimes find a mooring free near the entrance buoy. The row of moorings extends below and well above the Suffolk Yacht Harbour, and there is also a row on the opposite shore.

The next buoy, No 3 (Con G Fl G 2.5s), lies off the entrance to Levington Creek, which is marked by withies. This little drying gutway was once regularly used by trading barges and it is still possible to sound a way up to the old wharf at the head of the creek. Between Levington and Potter Point there is another pair of lit buoys – the Bay is conical green with a flashing green 5s light, while its opposite – a red can buoy No 4 – has a Q flashing red light.

There is the possibility of anchoring on the S side, just below No 4 buoy near Clamp House, where there will be shelter from the SW and landing is possible. This time-honoured anchorage, known as Buttermans Bay, is where the grain ships, barques and barquentines used to offload their cargoes into sailing barges. The mooring buoys are now used by the Sail Barge Association. A footpath to Pin Mill leads through the National Trust woods at Clamp House, while behind the woods on the opposite shore is Broke Hall, once the home of Admiral Broke of the Shannon.

PIN MILL

For the East Coast cruising man, the Orwell means Pin Mill and it is this unique hamlet, with its waterside inn and the prospect of a collection of spritties on the hard, that brings us back time and time again. Arthur Ransome sailed from Pin Mill and described it as '...that most charming anchorage'. The opening chapters of both *We Didn't Mean to Go to Sea* and *Secret Water* are set at Alma Cottage, just up the lane from the Butt and Oyster.

It is preferable to find a mooring rather than drop an anchor at Pin Mill. Visitors' buoys are generally located in the trot of moorings nearest to the channel, starting approximately 400 yards up river from Fox's Bottom buoy and again from just above the Butt buoy. Visitors should pick up a mooring with the name *Ward* on it, which also usually shows a mobile telephone number with which to contact the harbour master Tony Ward. In 2003 the charge was £6 per night; yachts of up

to 34ft can normally be accommodated.
Commercial shipping rounding Potter Point
passes very close to the outer rows of moorings
and occasionally leaves considerable wash.

The very long hard at Pin Mill is still not long
enough to provide landing at low water springs.
You may have to wait an hour or more to avoid
the mud, and boots are advisable. When the tide
is rising it is as well to haul the dinghy well
up the gulley formed by the Grindle, a stream
running down the side of the hard.

The upper hard at Pin Mill is no half-hearted
affair, but a fine expanse of firm shingle on which
there are sometimes barges undergoing repair.
Scrubbing, too, is made easy by reason of the
several stout posts that are available. At the top
of the hard is the Butt and Oyster Inn, itself
awash at HW springs. The hard continues, almost
imperceptibly, straight into a lane that leads up
the valley to Chelmondiston.

Visiting yachtsmen are welcome at Pin Mill
SC, whose clubhouse is by the riverside just
beyond the yard of Harry King and Sons,
builders of *Selina King* for Arthur Ransome and
many other wooden boats, several to designs of
Maurice Griffiths.

*The Pin Mill foreshore – described by Arthur Ransome as
'...that most charming anchorage'*

PIN MILL PORT GUIDE

Harbour Master	Tony Ward Tel and Fax 01473 780621; Mobile 0771 4260568; email: moorings.pinmill@virgin.net
Water	Tap at The Sail Loft chandlery and alongside clubhouse at Pin Mill SC
Stores	Limited at chandlery. General store and butcher at Chelmondiston, EC Wed
Chandler	The Sail Loft on left at top of hard. Tel 01473 780945
Fuel	Only paraffin (pre-packed) from chandler
Repairs	Kings or Webbs boatyards
Scrubbing post	On hard. (For use, consult HM)
Transport	Bus service to Ipswich and Shotley from Chelmondiston
Club	Pin Mill Sailing Club
Telephone	In public car park, 100 yards up the lane
Food and Drink	The Butt & Oyster Tel 01473 780764. Chinese Take-Away restaurant in Chelmondiston

CHELMONDISTON

Chelmondiston – Chelmo for short – is about
three-quarters of a mile from the hard at
Pin Mill, and the walk up the lane seems to
belong to Devon rather than Suffolk. There is
Hollingsworths butcher's and general store, the
Venture pub (formerly the Red Lion), plus a
Chinese take-away in this busy little village.

Above Pin Mill the channel turns more
northerly into Potter Reach, and about two cables
beyond the buoy marking Potter Point, on the
eastern shore, is a hard that can be used at most
states of the tide to land in Orwell Park. No 6
buoy (R can Fl 2.5s) marks the mud off Hall
Point, while a green conical buoy (Fl G 5s) on the
other side of the channel is located in Park Bight,
together with a continuous line of moorings used
by craft based on Woolverstone Marina.

WOOLVERSTONE

The dredged channel now approaches the W
bank of the river to within a cable, abreast the
'Cathouse' buoy (Con G Fl G 1s). Under no
circumstances should a boat anchor inside the
buoyed channel, as vessels up to 9,000 tons use
the river regularly. The Cathouse is a 200-year-old

gothic cottage built by the riverside in the grounds of Woolverstone Hall. Legend has it that a silhouette of a cat was placed in the window overlooking the Orwell to show approaching smugglers that the coast was clear. A footpath from Cathouse Hard winds through Woolverstone Park and along the shoreside to Pin Mill.

On the S bank below Cathouse Hard, the Royal Harwich Yacht Club has serviced pontoon berthing for members' yachts: berths on the outside pontoons are designated for visitors and overnight stays are possible. The club was formed in 1845 and by 1848 was holding the first Eastern Coast Regatta in Harwich Harbour, its head-quarters for the next hundred years. In 1946 the club moved up-river to its fine present-day site at Woolverstone where its members sail cruisers, dinghies, Ajax keelboats and the 60-year-old RH One-Designs. The RHYC is happy to allow visiting yachtsmen to use its clubhouse and facilities which, during the season, consist of showers, restaurant and a bar.

Immediately upstream, just S of the dredged channel, is the Woolverstone Marina where 300 pontoon berths are accessible at all times. Visitors can berth on the ends of any pontoon or on Pontoon 'F', the last one upstream. A Marina Master is on duty seven days a week throughout the year, while facilities include a fuel barge at the end of the short pier, a chandlery and stores as well as the on site Schooner Club restaurant.

No 7 buoy (Con G Fl G 5s), together with a red can (Fl R 5s), mark the commencement of Downham Reach and here the dredged channel becomes less than a cable wide so that the buoys must be strictly observed unless it is near HW. Another unlit green conical buoy marks the eastern edge of the channel through Downham Reach; the western edge is indicated first by a lit red can (Fl R 5s) and then by No 8, a red can light buoy (Fl R 5s) abreast the prominent tower in Freston Park. Just above No 8 buoy there is a green conical buoy (Fl G 5s) called the Priory, on the east side of the channel. The next pair of lit buoys are the Hill (Fl R 5s) and No 9 (Fl G 2.5s).

Along here are a number of small boat moorings just outside the channel on both sides. They belong to the Stoke SC whose clubhouse is just below Freston Tower. From Freston Hard it is a short walk up the road to the Boot Inn on Freston Hill where they serve freshly cooked

WOOLVERSTONE PORT GUIDE		
Woolverstone Marina		
	Tel 01473 780206; email: woolverstone@mdlmarinas.co.uk	
Berths	300	
VHF	Chs 80 and M (ex-37)	
Water	From end of pier	
Diesel fuel	From end of pier	
Gas	From Marina Master's office	
Repairs	Medusa Marine 01473 780090 Yard equipped for all services. Slipway, 25-ton mobile crane	
Showers and Launderette	On site	
Chandler	On site	
Stores	From Pantry on site	
Clubs	Royal Harwich Yacht Club Tel 01473 780319; www.rhyc.demon.co.uk A limited number of visitors' berths on pontoons; showers, restaurant and bar daily during season except Mondays Stoke SC 01473 780815	
Telephone	Kiosk on hard	
Food and Drink	Schooner Club at marina. Royal Harwich YC restaurant and bar. The Boot Inn, Freston Tel 01473 780277	

food and in front of which buses stop on the Shotley-Ipswich route.

By now the Orwell Bridge will dominate the view ahead, but since it provides a clearance of 125ft (38m) and the width between the only navigable span is 300ft (92m) it should inconvenience yachtsmen very little. No ship can hit any of the eight piers that rise from the river bed because their bases are all protected by artificial islands.

However, the bridge crosses the navigable channel at an angle so that the pilot of any commercial vessel about to pass under it will have his attention fully occupied without having to worry about any nearby yacht. Common sense therefore dictates that whenever possible the yachtsman should avoid being in the vicinity of the bridge if a commercial vessel is passing through.

There is an unlit port hand buoy, No 10, opposite the green conical No 11 buoy very near the bridge where the dredged channel is only about half a cable wide.

A green conical buoy, the E Fen (QG), marks the east side of the channel above the bridge, with lit buoys West Power and No 12 Cliff Reach Buoy (Can R Fl R 5s) on the west side.

The River Orwell is lined with delightful wooded banks and sandy foreshores from Collimer Point to the Orwell Bridge

The Orwell YC has both drying and deep water moorings on the W side of the river up to the West Bank Container Dock; there is a visitor's mooring near No 12 buoy. The last buoy with a light is the red can Factory buoy (QR) off the container terminal, although there are several more unlit buoys leading right up to the entrance to the Wet Dock.

OSTRICH CREEK AND FOX'S MARINA

Just before the No 12 red can channel buoy, a small RWVS barrel buoy indicates the entrance to Ostrich Creek through which a little stream, Belstead Brook, enters the river Orwell after flowing under Bourne Bridge. Having passed the RWVS barrel buoy, a port-hand beacon indicates the way into the creek, where the Orwell Yacht Club and Fox's Marina are situated.

In a small pool on the starboard-hand are three posts to which visitors may moor overnight – given permission from the yacht club. Beyond the posts is the club's floating pontoon, accessible at all times.

Fox's 100-berth marina and boatyard is situated next to Bourne Bridge. Entrance is through a dredged gutway off Ostrich Creek, marked on both sides by beacons. Facilities include travel lifts, workshops and a very large chandlery. The Oyster Reach Beefeater pub, formerly The Ostrich inn, is nearby.

BOURNE BRIDGE PORT GUIDE	
Fox's Marina	Tel 01473 689111; VHF Ch 80 and M (ex-37)
Berths	100
Water	Marina pontoons; at Orwell YC
Stores	Shops nearby
Petrol and Oil	Garage adjacent to clubhouse
Gas	From marina
Chandlery	At marina, open 7 days a week
Repairs	Travelifts and extensive facilities at marina boatyard
Transport	Buses into Ipswich ($1\frac{1}{2}$ miles). Good train service from Ipswich to London
Telephone	At marina, at club, or box nearby
Clubs	Orwell Yacht Club Tel 01473 602288; Fox's Marina YC

Chapter 7

IPSWICH DOCK

When it was opened in 1850 the Wet Dock at Ipswich was the largest in Europe and right up to the 1930s it was being used by square rigged grain ships. Now there are two marinas in the dock and much of the quayside is being developed.

The 100-berth Neptune Marina is at Neptune Quay on the Historic Waterfront, to the east of the Old Custom House. Yard facilities include a 40 ton travel hoist while shops and restaurants are nearby and Ipswich town centre is within a 10-minute walk.

Established in 2000 by Associated British Ports, the Ipswich Haven Marina has since been extended to offer over 200 pontoon berths and is situated on the south side, opposite the Old Custom House on the peninsula between the New Cut and the Wet Dock. Haven Marina has toilets, shower and laundry facilities, a 70 ton boat hoist and a repair shop. The Last Anchor waterfront bar and restaurant is on site, open seven days a week from 8am, and the town centre is only a short walk away.

New lockgates were installed in 2000 allowing most vessels 24-hour access to the dock; in practice this means the gates will be opened on demand during working hours and at other times by prior arrangement. When planning to enter the dock a yacht should contact Orwell Navigation Services before passing under the Orwell Bridge.

The duty officer will give navigation and lock times information. There is a pontoon against which a boat can lie outside the lock while awaiting its opening. For berthing information contact your chosen marina.

The dock is approached along a closely buoyed channel past the Ro-Ro terminal on the port-hand opposite Cliff Quay. Red and green traffic control lights are located above the Orwell Navigation Service building on the E side of the lock.

Yachts should not berth alongside any of the commercial quays without first obtaining permission from the Port Authority.

NEW CUT

Above the lock and to port is New Cut, with Debbage's yard just upstream providing drying pontoon moorings, water and diesel fuel,

Ipswich Dock is entered via a lock with 24-hour access. Once inside there are two marinas – Ipswich Haven and Neptune – both convenient for Ipswich town centre

The navigable head of the River Orwell looking towards the Wet Dock at the top centre right. In the foreground is Fox's Marina at Bourne Bridge

repairs and a 20-ton crane. Shops are nearby (EC Wed). Ipswich station is about half a mile away. There is a water velocity control structure within the entrance to New Cut: when three vertical red lights show, the structure is raised and vessels may not proceed.

IPSWICH

Beginning with the arrival of the Vikings, Ipswich has a long maritime history. When Defoe came in 1668 he described it as 'the greatest town in England for large colliers or coal ships employed between Newcastle and London...' Later, the spritsail barge fleets of Cranfield and Paul carried wheat, while others brought coal or potash for Fisons, loam for the foundries, or cattle feed. Outward-bound they would pick up a (hay)stack, carrots or mangolds (mangelwurzels) from little quaysides at farms up and down the rivers and creeks of the East Coast.

There are themed walks and signed heritage trails around the Wet Dock, along the riverside and through the lanes and streets of Ipswich. Details of the leisure activities, art galleries, museums or Tolly Cobbold Brewery tours are available from the Tourist Information Centre in St Stephen's Church near the Buttermarket shopping centre. Most are within walking distance of the Wet Dock.

IPSWICH PORT GUIDE	
Harbour Master	Tel 01473 211771
Orwell Navigation Service	VHF Ipswich Port Radio Ch 68
Neptune Marina	Tel 01473 215204 (dockside) 780366 (office) VHF Ch 80 or M
Berths	100 plus visitors
Ipswich Haven Marina	Tel 01473 236644; Fax 236645; VHF Ipswich Marina Ch 80 or M; email: ipswichhaven@abports.co.uk
Berths	210
Debbage's Yard	Tel 01473 601169
Stores	Nearby and in town centre
Water	Both marinas
Fuel	Diesel and gas at both marinas, petrol (own cans) nearby
Repairs	Travel lift, cranes, shipwrights, engineering, rigging and full yard facilities at Neptune. Hoist and cranage, repairs by arrangement at Ipswich Haven
Transport	Good train service Ipswich–London (station 10 minute walk from Ipswich Haven Marina)
Telephone	Near Neptune Marina
Food and Drink	The Last Anchor restaurant at Ipswich Haven Marina open from 8am daily; Tel 01473 253106. Numerous other pubs and restaurants on the quayside and nearby

Chapter 7

THE RIVER STOUR

Tides (Wrabness)	HW Dover +01.05 Range: Springs 3.7m Neaps 2.3m
Charts	Admiralty 2693, Stanford No 6, Imray Y16, OS Map No 169
Waypoints	Guard Buoy 51°57'.08N 01°17'.86E; Stour No 12 Buoy 51°56'.93N 01°05'.99E
Hazards	Ferries turning off Parkeston Quay

The River Stour has never been as popular with yachtsmen as the Orwell, for several reasons: Parkeston Quay with its attendant movements of large ferries, the absence of any waterside hamlet to compare with Pin Mill and the difficulty of lying afloat out of the fairway anywhere above Wrabness.

Yet the Stour is quieter and more spacious than the Orwell and, moreover, its twin towns – Mistley and Manningtree – have been called 'two of the best-looking places in Essex.' There are RSPB sanctuaries on the north bank between Shotley and Erwarton Ness and on the south shore between Parkeston and Wrabness.

Frequent ferries and a high speed Sea Cat operate from the Ro Ro terminals at Parkeston Quay, but it is not difficult to keep clear of them, since even at low water the channel is almost half a mile wide. There is still some coaster traffic up the Stour to the Baltic Wharf at Mistley.

However, beyond Wrabness the width of the low-tide channel narrows rather abruptly.

Although well buoyed, it does involve a risk of grounding, particularly when a first passage is attempted whilst the wide mud flats are covered. But this objection is not peculiar to the Stour, since much the same conditions are found in the upper tidal reaches of almost all the rivers of the Thames Estuary.

CHANNEL WIDTHS

The navigable channel extends from Harwich to Manningtree, some nine miles. The Stour separates the counties of Essex and Suffolk, and its general direction is westerly throughout the eight miles or so to Mistley. At high tide the river appears to be a mile or more wide throughout the whole of its length. In fact its width at LW, while

A south cardinal bn marks Erwarton Ness. Upstream, near the derelict quay, there is a good anchorage if the wind is anywhere in the north

nearly half a mile abreast Shotley Pier and much the same from there to Harkstead Point, diminishes rapidly thereafter to about two cables off Wrabness Point and up as far as Stutton Ness. Then, along the mile or so of Straight Reach, the channel again narrows to less than a cable just below Ballast Hill. The final reaches between Ballast Hill and Mistley Quay become narrower still, until abreast the quays the channel at LW is less than 50 metres wide.

The most useful anchorage in the entrance to the Stour is over on the north bank of the river close to Shotley Pier. Anchorage is prohibited in the vicinity of Parkeston Quay. The first useful small boat anchorage above Harwich Harbour is off Erwarton Ness, about a mile and a half west of Parkeston.

There are three starboard hand marks between Parkeston buoy and Harkstead Point; first Ramsey green conical buoy (LFl G 10s), then a S Cardinal beacon (Q (6)+ LFl(2)15s), followed by a green conical buoy (QG). The depth of the water in the channel is never less than 5m, until about a mile below Harkstead Point, when the mid-river water shallows gradually from about 5m to 3.5m abreast the Point.

ERWARTON NESS

With any north in the wind there is a good anchorage off Erwarton Ness about a cable from the derelict quay in line with the S cardinal beacon (Q F1(6) LF1 15s). There is good holding in mud, but no protection from either easterly or westerly winds. Landing is possible near the ruined staithe between half flood and half ebb. Erwarton village is about a mile away, although the inn, the Queen's Head, is a little nearer.

HOLBROOK BAY

Continuing up-river from Erwarton Ness, Harkstead Point is the next low headland on the north shore, while on the south bank, Wrabness Point is notable for its height (40ft) in East Coast waters. Once clear of Harkstead Point and the S cardinal Holbrook beacon (Q Fl(6) LFl 15s), the scene to the north will open out to disclose the extensive buildings and conspicuous central spire of the Royal Hospital School. This impressive piece of neo-Wren-style architecture was built in the 1930s, when the school moved from Greenwich; and from the high ground at Holbrook it commands sweeping views over the Stour.

Looking NE from over Holbrook Bay into Holbrook Creek at LW, where there are few boats on drying moorings. It is possible to land at the head of the creek near HW

Chapter 8

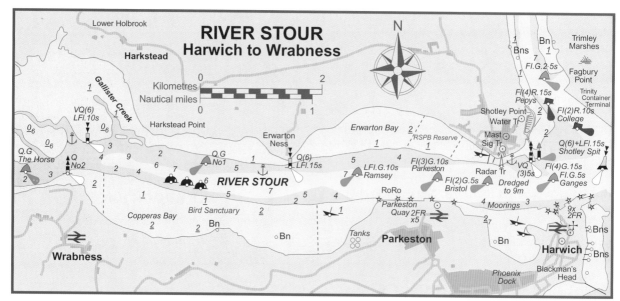

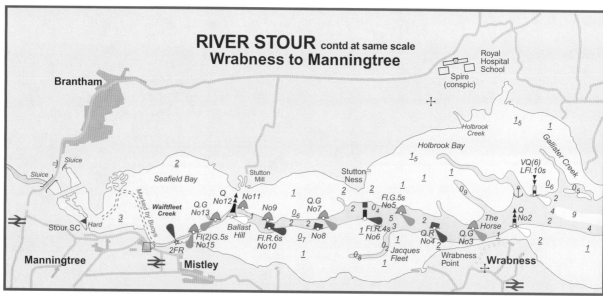

When the tide has no more than half flooded, the extensive mud flats of Holbrook Bay cover an area roughly two miles long and a mile deep. Two or three ill-defined creeks lead across these flats, the more important of them being Gallister Creek and Holbrook Creek. You may see a small fleet of Cornish Shrimpers with an accompanying RIB in this vicinity, crewed by pupils from the Royal Hospital School learning to sail in Holbrook Bay.

GALLISTER CREEK

Some small boat moorings are situated near the entrance, but there is enough water and just enough space to lie quietly to an anchor a cable or so inside Gallister Creek. For landing it is probably better to use Holbrook Creek.

HOLBROOK CREEK

This creek is marked by withies along its western edge and there is enough depth and space to allow anchoring for a quarter of a mile inside. Any exploring further up the creek should be done just before the mud banks are covered and while the gutway can be followed.

Clean landing is possible at the head of Holbrook Creek near HW, from where Holbrook village is about a mile away.

WRABNESS POINT

There used to be a horse (a shoal) in mid-stream off Wrabness, but following extensive dredging for shingle this seems to have merged with the flats on Holbrook Bay so that the only channel now runs close to the point, past a port hand N cardinal beacon (Q) and a conical green (QG) starboard-hand buoy. Because of previous dredging for shingle, the holding ground in the channel off Wrabness is not as safe as it used to be and if there is no vacant mooring, it will usually pay to move a bit further upstream towards the next port-hand buoy. In any case beware of anchoring in mid-channel because of the commercial shipping using Mistley Quay. If stopping overnight, a riding light is essential.

There is no yard or club at Wrabness, so it would be unwise to leave a boat on a vacant mooring.

The village of Wrabness is reached by climbing a pathway up the cliff and following the lane past the church towards the railway station. The church is one of the two in this district which have their bells in a wooden cage-like belfry in the churchyard.

A television mast on the south side of the river provides a conspicuous mark by day and by night.

When continuing up-river from Wrabness a stranger to the Stour will do well to set off before the mud flats are covered and while the course of the channel is visible as well as the buoys which mark it. In these narrow upper reaches the buoys must be given a wide berth whenever it appears that they are being swept by the tide over the banks they are intended to mark.

From the anchorage off Wrabness the channel turns a little N of W for about a mile, past a port-hand buoy (QR) and a conical green buoy (Fl G 5s) to starboard. Jacques Fleet and the bay of the same name are to the south; a few barges may sometimes be lying here.

The next mark is No 6 Beacon (Fl R 4s) with a tide gauge, marking Smith Shoal; it is located about three cables south of Stutton Ness, and the best water here is no more than two cables from the Suffolk shore.

West of Stutton Ness the channel continues for a mile along Straight Reach, becoming narrower and shallower. There are three conical green buoys to be left to starboard and two red cans to be left to port along this reach. Then comes a bottleneck at Ballast Hill, where for a short distance there is a depth of only 1m and a width of less than a cable at LW. The port hand at Ballast Hill is the N cardinal No 12 (QR).

Use of the sounder offers the best chance of getting through here early on the tide. Once past the shingle patch that forms Ballast Hill, there is an isolated widening and deepening of

Mistley is famous for its twin towers, all that remain of the church designed by Robert Adam in 1776

the channel in Cross Reach. This hole provides the only spot in which a boat drawing 1.5m of water can remain afloat within reasonable distance of Mistley.

After Cross Reach the channel turns south-westerly along Waiftfleet Reach and Miller Reach and from hereabouts the warehouses and maltings and the twin towers of the ruined Adam church at Mistley will all come into view.

MISTLEY

The buoyage and marking of the winding channel of the river between Wrabness and Mistley Quay changes considerably over the years, and this makes it very difficult to provide information that will remain reliable throughout the life of an edition.

There is good holding in the channel at Mistley, but the tide runs very hard during the first half of the ebb when the rate can be as high as 4 knots. At Mistley it is HW

Chapter 8

50 minutes later than at Harwich.

Drying moorings, administered by Mistley Marine, are on the port hand side, downstream of Baltic Wharf, which is the commercial part of the quay. It may be possible to moor alongside barges or the quay wall itself, but visiting yachtsmen are advised to contact David Foster at Mistley Marine beforehand.

It is worthwhile going ashore to walk to the top of Furze Hill and enjoy the fine view of the river from there, as well as to see the famous twin towers remaining from the church which Robert Adam designed in 1776.

Mistley has traditional links with sailing barges

classes belonging to the members of the Stour Sailing Club race around a course which takes them right across Seafield Bay to within a cable or so of the Suffolk shore.

At Manningtree, the Stour Sailing Club provides a visitor's mooring – a white buoy located in the creek near the bottom of the hard. Visiting yachtsmen are made welcome at the clubhouse, which incorporates a shower facility. Several shops and a supermarket are situated close to the waterside.

It is only a 10 or 15 minute walk to Manningtree from Mistley along a pleasant riverside road.

ABOVE MISTLEY

With local knowledge, Manningtree can be reached in craft drawing as much as 2m, provided the buoys are carefully observed and you are prepared to take the ground soon after arrival at Manningtree. The quay is not so extensive as at Mistley and there is no water at all at low tide.

In a shallower draught boat, drawing no more than 1m, it is also possible, just before HW, to take the North or Second channel across Seafield Bay direct from Ballast Hill to the bend in the channel known as the Hook. But if you are sailing across the flats off Mistley, look out for the wreck that lies there. The local centreboard

MISTLEY PORT GUIDE	
Mistley Marine	Drying moorings by arrangement, contact David Foster Tel 0850 208918; VHF Ch 71
Water	From the quay
Stores	Several shops in main street near the quay. EC Wed
Fuel	Diesel from Mistley Marine, petrol from garage
Repairs	Lift out and cranage
Transport	Train to London from main line station at Manningtree
Club	Stour Sailing Club
Food and Drink	The Thorn pub – near quayside

At Mistley, Baltic Wharf, to the left in the picture, is still used commercially. The quay walls are not yacht-friendly, although at High Water it may be possible to go alongside temporarily

WALTON BACKWATERS

Tides	Stone Point HW Dover +0040 Range: Springs 3.6m Neaps 2.1m
Charts	Admiralty 2695 Small Craft Edition, Stanford No 6, Imray Y16, OS Map No 169
Waypoints	Stone Banks Buoy 51°53'.19N 01°19'.22E, Pye End Buoy 51°55'.04N 01°17'.88E

The map that Arthur Ransome's *Swallows and Amazons* drew of their secret waters would still serve quite well for navigating the Walton Backwaters, for little has changed except the number of boats. All the creeks give good protection in almost any weather, and the Backwaters are an excellent base from which to make a number of modest cruises to the nearby Stour, Orwell or Deben.

APPROACHES

The entrance to the Backwaters is located about half a mile off the Dovercourt foreshore and half a mile or so south of the mouth of Harwich

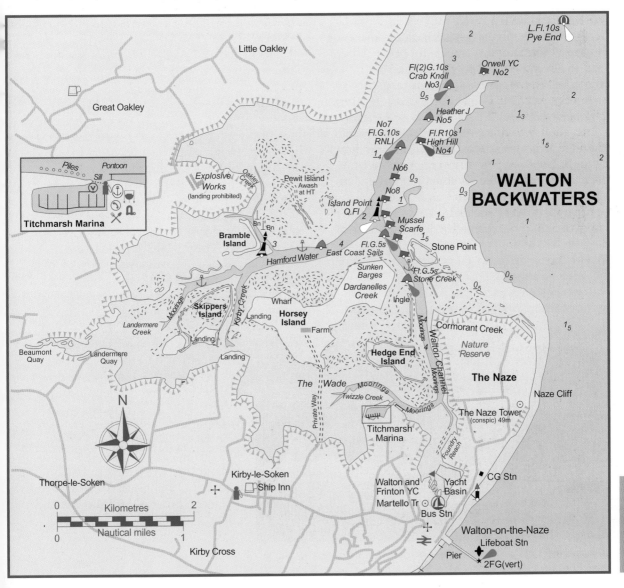

Harbour. Whether approaching from the north or the south, it is necessary to find Pye End buoy (Sph RW L Fl 10s) marking the northern extremity of an area of hard sand known as Pye Sand and the Sunken Pye.

When approaching Harwich from the south through the Wallet and the Medusa channel the most prominent landmark is the Naze Tower, erected by Trinity House in 1720 and standing 160ft above the cliffs just north of Walton-on-the-Naze.

Another conspicuous landmark was added in 1992 in the form of the 187ft radar mast located on the cliff-top between Frinton and Clacton.

The Medusa buoy (Con G Fl G 5s) lies just over two miles E of Walton pier and, from a position midway between the pier and the Medusa, the Naze Tower will bear approximately NW while the next mark, the Stone Banks buoy (Can R can topmark), will lie about three miles away to the NNE. Any less than a mile offshore around the Naze will probably have you bumping the bottom. There is considerable erosion of the cliffs, and as a result a shoal patch seems to be spreading out beneath the tower.

Another problem hereabouts is the multitude of lobster pots that are set by inshore fishermen. However hard one tries it is difficult to avoid them in poor visibility and practically impossible at night. So if you find your progress seems slower than usual, see whether you have a line and pot caught by your rudder or prop.

In good visibility such landmarks as the tall spire of St Nicholas Church at Harwich and the large cranes at the Port of Felixstowe will be seen before the Stone Banks buoy comes up. This buoy, as its name suggests, marks a number of isolated clumps of stones and rocks with no more than 2m over them at LWS. A course only slightly W of N

The Pye End Buoy

from the Stone Banks buoy will bring Harwich breakwater (awash at HW) in view ahead. When about a mile from the breakwater and the entrance to Harwich Harbour, it should be possible in conditions of reasonable visibility to spot the Pye End buoy (Sph RW LFl 10s) which is located approximately one mile due S (°M) from the end of the breakwater and is now the responsibility of the Harwich Harbour Board.

The buildings along the shore of Dovercourt Bay provide a background which makes it rather difficult to locate the buoy. Dovercourt Bay is a designated area for powered craft which launch from a ramp at Harwich Green.

The shallowest part of the approach to the Backwaters is the area known as the Halliday Rock Flats where there is less than 2m in places during LWS. This shoal water will prevent many craft from attempting the entrance before two or three hours of flood. It is spring tide HW hereabouts at approximately midday and midnight. Springs rise 4m and neaps 3m.

When approaching the Backwaters from the north, the well-buoyed big-ship channel should be crossed as quickly as possible and then followed, outside it, as far as the Landguard buoy (N Card YB Q) from which a course of approximately 245°M will lead to the Pye End buoy less than a mile away. This same course, if continued, should find the No 2 red can buoy at the entrance to the channel into the Backwaters.

The narrow channel into the Walton Backwaters over the Pye Sands has been marked for the past 75 years by buoys supplied and maintained by the Walton and Frinton Yacht Club, and in order to ease the cost of laying and raising them the Club has arranged for local firms to sponsor some of them. To assist local craft using the channel at night the No 3 Crab Knoll green conical, No 4 High Hill red can, No 7 green conical, the N Cardinal Island Point buoy and the next two green conicals are all lit.

However, even in bright daylight, the newcomer will look to the SW from

The steep-to shingle and sand landing place at Stone Pt makes the anchorage a popular destination on fine days

Island Point N cardinal

East Coast Sails Buoy

abreast the Pye-End buoy and find it difficult to believe that any kind of deep water channel lies ahead. But after sailing in a generally south-westerly direction for a quarter of a mile or so, the next buoys – No 2, a red can buoy, and No 3 (Crab Knoll), a green lit buoy (Fl G) with iron strapping to form a conical top, will come into view. The Dovercourt shore shelves gradually and is the safer side to work until this first pair of buoys have been reached, after which the channel becomes narrower and deeper and the sand is steep-to on either hand.

The next green conical buoy, No 5, is about half a mile further to the SW, marking the western edge of the channel where it narrows to a bottleneck, little more than a cable wide, at a point known as High Hill. This is identified by a lit red can buoy bearing that name (Fl R 10s radar reflector). There are eight or nine metres of water in the channel here, but since the sand on either side is quite steep-to, short boards are essential whenever it is necessary to turn to windward, and continuous use of the echo sounder is the only sure guide to the limits of the channel when the tide has covered the banks and there are no ripples. It is also as well to remember that spring tides run out of here at 2.5 knots during the first part of the ebb. From High Hill onwards, the channel widens to two or three cables and is marked on the W side by No 7 RNLI green conical buoy (Fl G 10s) and on the E side by red cans (Nos 6 and 8). From hereabouts it is usually possible to see the N Cardinal Horsey Island Point buoy (Q) at the junction of Hamford Water and the Walton Channel.

ENTRANCE TO WALTON CHANNEL

When bound for the Walton Channel there are three more unnumbered red can buoys to be left to port round Mussel Scarfe. This series of buoys should not be passed too closely because under certain conditions of tide and westerly wind they can be over the bank they mark. Neither should the Island Point buoy be approached too closely when entering or leaving the Walton Channel, as there is an extension of the mud bank to the E, just south of the buoy. A green conical buoy, East Coast Sails (Fl G), marks this hazard.

The last port-hand buoy marks the W edge of Stone Point. There is sometimes an outer (more northerly) port-hand buoy indicating the SW end of a channel known as 'The Swatch', which is occasionally used (near HW) by local craft bound for the fishing grounds off the Naze.

STONE POINT

The steep-to shingle bank at Stone Point provides a popular landing place at all states of the tide, while the anchorage nearby offers excellent protection. It is not advisable to anchor in the fairway where the depths are considerable and the ebb runs hard in midstream, as much as 3 knots during springs. It is preferable to anchor close to the E bank, where there is a slight contra-flow eddy during the first part of the ebb.

On a fine day in summer, Walton Stone Point is a good spot for a bathe and picnic, but be aware that it is adjacent to a privately-owned bird sanctuary and nature reserve. Unfortunately some unthinking people light fires, leave rubbish, disturb nesting terns and trample down the plants and grass that are so important to the wild life of the area. If this kind of thoughtless

Approaching Stone Point and the Walton Channel, leaving East Coast Sails green conical to starboard

behaviour were to continue, Stone Point might be prohibited to yachtsmen. Fortunately the Point is under the management of the Walton and Frinton Yacht Club, which needs our support. Should you intend to come to Stone Point as part of an organized group or club cruise, the W&FYC would appreciate being contacted in advance of your visit.

Chapter 9

Except for the Ingle lit green conical, the Walton Channel is not buoyed between Stone Point and the Twizzle. The best water is to be found between the moorings, except near the mouth of Stone Creek, where mud extends to the W and the channel is nearer the Horsey Island shore, marked by the aforementioned Ingle buoy. The depths in the channel decrease from 7m off Stone Point to rather less than 5m where the creek changes direction and name and becomes the Twizzle, at the entrance to which there is a shoal area.

WALTON AND FRINTON YACHT CLUB

The landing at the clubhouse, built in 1920 on the site of an old windmill, can be reached by dinghy for all but an hour on either side of LW. Visitors to the Backwaters are always welcome at the club – ask for the resident steward and he will sign you in. The bar and restaurant are open at lunchtime and evenings on most days of the year, the rest of the club and toilet facilities are accessible at all times.

The seaside resort of Walton-on-the-Naze with its shops, pubs, restaurants, ten-pin bowling and good beaches, is less than a mile away.

The Walton-on-the-Naze Yacht Basin is adjacent to the Walton and Frinton Yacht Club in Mill Lane, and is run by the Walton and Frinton Yacht Trust on behalf of the club. This yacht basin has a retaining gate that is opened around the time of high water (approximately 20 mins after HW Harwich) when there is a depth of about 2m over the sill in the entrance at neap tides and about 2.5m at springs. There

is a tide gauge to the left of the gate. It is not always possible to open the gate on very low neap tides, particularly if these coincide with high barometric pressure, besides which it is opened only during working hours.

Arrangements for gate opening should be made in advance with Bedwells, one of the two boatyards in Mill Lane – the other is Frank Halls. Inside the basin, yachts are moored fore-and-aft between staging and buoys.

THE TWIZZLE

The Twizzle, or Twizzle Creek, which runs in a generally westerly direction, is really a continuation of Walton Channel, offering complete protection in an average depth of 2m at LW except near its entrance. Craft are moored on both sides of the Twizzle and anchoring is certainly not advisable because many of the ground chains are laid across the channel. After enquiry at the clubhouse or one of the local yards, it is sometimes possible to borrow one of the moorings for a short period. Those marked with a 'B' belong to Bedwells, while those with an 'H' are owned by Halls.

TITCHMARSH MARINA

The Titchmarsh Marina (450 boats) is on the S side of the Twizzle, a little to the W of Colonel's Hard. Dredging over the years since this marina was established means that there is now 1.3m of water over the entrance sill at LWS. A pontoon is situated outside in the Twizzle, part of which is owned by the marina, where boats can lie while they wait for water over the sill. There is no longer a Customs Post at the marina, but the Customs boat, *Lynx*, is based here.

The marina is a fair way from the town of Walton-on-the-Naze, so you may need to call a taxi. There are good facilities on site including a chandlery and the Harbour Lights bar and restaurant, which overlooks the pontoons and provides breakfasts, bar meals, restaurant with silver service and, in summer, barbecues on the terrace.

The Twizzle is navigable at LW by craft drawing 1m as far as the western end of Hedge End Island. Further W, the Twizzle becomes a narrow, winding gutway through the extensive mud and saltings of Horsey Mere. The withies here indicate oyster layings rather than a channel. The creek finally peters out to the E of the rough roadway known as the Wade, which crosses Horsey Mere to join

WALTON-ON-THE-NAZE PORT GUIDE	
Water	From alongside the clubhouse
Stores	Shops 0.25 mile from clubhouse. EC Wed
Fuel	Diesel from yard, nearest petrol from garage in Frinton, or Kirby-le-Soken
Repairs	Yards in Mill Lane: Bedwells Tel 01255 675873; Franks Halls Tel 01255 675596
Chandlery	Mill Lane
Transport	Trains to London via Colchester. Buses to Colchester, Clacton and Harwich
Walton Yacht Basin	Contact Bedwells Tel 01255 675873
Club	Walton and Frinton Yacht Club, Mill Lane, Walton-on-Naze, Essex CO14 8PF. Tel 01225 675526. Bar and restaurant (lunchtime and eves)
Telephone	At clubhouse

The entrance to Titchmarsh Marina is on the port-hand side of the Twizzle. Here a yacht is leaving the marina on a misty morning

the mainland with the farm on Horsey Island.

There are oyster beds at the extreme W end of the Twizzle, so care must be taken not to go aground in this area.

Those who have read Arthur Ransome's *Secret Water* will remember the exciting race the 'Explorers' had when they crossed the Wade during a rising tide.

It is possible to sail straight across Horsey Mere from the Twizzle to Kirby Creek, provided the boat does not draw more than about 1m and the trip is made about an hour before HW, on a day near to, but before, spring tides.

TITCHMARSH MARINA PORT GUIDE

Harbour Master	Tel 01255 851899; VHF Channels M (ex-37) and 80
Marina Office	Tel 672185; www.titchmarshmarina.com
Water	On pontoons
Stores	Small selection at chandlery Local delivery service from Walton
Diesel	Fuel pontoon just inside marina entrance (open daylight hours)
Gas	From harbour master
Chandlery & Cycle Hire	Tel 679028
Repairs	35 ton travel-lift, French Marine Motors Tel 850303; Electronics: Hurst Marine Services Tel 673171
Food and Drink	Harbour Lights restaurant and bar Tel 851887 (open all week)

HAMFORD WATER

Hamford Water is also known as the West Water. It runs in a generally south-westerly direction from the Island Point buoy moored off the mud spit extending from the north-eastern corner of Horsey Island, to the north-eastern end of Skipper's Island, where the channel divides. There is plenty of water in this main reach of Hamford Water – 7m near the entrance and 5m about a mile inside, but depths are variable. The width of the channel is nearly two cables at LW and the N side of it is marked by a green conical buoy.

This is a very popular anchorage, with both excellent protection and holding, unless you are unlucky enough to drop your hook on top of one of the massive growths of pipe weed that have infested these waters in recent years. When any kind of anchor lands on a patch of this stuff its holding power becomes negligible. It is therefore a good idea to test (under power if necessary) that your anchor is holding before settling down for the night and certainly before leaving the boat.

During the summer months the Walton Backwaters warden is often on duty in the Tendring District Council launch, *Gamebird*.

OAKLEY CREEK

Oakley Creek branches to the north, out of Hamford Water and between Bramble and Pewit Islands. The spit off the W side of the entrance is marked by an E cardinal buoy. There is enough water for light draught craft to lie afloat for nearly a mile within, but it is probably best to resist any temptation to anchor here because the creek is used once or twice a week by freighters which load at the wharf belonging to an explosives factory at Oakley, where landing is strictly prohibited.

LANDERMERE CREEK

By continuing west along Hamford Water, a boat drawing up to 2m can safely reach the division of the channel where Landermere Creek turns towards Landermere Quay. Several moorings lie just beyond here but there is usually enough space and depth to anchor clear of them. Landing from a dinghy is feasible at the quay from about half-flood.

At around high water it is possible to take a dinghy beyond Landermere up to Beaumont Quay, where a plaque will inform you that the stones used for its construction came from the old London Bridge. An overhead power cable spans the cut and prevents boats with masts from reaching the quay. The quay is only a quarter of a mile from a main-road bus route to Thorpe-le-Soken, where there are shops from which most stores can be obtained.

KIRBY CREEK

This creek joins Hamford Water on its S side, about a quarter mile beyond Oakley Creek, and offers a quiet anchorage, although there are some moorings in the creek. The Naze Oyster Company has some of its layings in Kirby Creek and, like anywhere else that oysters are cultivated, a yachtsman is responsible if, by anchoring or grounding, he damages any of the stock. Notice boards to this effect will be seen at the entrance to the creek.

If for some reason conditions in Hamford Water are uncomfortable, yachtsmen may be able to anchor just within Kirby Creek and above the layings, but then they must beware the treacherously long spit of mud that extends from the NE end of Skipper's Island.

Skipper's Island is used by the Essex Naturalists' Society, whose members have erected an observation tower from which they can watch the many species of birds that come to the Backwaters. For stores a landing can be made at a wooden staithe on the mainland opposite the SE corner of the Island. This is a good landing except right at low water, but the walk along the sea wall to Kirby-le-Soken is about a mile and a half.

From abreast the wooden staithe Kirby Creek turns sharply to the E, to emerge into Horsey Mere, and then turns S again up to Kirby Quay. The quay can be reached by dinghy towards HW, and the tortuous gutway is plentifully marked by withies, which are no doubt understood by local sailors but at first acquaintance are only likely to baffle the uninitiated.

The village of Kirby-le-Soken is no more than a quarter of a mile from the quay, where shops, a pub and a garage satisfy most yachtsmen's day-to-day needs.

Yachts at anchor in the entrance to Landermere Creek near the head of Hamford Water

THE RIVER COLNE

Tides (Brightlingsea)	HW Dover +0.55 Range: Springs 4.6m Neaps 2.6m (HW Colchester approx 20mins after HW Brightlingsea)
Charts	Admiralty 3741, Stanford No 4, Imray Y17, OS Map No 168
Waypoints	Knoll Buoy 51°43'.88N 01°05'.06E, NW Knoll Buoy 51°44'.35N 01°02'.17E
	Inner Bench Head Buoy 51°45'.96N 01°01'.75E
Hazards	Knoll, Colne Bar and Bench Head shoals near LW

The gentle wooded slopes that line the banks of the Colne below Wivenhoe give the river a pleasant rural feel which is unspoiled by the moorings and marinas that characterize many other local rivers. Colchester has been de-registered as a port and the Hythe and quays are being redeveloped for

housing or leisure use, as has already happened at Wivenhoe Dock. So, although the ballast quays at Fingringhoe and Brightlingsea are still busy with sand barges, by and large the river is as peaceful and quiet as it has ever been.

The river Colne is smaller and more intimate than its close neighbour, the Blackwater. Both these rivers join the sea at the NW Knoll buoy, midway between Colne Point to the E and Sales Point to the W. The distance from the Knoll buoy

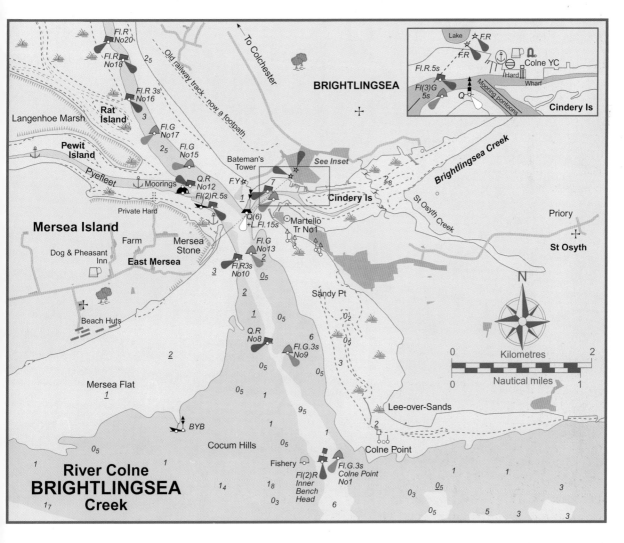

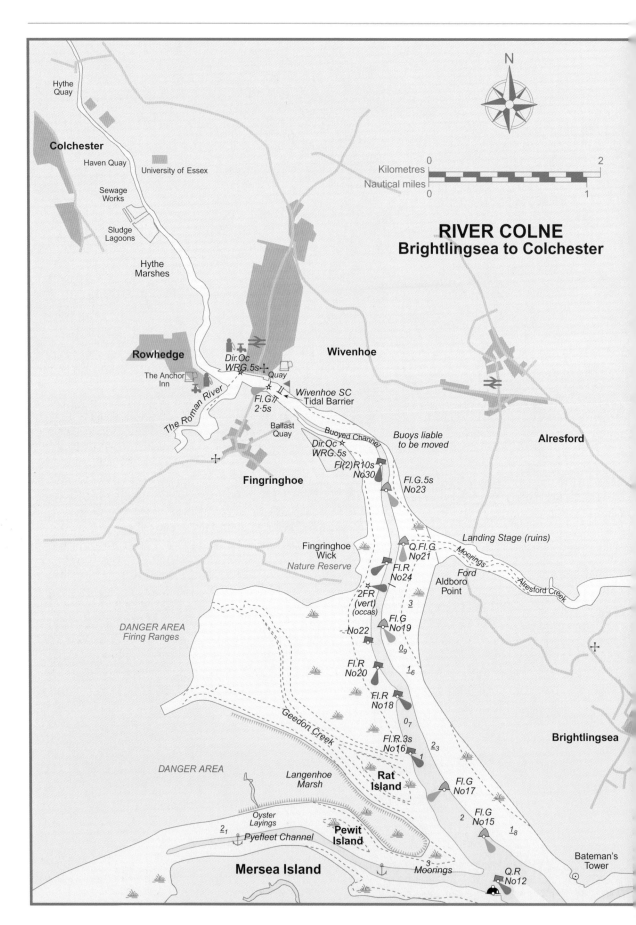

RIVER COLNE
Brightlingsea to Colchester

Hythe
Quay

Colchester

Haven Quay

University of Essex

Sewage
Works

Sludge
Lagoons

Hythe
Marshes

Rowhedge

The Anchor
Inn

The Roman River

*Dir.Oc
WRG.5s*

Quay

*Fl.G
2·5s*

Wivenhoe

Wivenhoe SC
Tidal Barrier

Ballast
Quay

Buoyed Channel

*Dir.Oc
WRG.5s*

*Buoys liable
to be moved*

Alresford

Fingringhoe

*Fl(2)R10s
No30*

*Fl.G.5s
No23*

Landing Stage (ruins)

Moorings

Fingringhoe
Wick

*Q.Fl.G
No21*

Alresford Creek

*Fl.R
No24*

Ford
Aldboro
Point

Nature Reserve

*2FR
(vert)
(occas)*

3

*Fl.G
No19*

DANGER AREA
Firing Ranges

No22

*0*9

*Fl.R
No20*

*1*6

*Fl.R
No18*

*0*7

Geedon Creek

Brightlingsea

*Fl.R.3s
No16*

*2*3

1

DANGER AREA

Langenhoe
Marsh

**Rat
Island**

*Fl.G
No17*

Oyster
Layings

*2*1

Pyefleet Channel

**Pewit
Island**

*Fl.G
No15*

2

*1*8

*3
Moorings*

Bateman's
Tower

Mersea Island

*Q.R
No12*

The entrance to Brightlingsea Creek is marked by a south cardinal buoy, and the course of 42°M is indicated by red and white striped leading marks onshore in the town

to the Hythe at Colchester is about 11 miles, most of which lies in a north-north-westerly direction.

APPROACHES FROM SEAWARD

When approaching the Colne from the S through the Swin Spitway or from the N, up the Wallet, make for the Knoll buoy (N Car Q) and then leave both the Eagle (Con G QG) and the Colne Bar (Con G Fl(2)G 5s) buoys close to starboard before shaping a course of 350°M into the entrance of the river. From a position near the Bar buoy a group of three more buoys will usually be seen in daylight – the Fishery buoy (Sph Y), the Colne Point buoy (Con G) and the Inner Bench Head (Can R Fl(2)R 5s).

Shoal draught boats can, provided it is not too near the time of low water, cross Colne Bar north of the Eagle and as much as a mile inside the Bar buoy. When coming south a sudden increase in depths will indicate when the bar has been crossed.

From the Inner Bench Head light buoy inwards, the channel is buoyed on both sides – even numbered red cans to port and odd-numbered green conical buoys to starboard. There is a depth of some 9m between the first pair of channel buoys, and there is not much less than 6m anywhere within the channel until abreast the entrance to Brightlingsea Creek. However, carefully observe the buoys on both hands, since the water shoals quite rapidly, particularly to the W.

When sailing to the Blackwater from the Colne it is safe, except near low water, for craft drawing 2m or less to cross from the deep water of the Colne on a course that has St Peters Chapel (near Sales Point) bearing 240°M. This will lead about midway between the Bench Head and Cocum Hills shoals.

In clear weather, from a position abreast the Inner Bench Head, it is possible to see Brightlingsea Church tower on high ground, due N (°M), from a distance of four miles. Another mark that will help the newcomer get his bearings is the very large building shed at Brightlingsea, which may be seen over the low-lying shore from several miles away.

Once inside Brightlingsea Creek, a green conical buoy keeps you off the spit extending from St Osyth Stone Point

BRIGHTLINGSEA CREEK

The buoy at the entrance to Brightlingsea Creek is a South Cardinal yellow and black buoy (QFl(6)+LFl 15s). The entrance it marks is very shallow, with not much more than 1m best water at LWS. A conical green buoy (Fl(3)G 5s) inside the entrance is intended to keep you off the spit that extends from St Osyth Stone Point, while a red can (FlR 5s) marks the northern edge of the channel.

The correct course into the creek itself is 42°M and by day this line is indicated by two leading marks (red and white stripes) known locally as the 'cricket stumps' and set up on poles in the town. By night these leading marks bear two fixed red lights.

Batemans Tower, although condemned at one time, is now safe and lit with an orange sodium lamp.

In recent years most of the old fore and aft moorings between the two lines of piles running S of Cindery Island have been replaced by pontoons. Some local Brightlingsea boats have permanent berths here but more visitors than previously can now be accommodated. This is a popular port of call in the summer months so it is advisable to enquire beforehand as to availability of berths. Around high water the harbour master can usually be found in his launch, or he can be contacted on VHF. It is the custom for regular berth holders to leave a note when they vacate their mooring saying whether they will be back that day, but do not leave your boat unattended on any berth without checking first. From April to October on weekends from Friday evening to Sunday night there is a regular and inexpensive water taxi service to the Colne YC pontoon, and also to East Mersea.

The little water there is in the creek runs to the N of Cindery Island and on up to the head of the creek where there is a jetty used by sand barges.

Pontoon moorings at Brightlingsea

Small freighters also use the commercial wharf beyond the Colne YC. Some of this traffic can be at night, so there are no moorings to the N of Cindery Island and a fairway must be maintained here at all times.

Brightlingsea offers excellent facilities to the yachtsman. There is a fine hard on which almost any boat can stand upright against one of the several posts available. Arrangements for using the posts should be made with the Hard Master whose office is near the YC jetty; he is in attendance from Monday to Friday in the mornings only.

The Colne YC has a catwalk and pontoon as well as a clubhouse with commanding views, just E of the town causeway. Visiting yachtsmen are welcome, and meals and showers can usually be obtained. Just beyond the YC pontoon is the Aldous Heritage Smack Dock, HQ of the Colne Smack Preservation Society and home to a fleet of restored fishing craft, many of which were built in Brightlingsea over 100 years ago.

ST OSYTH CREEK

Above Brightlingsea there are two tidal islands – W and E Cindery Islands, dividing Brightlingsea Creek into two branches, abreast the junction with St Osyth Creek. This latter creek is no more than a mile long and is very narrow, particularly near the entrance where the best water (perhaps as much as 1.5m at LW) will be found between a tiny hummock of land known as Pincushion Island and the S bank. Shallow draught boats can safely reach the head of the creek for about an hour or so either side of HW. The creek is sparsely marked by withies.

St Osyth itself is worth visiting to see the remains of the twelfth century Priory, although all signs of the tide-mill have now disappeared. There is a boatyard with a crane and slip and a chandler near the quay, which is wooden faced and has several ladders. This is a popular venue for owners of Essex smacks.

The E Coast Sail Trust's sailing barge, Thalatta, *anchored at the entrance to Pyefleet Creek*

EAST MERSEA POINT

Opposite the entrance to Brightlingsea Creek is Mersea Stone Point – the eastern extremity of Mersea Island. There is a good landing on the shingle here, and one can walk to the Dog and Pheasant, about a mile away.

Good holding ground in 5m, well protected from all but south or south-easterly winds, can be found clear of the few moorings and between Mersea Point and the old wreck that dries out just below the entrance to Pyefleet Creek. This wreck, of a ship called *Lowlands*, is marked by a red can buoy (Fl(2)R 5s).

Since chartered sailing barges and coasters frequently bring up off the entrance to Brightlingsea Creek, it is essential to use a riding light when anchored at night.

PYEFLEET CREEK

A cable or two above the wreck on the W side of the river is the entrance to Pyefleet Creek, which provides an excellent anchorage with good protection. In fact, an anchorage in Pyefleet is usually more comfortable than a berth within Brightlingsea Creek, because of the swell that often enters the creek at the turn of the tide.

Pyefleet Creek is one of the most popular Saturday night anchorages on the whole of the East Coast. Perhaps this is because it offers that sense of remoteness for which so many of us feel a need. There are no landing places and no cars in sight and, although there may be 20 or 30 craft at anchor, everyone (except the

waterskiers) is there for the peace and quiet and acts accordingly.

Oysters are still cultivated in Pyefleet Creek, as they were when the Romans were at Colchester. Every October the Mayor, accompanied by officials of the Colchester Oyster Company, celebrates the start of a new season while moored in the Creek. At weekends during the summer it is possible to buy cooked crabs and lobsters at the Colchester Oyster Company shed (Tel 1206 384141), which is open all day on Sundays and early on Saturday mornings. However, do remember that the hard and the East Mersea foreshore hereabouts are private.

The deep water in the entrance to Pyefleet is indicated by a line of mooring buoys, belonging to the Oyster Company, which may charge for their use. There is plenty of room and plenty of water for a mile or more up the creek, and yachts may bring up either just within the entrance or anywhere up to or even above Pewit Island, with its old oyster packing shed. Great care must be taken to avoid anchoring or grounding on any of the oyster layings (beds) in the Pyefleet. Craft drawing up to 2m can remain afloat as far up as Maydays Marsh, where the channel divides; the S branch leading to the Strood which joins Mersea Island to the mainland.

The only disadvantage of the Pyefleet anchorage is that no supplies are available nearer than Brightlingsea, which can seem a long way when a strong wind is blowing up or down the Colne.

Returning to the Colne river buoyage, a red can buoy, No 16 (Fl R 3s), marks the mud spit formed by the small creek which enters the river N of Rat Island. Above Rat Island the channel continues

Above the small boat moorings and the ford, Alresford Creek virtually dries out at LW

in a NNW'ly direction before turning NE'ly round Aldboro Point. Two red cans and a green conical buoy mark the course of the channel round this bend.

ALRESFORD CREEK

Fingringhoe Marshes, a nature reserve controlled by the Essex Wildlife Trust, are now on the port hand and a disused jetty will come into view on the same shore. The next buoy (No 21 green conical Q Fl G) will be found off the entrance to Alresford Creek. The entrance is marked by a pair of small pillar buoys, with further pairs of similar buoys marking the gutway. For a quarter of a mile inside the creek there are small boat moorings up to a ford, at which landing can be made on either bank. From the ford up to Thorington Mill at the head of the creek is a little over a mile, but most of the creek dries out at LW. Out in the river there is enough water for large boats to lie afloat at LW out of the channel opposite Aldboro Point.

Above Alresford Creek the channel continues in a northerly direction and is well marked with both lit and unlit buoys round the sweeping bend known as Marriages Bight. The mud flat stretching from the Fingringhoe shore is extensive and the narrowing channel leads right over to within half a cable of the pleasantly wooded Alresford shore, before turning NW'ly again towards the other bank.

The next channel buoys are located just below the ballast quay on the Fingringhoe shore (from which small sand barges operate). Above this point the best water lies roughly midway between the banks,

and the buoyage sequence is liable to change. There are fore-and-aft mooring trots on either hand just below the Wivenhoe Tidal Barrier, which will now be seen. This is normally open and if so causes no problem. However, if 3FR(vert) lights show on the N pier, up or downstream, either the gates are shut or a large vessel is negotiating the barrier. Immediately below the barrier on the starboard-hand is Wivenhoe SC which, with its slipway and pontoons, has access from around one hour before to one hour after HW on average tides. Yachts of up to 6ft draught can lie in soft mud alongside and visitors are welcome to stay overnight.

WIVENHOE

The river front at Wivenhoe has a pleasant and unusual atmosphere, especially at high water with the sun shining on the quayside houses. Most of the boats at Wivenhoe dry out at about half-ebb, when they settle in soft mud.

The village became a yachting centre after the local boatbuilder and smuggler, Sainty, had been commissioned to build the famous *Pearl* for the Marquis of Anglesey in the 1820s. Many more successful schooners, yawls, cutters, fishing smacks and other craft were then launched from yards in Wivenhoe in its heyday, including Sir Thomas Brassey's *Sunbeam*, Edward Fitzgerald's *Scandal* and the lovely clipper-bowed *Creole*. The last yard closed in 1930, huge sheds were then built by Vospers during the Second World War to house MTBs, but now the only building is of new houses on the docksides.

WIVENHOE PORT GUIDE	
Water	From quayside hose
Fuel	Garage 0.75 mile (cans)
Stores	Local shops including PO. EC Thurs
Transport	Train service to Colchester and London
Club	Wivenhoe Sailing Club, open Fri evenings and Sun lunchtimes, or when tide suits (showers, toilets, telephone etc) Tel 01206 822132
Essex Wildlife Trust, Fingringhoe	Tel 01206 729678

Across the river from Wivenhoe is the entrance to Fingringhoe Creek or the Roman River – a reminder that the Romans settled in these parts nineteen centuries ago. In the summer months a ferry service runs between Rowhedge, Fingringhoe and Wivenhoe from about two hours before to two hours after HW.

ROWHEDGE

Up-river on the W bank is Rowhedge, described by Hervey Benham as '...once the roughest of all the Colne and Blackwater villages.' Alain Gerbault's famous *Firecrest* was built here in 1892 – at a time when some 40 smacks sailed out of Rowhedge mixing fishing with salvaging, wrecking – and yachting in the summer! The Dixon Kemp-designed *Firecrest* was one of hundreds of vessels built in the village – the Rowhedge Ironworks built minesweepers and MFVs and later maintained RNLI lifeboats. Today, as at Wivenhoe, there are new houses on the quayside and scarcely any signs remain of the once strong maritime links of this Colne-side village.

Access to the quay at Rowhedge, near the riverside pub, is possible from about 2 hrs before and 1½ hrs after HW.

The remaining three miles of river between Rowhedge and the road bridge above the

Wivenhoe Yacht Club is just downstream of the tidal barrier on the north bank where there is an extended club mooring pontoon and a visitor's buoy for staying on the tide

Hythe at Colchester should only be attempted after about four hours of flood. The best water, which will vary from 2m to 3m at the top of the tide, will generally be found midway between the banks. At night, during HW, one bank is lit by a continuous line of street lamps.

COLCHESTER

Colchester is a de-registered port and the Hythe quayside area is being re-developed. Brightlingsea Harbour Commissioners are to take over responsibility for buoyage in the River Colne.

The waterfront at Wivenhoe is lined with attractive old buildings and usually has a variety of craft berthed in the mud along the quayside

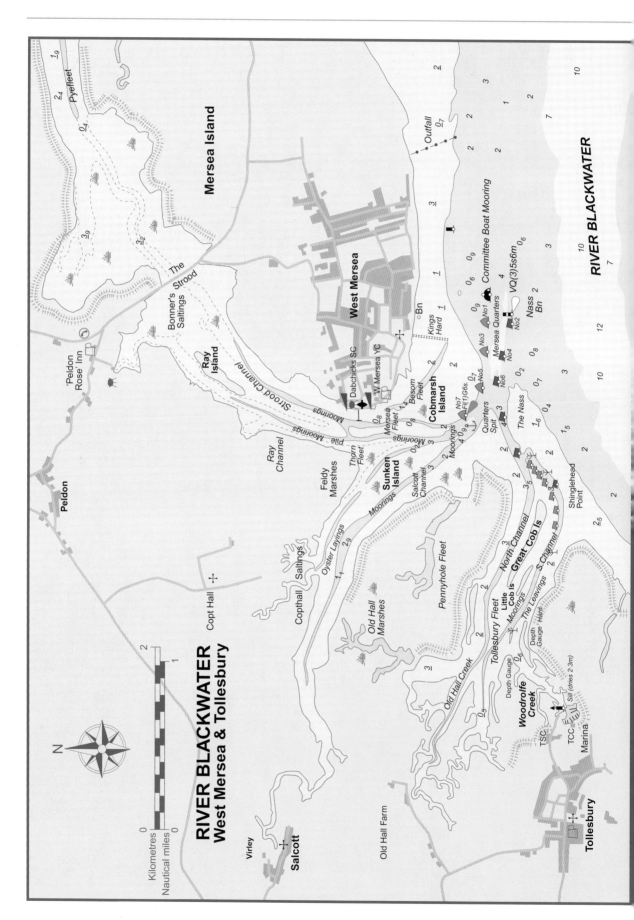

RIVER BLACKWATER
West Mersea & Tollesbury

N

Kilometres
Nautical miles

RIVER BLACKWATER
Copt Hall

Peldon

'Peldon
Rose Inn'

Virley

Salcott

Old Hall Farm

Copthall
Saltings

Oyster Layings

Old Hall
Marshes

Pennyhole Fleet

Old Hall Creek

Tollesbury Fleet

Little
Cob Is

Great Cob Is

The Leavings

Depth Gauge

Depth
Gauge Hard

Woodrolfe
Creek

Depth Gauge

TSC

TCC

Sill (dries 2.3m)

Marina

Tollesbury

North Channel

S. Channel

Shinglehead
Point

The Nass

Nass
Bn

VQ(3)5s6m

Mersea Quarters

Committee Boat Mooring

RIVER BLACKWATER

Outfall

No1

No2

No3

No4

No5

No6

No7

Fl(1)G6s

Quarters
Spit

Salcott
Channel

**Sunken
Island**

Feldy
Marshes

**Cobmarsh
Island**

Bn

Kings
Hard

Besom
Fleet

Mersea
Fleet

Thorn
Fleet

Moorings

Pile Moorings

Moorings

Dabchicks SC

W Mersea YC

West Mersea

Ray
Channel

**Ray
Island**

Moorings

The
Strood

Bonner's
Saltings

Mersea Island

Pyefleet

EAST COAST RIVERS CRUISING COMPANION

THE RIVER BLACKWATER

Tides (Nass Beacon)	HW Dover +00.30 Range: Springs 4.6m Neaps 2.6m (HW Maldon approx 25mins after HW West Mersea)
Charts	Admiralty 3741, Stanford No 4, Imray Y17, OS Map 168
Waypoints	Bench Head Buoy 51°44'.69N 01°01'.10E, Nass Beacon 51°45'.84N 00°54'.84E
Hazard	Thirslet Spit

Arnold Bennett owned a Dutch barge-yacht called *Velsa*, which he kept in Walton Backwaters but also sailed to other Essex and Suffolk rivers as well as to Holland. In the *Log of the Velsa* he wrote: 'Time was when I agreed with the popular, and the guide book, verdict that the Orwell is the finest estuary

in these parts; but now I know better.

I unhesitatingly give the palm to the Blackwater. It is a noble stream, a true arm of the sea; its moods are more various, its banks wilder, and its atmospheric effects much grander. The season for cruising on the Blackwater is September, when the village regattas take place and the sunrises over leagues of marsh are made wonderful by strange mists.'

The entrance to both the Blackwater and the Colne is generally considered to be at the Bench

Head buoy, some 15 miles down-river from Maldon. Coming up from the south, most yachts follow the example of the sailing barges and go through the Swin Spitway.

The deepest water through this swatch is in a line between the Swin Spitway buoy, a safewater pillar buoy with spherical topmark (Iso 10s Bell), to the SE of the swatch, and the Wallet Spitway buoy (Sph R W V S LFl 10s Bell), a mile away to the NNW. Quite often a yacht gets a fair wind through the spitway when entering the

The moorings at West Mersea looking towards the River Blackwater over Cob Marsh Island. The pile moorings in the Thornfleet can be seen in the foreground, with West Mersea itself in the top left corner

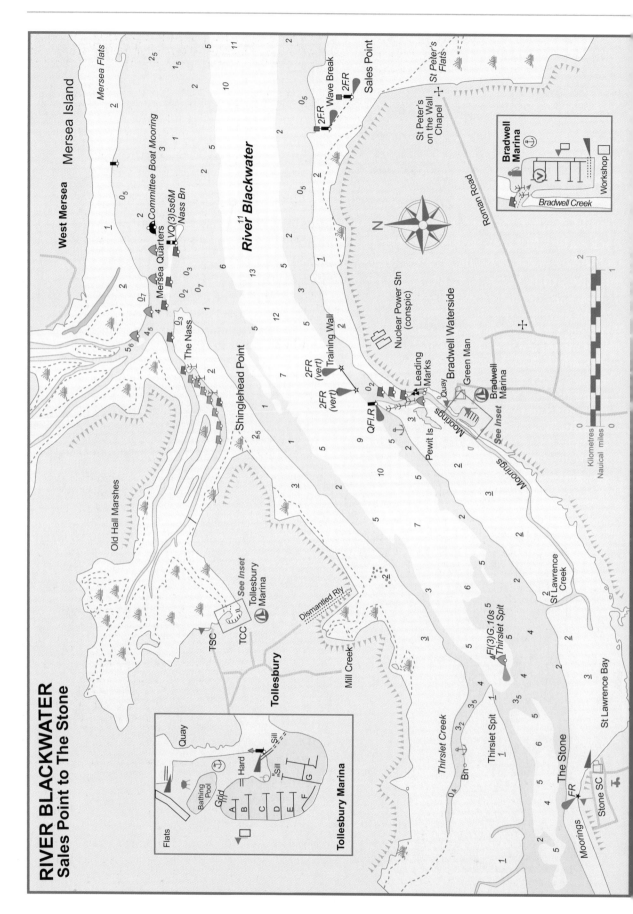

RIVER BLACKWATER
Sales Point to The Stone

West Mersea Mersea Island

Mersea Flats

Committee Boat Mooring

Mersea Quarters

VQ(3)5s6M
Nass Bn

The Nass

Shinglehead Point

River Blackwater

Old Hall Marshes

Mill Creek

Tollesbury

TSC

TCC
Tollesbury Marina

See Inset

Dismantled Rly

Tollesbury Marina

Flats

Quay

Bathing Pool

Grid

Sill

Hard

Sill

A B C D E F G

Grid

Thirslet Creek

Bn

Thirslet Spit

Fl(3)G.10s
Thirslet Spit

St Lawrence Creek

St Lawrence Bay

The Stone

FR
Stone SC

Moorings

Wave Break

2FR

2FR
Sales Point

St Peter's
Flats

St Peter's
on the Wall
Chapel

Training Wall

*2FR
(vert)*

*2FR
(vert)*

QFl.R

Nuclear Power Stn
(conspic)

Leading
Marks

Bradwell Waterside

Green Man

Quay

Pewit Is

Moorings

Bradwell
Marina

Moorings

Roman Road

**Bradwell
Marina**

Workshop

See Inset

Bradwell Creek

N

Kilometres
Nautical miles

Blackwater, but if ever it is necessary to beat through, then very short boards and constant use of the sounder are essential because the water shoals on to the Buxey Sands on the one hand and the Gunfleet Sands on the other.

From the Spitway, course is changed to bring the Knoll buoy (N Car B Y VQ) close to port after about two miles. Then, about a mile away is the Eagle (Con G Q G), to be passed close to starboard. With Eagle abeam, the red can of the NW Knoll light buoy (Can R Fl(2) R 5s) will usually be visible and is passed close to port. After this, without altering course appreciably, the unlit conical green Bench Head buoy can be left to starboard at the entrance to the Blackwater.

With the Bench Head astern, a newcomer will find it difficult to identify anything, except the conspicuous Nuclear Power Station at Bradwell, but a course of 295°M from the Bench Head will lead to the Nass beacon. This course is in fairly deep water – for the East Coast at least – and when the tide is running up against a westerly wind it is easy to tell where the channel lies because of the rougher water. After a while St Peter's Chapel should become visible on Sales Point to the SW, and at about the same time the trees and higher ground at West Mersea will take shape. The safest course is roughly midway between these two shores.

The Nass beacon, marking the entrance to Mersea Quarters, is a yellow and black steel post topped by a solar panel and a quick flashing light, so that it is often easier to find by night than by day. There is little water near the Nass beacon – perhaps no more than 2m at LWS.

The Nass beacon marks the entrance to both West Mersea and Tollesbury

WEST MERSEA PORT GUIDE

Moorings	WMYC Boatman Jeffrey Wass VHF Ch M callsign *YC ONE* or mobile 0976 962178 Peter Clarke's Tel 01206 385905 Launch Service Douglas Stoker VHF Ch M callsign *CC ONE*
Water	Standpipes at both ends of pontoon landing
Stores	Limited at Fleetview Stores near pontoon; shops inc Co-op in W Mersea village; EC Wed
Fuel	Diesel by can from AB Clarke's; petrol from Underwoods garage in village
Gas	Chandlery
Repairs	Peter Clarke's Boatyard: slipways, cranage, hoist, chandlery Tel 01206 385905; West Mersea Marine Tel 01206 382244
Marine Engineers	AB Clarke's near pontoon Tel 01206 382706
Chandlery	Wyatt's Chandlery Tel 01206 384745; Peter Clarke's Tel 01206 385905 Sailmakers Gowen Ocean Tel 01206 382922
Scrubbing posts	On foreshore (contact WMYC)
Transport	Buses to Colchester whence trains to London
Clubs	West Mersea YC (restaurant and bar weekends, and lunchtimes during week) Tel 01206 382947 Dabchicks SC bar usually open Wed, Sat and Sun evenings plus Sat and Sun lunchtime Tel 01206 383786
Telephone	Near Victory Inn on Coast Road
Food and Drink	WMYC open weekends and lunchtimes in the week; all-day breakfasts at Waterfront Cafe (Coast Road beyond Firs Chase); Soc & Sail bistro and/or Willow Lodge Tel 01206 383568; Victory Hotel Tel 01206 382907; The Company Shed (nr Wyatts Chandlery) oysters and shellfish, bring your own bread and wine; Tel 01206 382700

During the season there are a couple of mooring buoys in the vicinity of the beacon which are used by committee boats starting races for the West Mersea clubs. It should be noted that many Blackwater Joint Racing Committee racing marks exist in the estuary and these are regularly used throughout the season for local club racing, regattas and class championships. A series of four

Woodrolfe Creek looking up towards Tollesbury Marina at its head. The lightship in the saltings is operated as a residential outdoor centre by the Fellowship Afloat Charitable Trust which owns the salt marshes

starboard-hand green conical buoys mark the way through Mersea Quarters from the Nass beacon, the last of these, No 7, off Cobmarsh Island, being lit. To port are three red can buoys, with a fourth to the south indicating the entrance to Tollesbury creek. These navigation buoys are laid by the West Mersea YC.

WEST MERSEA

West Mersea is probably the most popular sailing centre on the River Blackwater and consequently it tends to be crowded. When Archie White, the marine artist, wrote: 'The creeks are crowded with yachts and smacks, the channels are narrow, and there is more mud than water...', he summed up Mersea rather nicely. One of the few East Coast sailing centres without a marina, Mersea retains a timeless quality, which could be why the magician of the swatchways himself, Maurice Griffiths, chose to spend the latter part of his life on Mersea Island.

The best ploy for visiting yachtsmen is to pick up a vacant buoy temporarily and contact Jeff Wass, the West Mersea YC boatman, who will advise further. Although there are no moorings actually designated for visitors, Jeff will usually be able to find you a vacant buoy, probably in the Salcott Channel or the Thornfleet. Peter Clark of The Boatyard on Coast Road, can also help with visitors' moorings.

It is not advisable to anchor further in than The Quarters because of the extensive moorings, and also there are oyster layings in Mersea Fleet running between Cob Marsh Island and Packing Marsh Island, as well as the Salcott Channel up to the little villages of Salcott and Virley. Space has become so scarce at Mersea that moorings are laid well inside Salcott Creek.

For getting ashore, contact Jeff Wass, who runs the WMYC launch, or Douglas Stoker who also operates a launch service.

The all-tide pontoon landing is the centre of sailing life at West Mersea – a hub of activity with sailing folk coming and going according to the tide – much as the village fishermen must have done when the posh pontoon was just a muddy hard.

TOLLESBURY

Tollesbury Creek leads directly out of Mersea Quarters and soon divides into the South Channel, which holds the more water, and the North Channel, with the Cob Islands between.

A red can indicates the junction of the Creek with the Quarters and this is followed by a further series of red cans up to the spit extending from Great Cob Island. The entrance to the South Channel is indicated by the first of a series of green cans (which sometimes appear blue). Keep close to these until you reach a line of moorings which, combined with some port-hand withies, show the way through The Leavings (where the fishing smacks were left while their crews went ashore) to the entrance of Woodrolfe Creek.

Near the entrance to the creek, which dries out, there are visitors' moorings belonging to Woodrolfe Boatyard, where you can lie afloat. A tide gauge here shows the depth of water over the sill at the marina. The sill has some 2m of water over it at HWS and about 1.5m at Neaps. Nearby is a hard from which it is about a mile along the sea wall to the marina and nearby Tollesbury village.

The way up Woodrolfe Creek to the marina is marked initially by pairs of red and green cans; after which keep to the centre, passing the ex-Trinity House lightvessel (now a residential outdoor centre) in the saltings on your starboard hand. On the bend where the creek turns to starboard, you will see the marina entrance to the south of the Woodrolfe Boatyard buildings.

At HWS there is some 2m over the sill, but only about 1.5m at neaps. Having entered the basin, moor temporarily at the jetty beneath the crane. While in the yacht harbour, visiting yachtsmen are welcome at Tollesbury Cruising Club where facilities include a heated, covered swimming pool, tennis courts and restaurant.

On leaving the Quarters and rounding the Nass into the deep water of the Blackwater, the course when proceeding up to Osea Island or Maldon is approximately 250°M. Frequently, quite large ships are laid up in the main channel between the Mersea and Bradwell shores.

TOLLESBURY PORT GUIDE

Tollesbury Marina/Woodrolfe Boatyard
Tel 01621 869202; Fax 868489; VHF Ch M and 80; email: marina@woodrolfe.demon.co.uk; www.tollesbury-marina.co.uk

Berths	240
Water	On pontoons
Showers and Laundry	
	On site
Stores	Shops in village 10 minute walk. EC Wed
Fuel	Diesel and gas from pontoon, petrol from garage in village
Chandlery	At yard
Repairs	Three slipways, lifts, cranage, workshops
Transport	Bus to Colchester rail station
Club	Tollesbury Cruising Club (in marina) Tel 01621 869561 Tollesbury SC www.tollesburysc.co.uk bar open Wed, Fri, Sat evenings and Sun lunchtime
Food and Drink	Tollesbury CC restaurant offers home cooking. The Hope and the King's Head pubs in High Street

The head of Salcott Creek at low water, looking towards the village of Salcott and the hamlet of Virley at the top of the picture, with Old Hall Marshes to the bottom left

At Bradwell Quay there are two scrubbing posts alongside a public ramp. The Bradwell Quay YC clubhouse can be seen beyond the bilge keeler being scrubbed on the foreshore

BRADWELL CREEK

About a mile up-river from the Nass, on the south shore is Bradwell Creek. The entrance is difficult to see but is in fact only about a quarter of a mile SW of the Barrier wall off the Nuclear Power Station.

Entrance to the creek is marked by a substantial beacon bearing a tide gauge that shows what water there is over the sill into the marina. Because of silting near the end of Pewit Island, the creek is only accessible within four hours either side of HW. The beacon is considered to be a port-hand mark in the River Blackwater, so its light flashes red. However, it MUST be left to starboard on entering the creek.

From the beacon a line of red can buoys indicates the port side of the gutway and a line of withies marks the other side. Best water will be found near the withies.

When the last of the can buoys has been left to port, the channel changes direction towards the SE, as indicated by two orange-painted triangular topped leading marks that will be seen rather low down in the saltings under a concrete slabbed section of the sea wall. After steering on these beacons for about a cable, the last mark – a green conical buoy – should be left to starboard before continuing along the line of moored craft that extends past the old quay. A concrete slip is situated near the quay end.

At the quay itself, a few remaining gnarled old tree-trunk piles remind us of the days when the creek was always busy with sailing barges,

loading from the farms around. There are still two scrubbing posts alongside the public ramp which were erected by the Bradwell Quay YC. The club is quite willing for visitors to use them provided they book a time and pay a small fee. Visiting yachtsmen are welcome to use the nearby clubhouse facilities, which include a bar, a barbecue unit and decking area. The Bradwell Quay YC stewardess can provide meals at reasonable prices particularly for groups, class associations or club visits, so long as she is given ample notice.

The Essex County Council has based its Field Studies and Sailing Centre here at Bradwell Waterside, and there is usually a good deal of youthful activity afloat and ashore as a result.

BRADWELL PORT GUIDE	
Marina	Tel 01621 776235; Fax 776391; VHF Ch M (ex-37) or 80
Coastguard	Tel 01621 776310
Water	In Marina or from Bradwell Quay YC (near top of hard)
Stores	Shop in village
Fuel	Diesel, petrol and marine LPG at marina
Chandlery	At Marina, Tel 01621 776147
Repairs	At Marina, slip up to 20 tons, hoist up to 16 tons
Transport	Railway station Southminster; buses to Maldon; taxis
Telephone	Quarter of a mile from quay
Food and Drink	Bar and restaurant at marina, Green Man PH restaurant (Tel 01621 776226) just up the road from Waterside
Clubs	Bradwell Cruising Club (Marina) Tel 01621 892970 Bradwell Quay Yacht Club Visitors welcome, bar open weekends and BH evenings, barbecue unit available, meals provided by arrangement. Tel 01245 258420 (Gerry Askham, BQYC Commodore), or www.bradwellquay.fsnet.co.uk

BRADWELL MARINA

The entrance to the marina is indicated by a red can buoy – Bradwell Marina – and the way in is marked by withies on either hand. Depths in the marina are slightly more than in the creek, which has access approximately four hours either side of HW. Once inside, a visitor should berth on the ends of A or B pontoons.

The village of Bradwell (Bradwell Juxta-Mare) is about a mile from the quay and the Chapel of St Peter's on the Wall, a Saxon chapel built in 654 AD on the site of the Roman shore fort of Othona, is another mile away along a track towards the sea. This ancient building, possibly the oldest in England from which Christianity was preached, has been used over the centuries as a mariners' beacon and as a barn, and was re-consecrated in 1920.

THIRSLET CREEK AND GOLDHANGER CREEK

Out in the river again, the next thing to watch for is the green buoy (Fl(3)G 10s) marking a spit of hard sand which protrudes into the river on the north side at the entrance to Thirslet Creek.

Until the buoy is located, there is nothing to indicate how far into the river the spit extends, and many yachts have sailed headlong on to the hard sand while aiming, as they thought, straight up the middle of the river! When coming down-river, a safe course results from steering on Bradwell Power Station. Although the water is deepest along this northern shore, the sand is dangerously steep-to and care must therefore be taken not to stand over too far. It is safer to keep well over to the south shore until abreast St Lawrence Bay.

A couple of miles above Thirslet Creek, also amid the northern flats, is the entrance to Goldhanger Creek, marked by a conical green buoy. This also serves as a main river channel buoy and must, therefore, be left to port when entering the creek. The creek leads up to a hard near Goldhanger village, but this is only really accessible by dinghy since there is very little water at the head of the creek, even at HWS.

But for those who appreciate the quiet of remote anchorages, there is enough water in which to lie afloat overnight for half a mile or more within the entrances to both Thirslet and Goldhanger Creeks. A reasonably hard foreshore exists near the top of Goldhanger Creek and a path along the sea wall can be used to reach the village and the Chequers inn, a mile or so away. There are oyster layings in the creek.

STONE ST LAWRENCE

Over on the south shore is Stone St Lawrence, easily located by the many boats moored in the bay as well as the bungalows and caravans on shore. Stone Sailing Club at the top of the shingle beach is home to fleets of performance dinghies and catamarans which use the wide expanses of the Blackwater for their racing.

Another club, Marconi SC, has its clubhouse half a mile further up-river and at night a fixed white light is shown from a corner of the building. There are four rows of moorings along with one for visitors opposite the club. Here water is obtainable at the top of the slip. A red port-hand lit buoy, Marconi, marks the south side of the river where it narrows between Stangate Point and Osea Island.

From St Lawrence Bay the remains of the little pier at Osea Island can be seen in daylight and its two fixed green lights at night. It is safe for any but deep draught boats to set a course direct to the end of the pier. Larger boats must watch out for a shallow patch known as the Barnacle just E of the pier.

OSEA ISLAND

The southern side of Osea Island has been used as an anchorage for centuries. Almost certainly the longboats of the Vikings lay there before the battle of Maldon in 654 AD and throughout the 19th century collier brigs would have waited off the island for water to take them up to the Hythe at Maldon.

The anchorage off Osea Island with a smack careened on the beach

MAYLANDSEA BAY PORT GUIDE

Blackwater Marina	Tel: 01621 740264
	VHF Ch M (ex-37)
Water	From pontoons at yard
Stores	Limited provisions from nearby shops
Services	Shower and toilet facilities
Fuel	At yard
Repairs	Yard with slipways, hoists, workshops
Chandler	At yard
Transport	Buses to Maldon and Chelmsford
Telephone	At marina clubhouse
Clubs	Maylandsea Bay Yacht Club; Harlow Blackwater Sailing Club
Restaurant/bar	Blackwater Marina

LAWLING CREEK AND MAYLANDSEA

Half a mile or so across the river from Osea lies Lawling Creek, the entrance to which is marked by a red can (Fl 3s). Once over the shallow bar (1m LWS) and past the yellow Blackwater Marina buoy, there are some small red and green spherical buoys, but more useful are the mooring buoys – showing a letter C – that have been laid in the middle of the channel. A yacht can reach the yard for about half the tide, but in a dinghy it is possible at almost any time. As well as the many swinging moorings that extend throughout the length of the creek, the yard has serviced floating pontoons and three slipways. All forms of repair and rigging can be undertaken and there is a launch service available.

It is a good thing for yachtsmen that the Maldon District Council buoy the Blackwater above Osea Island because the channel follows a much less obvious course in the upper reaches of the river. Just above the remains of Osea pier a green conical buoy guards a mudbank – known as the Doctor.

Above the Doctor the channel turns to the NW, past a port hand red can buoy. If a boat draws four or five feet, this is about as far up-river as she can expect to reach and remain afloat at LW. Two more buoys, one a green conical (Fl G 3s) and the other a red can – known locally as the Doubles – are located just above the entrance to Southey Creek.

By this time the maltings and mill buildings beyond Mill Beach should be seen about a mile ahead, and to the west of them a long, low, white building. This is the clubhouse of the Blackwater SC and it will serve as a mark on which to steer until the red can buoy marking Hilly Pool Point at the northern end of Northey Island is seen to port. A light (Iso G 5s) is shown from the roof of the Blackwater SC.

HEYBRIDGE BASIN

After rounding the Point and turning sharply southwards into Collier's Reach, the cluster of houses round Heybridge Lock will come into view about half a mile away. It is never very easy to tell whether the lock gates are open or shut until close to and in line with them, but if it is necessary to wait, there is good holding ground in the river outside the lock.

From an hour before to an hour after high water a boat drawing six or seven feet should have no great difficulty in getting into or out of Heybridge Lock. Because of the need to retain water in the canal during the summer months, the lock is worked for only one hour before HW during neap tides. At springs the lock will be worked over a longer period. Prior notification and confirmation with the lock-master is required if the lock is to be used at night.

The Basin is managed by The Chelmer and Blackwater Navigation Company, which provides berthing for visitors immediately inside the lock,

Approaching Colliers Reach, the maltings and mill buildings can be seen beyond the moored boats off Mill Beach

with adjacent facilities. There are two pubs and a cafe near the lock, and a daily launch service is available up the canal to Heybridge and Maldon where there are shops and superstores. The Basin has always been a stronghold for traditional boats and there are usually several classic old-timers together with local smacks undergoing restoration work alongside the towpath.

Preparing to come alongside the Hythe Quay at Maldon where there will usually be several barges and the pontoon for visiting yachts is heavily used

Heybridge Basin and the 14 mile Chelmer and Blackwater Navigation Canal were constructed in 1797 for the purpose of lightering coal into Chelmsford – hence Collier's Reach. A licence is necessary for boats navigating the canal.

From off the entrance to the lock, the river continues in a south-westerly direction for about a quarter of a mile before turning N round

Herring Point. From here up to Maldon the winding channel is well marked with conical green buoys on the starboard side and red cans on the port hand side.

MALDON

Towards the top of the tide you can sometimes find yourself approaching the town in company with one or more sailing barges, not to speak of smacks and other yachts. Bear in mind that the barges come alongside the quay with their bows pointing downstream and will therefore need room to manoeuvre.

Apart from one or two holes, the river dries out almost completely at Maldon, and the local boats take the mud. In 1892 H Lewis Jones wrote in *Swin, Swale and Swatchway* '...it is rather an undertaking to stay at Maldon Hythe...' Nowadays the visitors' pontoon at the north end of Hythe Quay is accessible about one and a half hours either side of HW. The pontoon is about 70ft long and if you are prepared to take the mud, and probably raft up, you can stay overnight. This is a delightful spot to stop over but it can get crowded – check with Chris Reynolds-Hole, Maldon District Council's River Warden. You will find him at the Bailiff's Hut on the Quay near Cook's Boatyard. Facilities include toilets, showers, washing machines, dryers and garbage disposal nearby.

For a short stay you may be able to lie alongside one of the barges, but your yacht

HEYBRIDGE BASIN PORT GUIDE	
Lock-master	Colin Edmond Tel/Fax 01621 853506; VHF Ch 80
Visitors' Berths	Immediately inside inner gates, some rafting up
Water and Electricity	At visitors' berths
Services	Toilets, showers and laundry
Stores	Launch service am daily (pm by arrangement) to shops, Tesco at Heybridge/Maldon
Fuel	Diesel can be delivered by arrangement. Petrol, gas from garages at Heybridge
Transport	Infrequent buses to Maldon (whence good connections)
Telephone	110 yards from lock
Repairs	Chelmer & Blackwater Navigation Co operates repair service. Lift up to 6 tons
Club	Blackwater SC Tel 01621 853923 (quarter mile from lock) Chelmer and Blackwater Navigation Co 10 Bradford Street, Braintree Tel 01621 855433

should not be left unattended. Several barges are based at Hythe Quay including the Thames Barge Sailing Club's *Centaur* and *Pudge*; the annual Blackwater Barge Match usually takes place in early June.

Maldon's name derives from *Maeldun*, Anglo Saxon for cross on a hill top. Here the Saxons built a fort to defend the River Blackwater against marauding Norsemen – to whom they finally succumbed in 991 at the Battle of Maldon. As you pass the western end of Northey Island, give a thought to the heroic defence by Brythnoth's men against the Danes a thousand years ago. Access to the National Trust-owned island can be arranged by contacting the NT warden.

The town went on to prosper as a fishing and trading port, the Royal Charter was granted, and ships were built such as the 48-gun *The Jersey*, which served with Blake in the Mediterranean. She was launched at the yard where, several hundred years later, John Howard created a succession of beautiful Maldon barges and smacks. At that same yard during the last century, Dan Webb built the famous little Blackwater sloops, many of which are still sailing today.

MALDON PORT GUIDE	
The Hythe Quay	
River Warden	Chris Reynolds-Hole (Bailiff's Hut) Tel 01621 856487; Mobile 07818 013723
Water	Standpipe on quayside near pontoon
Stores	Many shops in town. EC Wed; Tesco at Fullbridge (10–15 minute walk)
Fuel	Diesel and petrol from Promenade Garage (own cans) Tel 01621 852821
Repairs Chandlery	Yards and slips above The Hythe Maldon Chandlery, North Street Tel 01621 854280
Sailmaker	Taylors, The Hythe
Transport	Bus to Chelmsford main line railway station
Clubs	Maldon Little Ship Club, The Hythe Tel 01621 854139; Maldon YC
Food and Drink	Queen's Head and Jolly Sailor on The Hythe; pubs and restaurants in High Street; local oysters and seafood at Essex Oyster and Seafishing Company behind Cook's Yard on quayside (occasional during summer). NT Northey Island 01621 853142

Maldon from the air at High Water. The swimming pool and promenade can be seen bottom left, with the Hythe and various boatyard jetties along the town bank leading up to Fullbridge, the navigable head of the Blackwater

THE RIVER CROUCH

Tides	HW Dover +1.10 Range: Springs 5.0m Neaps 3.2m (HW at Whitaker Beacon approx (Burnham on Crouch) 20mins before HW at Burnham)
Charts	Admiralty 3750, Stanford No 4, Imray Y15, OS Map 168
Waypoints	Wallet Spitway Buoy 51°42'.87N 01°07'.30E

<table>
<tr><td></td><td>Wallet Spitway Buoy 51°42'.87N 01°07'.30E</td><td>Swin Spitway Buoy 51°41'.96N 01°08'.32E</td></tr>
<tr><td></td><td>Whitaker Bell Buoy 51°41'.44N 01°10'.50E</td><td>Whitaker Beacon 51°39'.65N 01°06'.17E</td></tr>
<tr><td></td><td>Ridge Buoy 51°40'.13N 01°04'.88E</td><td>Sunken Buxey Buoy 51°39'.53N 01°00'.60E</td></tr>
<tr><td></td><td>Outer Crouch Buoy 51°38'.38N 00°58'.51E</td><td>Buxey Beacon 51°41'.16N 01°01'.30E</td></tr>
<tr><td>Hazard</td><td colspan="2">Shoal water between Swin Spitway and Whitaker Beacon</td></tr>
</table>

Some people say Burnham's popularity as a sailing centre has declined recently, but if you arrive in the Crouch during Burnham Week, you'll be thankful the place is no more popular than it already is. As a river, the Crouch can hardly be described as beautiful. Its higher reaches are certainly more pleasant than the five or six miles between Burnham and Shore Ends, where nothing much can be seen above the bordering sea walls except for a short while at high tide. Yet, because of these unobstructed shores, the Crouch offers racing yachtsmen the best possible sport and, with the smaller river Roach entering at right angles, a variety of courses can be laid to suit all wind conditions.

BUOYAGE OF RIVER CROUCH

Buoyage and marking of the River Crouch is the responsibility of the Crouch Harbour Authority. All the buoys were lit in the 1980s when there was considerable commercial traffic by a company importing and landing timber at Baltic Wharf, Wallasea. Some buoys were removed about 10 years ago when shipping declined, although there is still a working cargo terminal at the wharf.

From Battlesbridge, the navigable limit of the river, down to Shore Ends where the Crouch clears the land, is approximately 15 miles. From Shore Ends out to the Whitaker bell buoy, marking the extremity of the Whitaker Spit, is another nine or 10 miles.

Excluding the top-of-the-tide entrance through Havengore Creek and the river Roach, there are two approaches to the Crouch: through the Whitaker Channel from the Swin or the Spitway and through the very shallow Ray Sand (Rays'n) Channel between Dengie Flats and the Buxey Sands. The deep water approach will be considered first.

When coming from the N through the Swin Spitway, shape a course of 180°M from the Wallet Spitway buoy towards Whitaker No 6 buoy and, to avoid the eastward-extending Swallowtail shoal, continue until the Ridge buoy (red can with topmark) bears 255°M before altering course to pass just N of the Ridge buoy. From the Ridge and Foulness buoys, a course should be set to Buxey No 1 buoy, leaving the S Buxey (conical green) buoy to starboard.

The channel between the Ridge and Swallow Tail is wide and deep, but the channel to the north of the Swallow Tail, along the south-east shore of the Buxey Sand, is often used when sailing between the Spitway and S Buxey buoys. As a result a safe water mark, North Swallow, has been established here. The buoy is an unlit pillar buoy, red and white vertical stripes with a red ball topmark.

The Sunken Buxey shoal is marked on both sides, and many yachtsmen prefer to pass to the south of it, leaving the S Cardinal, Buxey No 1 (VQ(6)+L Fl 10s) buoy to starboard and the N Cardinal Buxey No 2 (FlR 10s) to port. This way in is probably easier with a fair wind or under power, but when beating, the northern side of the shoal will allow longer boards.

The Swin Spitway Buoy

When coming from the S round the Whitaker Beacon, deep water will be found about midway between Whitaker No 6 (N Cardinal) and the Ridge buoy, and when the latter bears 255°M, alter onto that course.

Continue as described above, and once the Outer Crouch buoy (S Cardinal VQ(6) + LFl 15s) has been located, course should be shaped to leave it close to starboard and thence into the river.

THE RAYSAND CHANNEL

Moderate draught yachts bound from the Blackwater to the Crouch can, at the right state of the tide, come through the Ray Sand or Rays'n Channel. There is little or no water in the southern end of the swatchway at LWS, in fact it is possible at low water extraordinary springs to walk virtually dry footed from the mainland to the Buxey Sands.

The time honoured Buxey Beacon still stands where it did when Maurice Griffiths wrote *The Magic of the Swatchways*, but no longer with its easily recognised sign-post topmark. Instead, a N Cardinal mark tops the beacon which, like the Whitaker, has a tripod base. Trinity House has now disowned this and several other beacons in the Thames Estuary, so we must hope that local authorities or yacht clubs will see that they are maintained in future.

The Dengie Flats were once used as a dive-bombing range and four derelict target craft still remain as a reminder. These wrecks are marked by unlit beacons; the two inshore having W Cardinal topmarks and the outer two with E Cardinal topmarks.

When bound from the Wallet past the Knoll buoy, the best course to hold into the Rays'n will be 235°M. The N Buxey buoy is no longer there to guide you, but sudden changes in depth near the

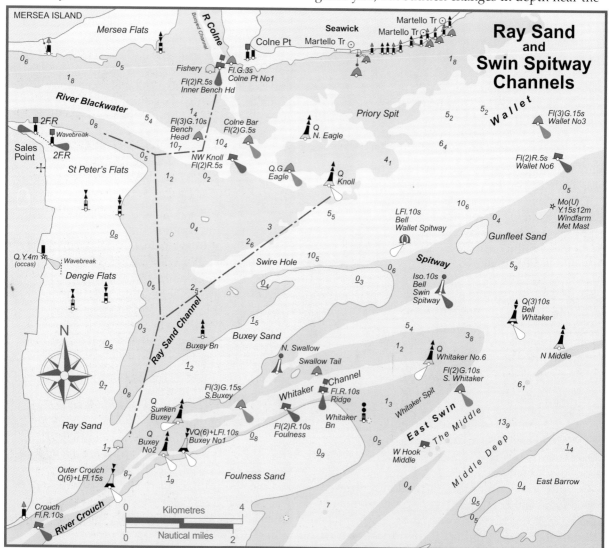

Keelboat moorings off the Burnham waterfront, where sailing activity is largely geared to racing. The clubhouse of the Royal Burnham Yacht Club is in the centre of the picture

Chapter 12

Swire Hole should serve to locate you on the chart. When the Buxey Beacon bears 180°M, change course to 215°M to pass it about half a mile away to port.

Finally, when the conspicuous pylons on Foulness Island come to bear 210°M, change on to this course until the deeper water of the Crouch is found – about a mile to the W of the Sunken Buxey buoy, with its double cone (N Cardinal) topmark.

Shallow draught boats, using a rising tide, can often sneak through the Rays'n closer inshore by following a course approximately 185°M and about a mile to seaward of the outer pair of wrecked target vessels. This is the area in which to change course to about N, if bound from the Crouch to the Blackwater.

A small spherical yellow buoy is laid in the S entrance to the Rays'n by the Burnham yacht clubs and is intended to indicate a way through the swatch. During the summer of 2003 the Rays'n buoy was in position 51°39.15N 00°59.30E, but it is liable to be moved. There was a shallow patch to the west of this buoy, which is best treated as if it were an east cardinal mark. Even so, do not expect to find any clear cut channel or gutway.

About one and a half miles SW of the Outer Crouch buoy and just inside the river itself is the Crouch red can buoy (Fl R 10s). After the Crouch buoy direction is changed to a westerly course, which can be held up-river as far as the junction

Fine Georgian buildings line the Burnham Town Quay, dating back to a time before yachtsmen arrived, with the railway line, in the 1890s

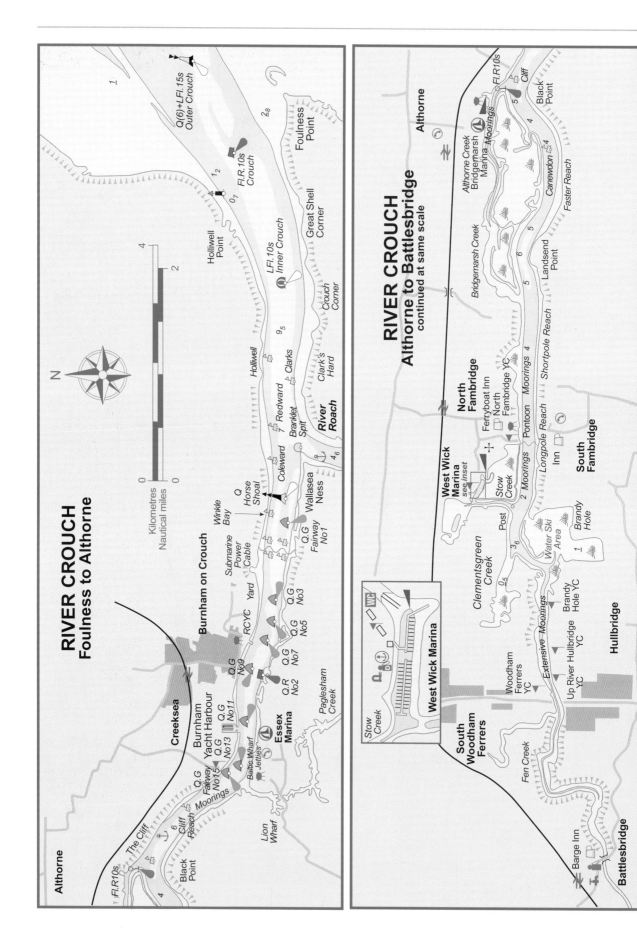

RIVER CROUCH
Foulness to Althorne

N

Kilometres
Nautical miles

Q(6)+LFl.15s
Outer Crouch

Fl.R.10s
Crouch

Holliwell
Point

Foulness
Point

Great Shell
Corner

LFl.10s
Inner Crouch

Crouch
Corner

Holliwell

Clark's
Hard

Redward

Clarks

Branklet
Spit

**River
Roach**

Coleward

Wallasea
Ness

Horse
Shoal

Winkle
Bay

Submarine
Power
Cable

Q.G
Fairway
No1

Q.G
No3

Q.G
No5

Q.G
No7

Q.R
No2

Q.G
No9

Paglesham
Creek

RCYC Yard

Burnham on Crouch

Q.G
No11

Q.G
No13

**Essex
Marina**

Baltic Wharf
Jetties

Burnham
Yacht Harbour

Q.G
No15

Fairway
Moorings

The Cliff

Cliff Reach

Creeksea

Lion
Wharf

Black
Point

Fl.R10s

Althorne

RIVER CROUCH
Althorne to Battlesbridge
continued at same scale

Fl.R10s

Cliff

Black
Point

Althorne

Althorne Creek

Bridgemarsh
Marina

Canewdon

Easter Reach

Bridgemarsh Creek

Landsend
Point

Shortpole Reach

Longpole Reach

Moorings

North
Fambridge

**North
Fambridge**

Ferryboat Inn

North
Fambridge YC

West Wick
Marina
see inset

Stow
Creek

Post

**South
Fambridge**

Inn

Moorings

Pontoon

Moorings

Moorings

Brandy
Hole

Water Ski
Area

Clementsgreen
Creek

Woodham
Ferrers
YC

Extensive Moorings

Brandy
Hole YC

Up River Hullbridge
YC

Hullbridge

**South
Woodham
Ferrers**

Fen Creek

Stow
Creek

West Wick Marina

WC

Barge Inn

Battlesbridge

of the river Roach about three miles away. Half-way between the Crouch buoy and the entrance to the Roach is the Sph RW Inner Crouch (L Fl W 10s), which can be passed on either hand. Two racing buoys may be seen on the northern side of the channel, just below the entrance to the Roach, and these should be left to the north to be sure of missing the mud of Redward Flats. The Branklet Spit buoy (Sph Y) marks an arm of mud that extends north-easterly from Wallasea Ness. West of Branklet Spit the deepest water is to be found near the N bank of the river. However, because the south shore is steep-to, it is often the safer one to work.

A North Cardinal buoy – Horse (Q Fl) – just west of the entrance to the river Roach, was originally intended to mark the S end of a dredged channel leading to the Burnham Fairway buoy; but it is doubtful whether the channel still remains.

BURNHAM

Burnham-on-Crouch has long been considered as the Cowes of the East Coast. When the Great Eastern branch railway line was built in the 1890s, boat owners migrated to Burnham from the then busy and dirty Thames and found the Crouch to be a better location for both cruising and racing. Thus it was that a quiet oyster-fishing village turned rapidly into a popular yachting centre, and has remained so to this day.

According to Francis B Cooke '...a year or two before the outbreak of the Great War ...there were more than eight hundred craft... lying off the town.' Boatyards, sailmakers, chandleries and stores flourished, and fleets of the elegant East Coast One-Designs, followed by the Royal Burnham and the Royal Corinthian One-Designs were launched. In the '60s, Tucker Brown, whose premises now house the local museum, produced

The Contented Sole restaurant in Burnham-on-Crouch

BURNHAM-ON-CROUCH PORT GUIDE

Crouch Harbour Authority
Harbour Master
Tel 01621 783602 Mon–Fri 0930 to 1130;
email: h.m@cha.valiant.co.uk
CHA Launch Weekends 0900 to 1700; VHF Ch 16 and M (ex-37)

Burnham Yacht Harbour
Tel 01621 782150; Fax 785848; VHF Ch 80

Berths	350 at Yacht Harbour
Swinging Moorings	Rice & Cole, Sea End Boathouse Tel 782063 RJ Prior & Sons Tel 0782160
Water	Yacht Harbour, Rice & Cole pontoon, stand-pipes near most landing places
Stores	Co-op near Yacht Harbour open late most eves and Sun am. Shops in High Street. EC Wed
Fuel	Diesel from yacht harbour; petrol from Essex Marina fuel barge at Wallasea or garage in town; gas from chandlery at yacht harbour
Repairs	100 ton slipway, 30 ton hoist, engineers, riggers at Yacht Harbour; Rice & Cole, Sea End Boathouse
Chandlery	On site at Yacht Harbour Fairways Yacht Chandlery, The Quay Tel 782659
Sailmakers	Lonton & Gray, 61c High Street Tel 786200
Transport	Train service to London via Wickford except on Sundays in winter months. (Station about 10 minutes walk from yacht harbour)
Clubs	Royal Corinthian Yacht Club (Tel 782105) Royal Burnham Yacht Club (Tel 782044) Crouch Yacht Club (Tel 782252) Burnham Sailing Club (Tel 782624)
Telephone	Near White Hart
Food and Drink	Swallowtail lounge bar and restaurant at Yacht Harbour (Tel 785505); bar and restaurant at Royal Corinthian and Crouch YCs; White Harte (Tel 782106) and other pubs on Quay and High Street; Contented Sole (Tel 782139) specializes in seafood; Dengie Shellfish stall near War Memorial off High Street

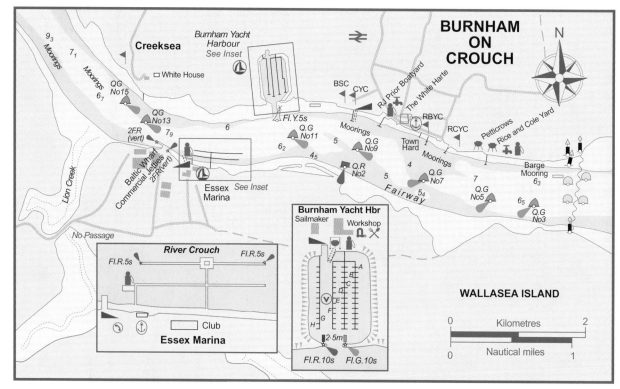

a galaxy of Stellas, and Priors built offshore racers such as Maurice Laing's *Vashti*. Nowadays Petticrows turn out glassfibre Dragons that are sold worldwide – the Burnham Dragon fleet is one of the strongest in the UK.

Approaching Burnham from the river, after the featureless seawall scenery in the lower reaches of the Crouch, you cannot fail to notice the clubhouse of the Royal Corinthian Yacht Club.

This edifice dominates the eastern end of the town's skyline from miles away. When it was built in 1931, J Wentworth Day, that staunch defender of traditional Essex, described it as '....a cross between a football grandstand and a town hall of Teutonic conception...' The concrete and plate glass construction seems out of keeping with the mellow Georgian houses further along the red brick quayside, yet it has become an

A lit yellow safe water buoy marks the entrance to Burnham Yacht Harbour. The pair of port and starboard, red and green, entrance beacons can also be seen on either side beyond the buoy

integral part of Burnham's waterfront image and is now a listed building.

The many yacht moorings off Burnham commence just above a group of four yellow spherical buoys marking submerged cables carrying 33,000 volts. The Burnham Fairway is on the S side of the river and although narrow, it is well marked by eight starboard-hand buoys (QG) and one port-hand can buoy (QR). There is at least 4 m of water throughout the length of the Fairway and the south shore is steep-to. When it becomes necessary to beat up-river and boards on the port tack are extended in among the moored craft, a close watch should be kept on the effects of the tide, for the ebb at spring tides can run at 3 knots past Burnham.

Anchoring is prohibited in the fairway, and the multitude of moorings makes it very difficult to bring up to an anchor anywhere in the area. For brief stops you may be able use one of the pontoons along the waterfront: from the east these are at Rice & Cole's, the Royal Corinthian YC, the Royal Burnham YC, Prior's and the Crouch YC. You can usually find a buoy off one of the clubs or yards, although during Burnham Week (which always starts near the August bank holiday weekend) this would need pre-booking. The Royal Corinthian Yacht Club has a visitor's mooring sited directly off their clubhouse, but if this is occupied, enquiries will usually lead to the provision of some other vacant buoy. It should be noted that the tide runs fast through the moorings, particularly on a spring ebb, so for longer stays the visiting yachtsman would be well advised to head for the 350-berth Burnham Yacht Harbour, accessible at all states of the tide, at the western end of the town.

The entrance is marked by a yellow pillar buoy with X topmark (Fl Y 5s) and a couple of posts with red and green flashing lights.

The little town is a pleasant place, there are facilities for yachtsmen close at hand and many of its people are in some way connected with sailing.

WALLASEA BAY

On the opposite shore and about a mile up-river from Burnham is Wallasea Bay. Here again the moorings are numerous, but this time located along the S as well as the N side of the river. Many of the yachts at Wallasea Bay remain afloat along the outside of the Essex Marina pontoons, in plenty of water at all states of the tide. The marina has finger-berth pontoons

The conspicuous concrete and plate glass Royal Corinthian YC

and some pile berths have been established along with toilet, shower and laundry facilities. The fuel barge is located on the upriver, or W end of the inshore pontoon near the slipway.

The western end of Burnham Fairway is marked by the No 13 buoy off the Baltic wharf, which is strictly commercial with no facilities to the public. There is shallow water on the north side of the river just below Creeksea.

The river now turns north-westerly through Cliff Reach; so called because of the modest (40-50ft) cliff just above Creeksea. Cliff Reach

WALLASEA BAY PORT GUIDE

Essex Marina	Tel 01702 258531; VHF Ch 80
	www.essexmarina.co.uk
Water	From pontoon
Stores	Shop near boatyard
Fuel	Petrol and diesel from fuel barge
Chandlery	In Harbour Master's office
Repairs	Yard with slipway, crane (13 ton),
	hoist (40 ton)
Meals	Restaurant nearby
Transport	Bus from Loftman's Corner (2 miles
	away) to Southend-on-Sea
Club	Essex Marina Yacht Club
Telephone	W end of sea wall

is important to the yachtsman inasmuch as it provides shelter from south-westerly winds, when most of the other reaches in the Crouch are made uncomfortable. Towards low tide a good look-out should be kept for a line of concrete sinkers that can be found along the low water line below the cliff. At the top of Cliff Reach the main stream turns south-westerly round Black Point, where the shore is steep-to, into Easter Reach. But a minor branch continues north-west.

ALTHORNE CREEK

A yellow racing buoy marked 'Cliff Reach' is usually located off Black Point, and it provides a point for entering Althorne Creek.

The entrance to the creek is now identified by a port-hand spar (FlR10s) and a series of three red can buoys. The course when entering is roughly N (°M), leaving the beacon and the first red can close to port.

At Bridgemarsh Marina (Tel 01621 740414) there are over a hundred boats moored to pontoons between piles along the centre of the creek, both above and below the spot where there was once a ford leading on to Bridgemarsh Island. There are six visitors' moorings, while on the N bank is a yard comprising two docks, a slipway, a crane and pontoons equipped with water and power, with toilet and showers provided. Althorne station is only about a quarter of a mile away, whence it is no more than an hour to Liverpool Street station in London.

NORTH FAMBRIDGE PORT GUIDE	
North Fambridge Yacht Station	Tel 01621 740370
West Wick Marina (Stow Creek)	Tel 01621 741268
Berths	180 at marina
Water	Near boat shed at Yacht Station, on pontoons at marina
Stores	Shop and PO at N Fambridge (0.5 mile)
Fuel	Diesel at marina
Repairs	Facilities and crane (5 ton) available at Yacht Station and Marina
Chandlery	Yacht Station and Marina
Transport	Trains to London from Fambridge station (one mile) except on Sundays in winter months
Club	North Fambridge YC, West Wick YC
Food and Drink	At Ferry Boat Inn Tel 01621 740208

It is possible in a small craft, with a rising tide and a commanding wind, to sail through Althorne Creek and Bridgemarsh Creek to join the Crouch again some two miles further up-stream; but the channel is extremely narrow and tortuous.

From the Cliff Reach buoy the river flows south-westerly through Easter Reach, where during the summer the last of the racing buoys – Canewdon – is located in mid-stream in about 5m at LW. Then, from abreast the point where Bridgemarsh Creek emerges from behind the western end of the island, the river flows westerly for two or three miles straight through Shortpole and Longpole Reaches up to and beyond North and South Fambridge. There is no less than 4m of water in mid-channel up as far as North Fambridge.

NORTH FAMBRIDGE

Francis B Cooke (whose many books on small boat cruising have become collectors' items) contributed an autobiographical note entitled: *Birth of a Great Yacht Station* to *Yachting Monthly* on the occasion of his 100th birthday:

'Anyone seeing Fambridge today for the first time could hardly imagine what a delightful waterside hamlet it was when I first discovered it (in 1893). The only buildings near the water were Fambridge Hall, the old Ferry Boat Inn, a tiny school, a row of four or five small timber built cottages, an old barn and the little church nestling among the trees. The road leading down to the Ferry hard was just a narrow country lane, with wild roses blooming in the summer. My friends the Viner brothers had decided to spend the summer there and asked me to join them. I readily agreed and we arranged with the landlady of the Ferry Boat Inn to board there. She agreed to take us for twelve shillings a week and hoped she was not charging too much, but of course that would include our laundry.'

There are four lines of moorings off Fambridge, with a fairway between them, and these are administered by the North Fambridge Yacht Station. The only possible places to anchor are above or below these moorings, but there is plenty of water (2.5m) even at Low Water Springs.

Landing is possible on the hard, or at the floating pontoon near the North Fambridge YC clubhouse on the N bank. Landing on the south bank is not easy.

STOW CREEK

Rather less than a mile above Fambridge, Stow Creek enters the river from the N side.

The entrance is marked with a beacon on a pile, and this should be left close to starboard when entering. The creek is then identified (occasionally) with starboard hand withies up to the entrance to West Wick Marina, just over a quarter of a mile from the entrance. Access is possible for about five hours either side of HW. Here, boats lie to pontoons, in about 1m at LWS.

Above Stow Creek the river narrows and shallows fairly rapidly. Clementsgreen Creek is navigable only around HW and, since it is dammed, it is of little interest to yachtsmen.

BRANDY HOLE

From abreast Clementsgreen Creek the river turns south-westerly through Brandy Hole reach into Brandy Hole Bay, which is a water-skiing area and very busy at weekends. Moorings begin again off Brandy Hole YC and continue for a mile or more up to the entrance to Fenn Creek, just above the ford at Hullbridge. Anywhere along here a boat will take the ground for an hour or two either side of LW. Watch out for a spit extending from the N bank just above Brandy Hole YC.

HULLBRIDGE

Hullbridge YC lies half a mile above Brandy Hole YC, and here there is a jetty and slipway. Shallow draught boats can lie against the jetty, which has a tide gauge at each end marked in feet. Water is available from the rear of the clubhouse where there are showers and toilets (keys in office); and there are scrubbing posts which can be used, tide permitting, by arrangement.

The other yacht club on the S shore at Hullbridge is the Up River YC, which has dinghy sailors as well as a cruising membership, while on the N bank near the road down to the ford is the Woodham Ferrers YC.

HW at Hullbridge is 25 minutes later than at Burnham.

BATTLESBRIDGE

Above Hullbridge the river becomes very narrow and tortuous, and in places is no more than 10 or 12m wide between the retaining walls, although there are some moorings in Long Reach. At springs, a boat drawing 2m can take the tide right up to Battlesbridge, where there is an antiques centre based in the old mill buildings and a typical Essex weather-boarded pub, The Barge, near the quayside. Unless the return trip is commenced almost immediately, it would be best to moor alongside the concrete landing quay, or a small pontoon on the S bank.

HULLBRIDGE (BRANDY HOLE) PORT GUIDE	
Brandy Hole Yacht Station	Tel 01702 230248
Water	At hard and clubhouses
Stores	At Hullbridge village
Fuel	Diesel at Brandy Hole Yacht Station, petrol at Garages (one mile)
Repairs	Boatyard adjacent to Brandy Hole Yacht Club
Transport	Buses from Hullbridge to Southend (from The Anchor)
Clubs	Brandy Hole YC. Up River YC Hullbridge YC. Woodham Ferrers YC

Hullbridge Yacht Club on the south bank of the Crouch above Brandy Hole boasts a jetty, a slipway and scrubbing posts

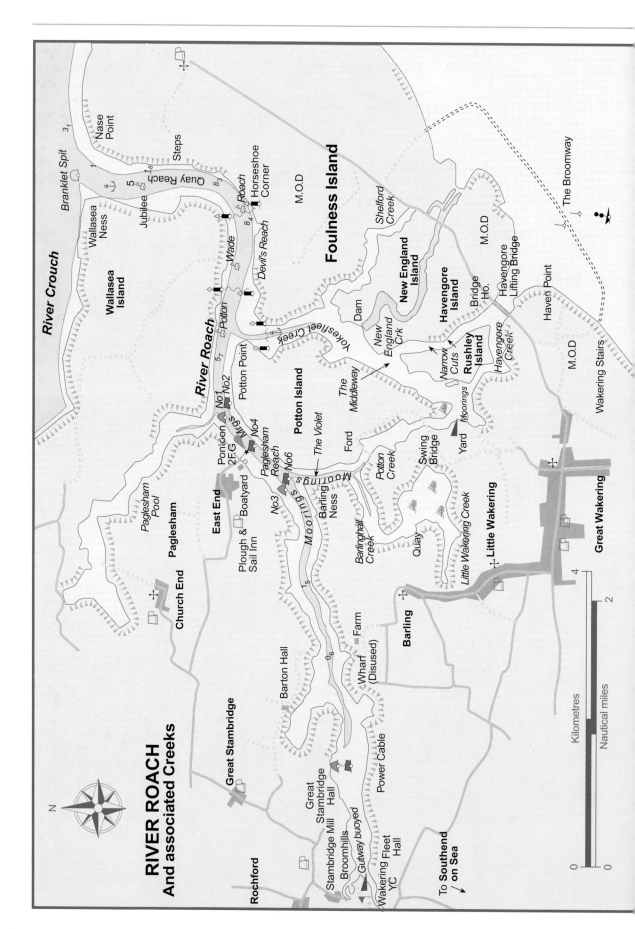

RIVER ROACH
And associated Creeks

N

River Crouch

Branklet Spit

Nase Point

3.1

1

Wallasea Ness

Jubilee Steps

Quay Reach

5

1.8

8.3

Reach

Horseshoe Corner

Wallasea Island

Wade

8.4

Devil's Reach

M.O.D

Foulness Island

Shelford Creek

Potton

Yokesfleet Creek

River Roach

Dam

New England Creek

New England Island

5.7

Potton Point

The Middleway

Havengore Island

Bridge Ho.

Havengore Lifting Bridge

M.O.D

No1

No2

Moorings

2 F.G

Pontoon

No4

Paglesham Reach

No6

Potton Island

The Violet

Ford

Narrow Cuts

Moorings

Rushley Island

Havengore Creek

Haven Point

M.O.D

East End

Plough & Sail Inn

No3

Barling Ness

Moorings

Swing Bridge

Yard

Wakering Stairs

Paglesham

Church End

Paglesham Pool

Barton Hall

1.5

Barlinghall Creek

Potton Creek

Quay

Little Wakering Creek

Little Wakering

Haven Point

The Broomway

Rochford

Great Stambridge

Great Stambridge Hall

Stambridge Mill Hall

Broomhills

Gutway buoyed

Wakering Fleet YC Hall

Power Cable

Farm

Wharf (Disused)

0.6

Barling

Great Wakering

To Southend on Sea

0   2   4
Kilometres

0   2
Nautical miles

THE RIVER ROACH AND HAVENGORE

Tides (Paglesham)	HW Dover +1.10 Range: Springs 5.0m Neaps 3.2m
Charts	Admiralty 3750, Stanford No 4, Imray Y 17, OS Map No 178
Waypoints	Branklet Spit 51°36'.98N 00°52'.15E, South Shoebury Buoy 51°30'.44N 00°52'.40E
Hazard	Havengore route – except on rising tide

Yachtsmen who are based on the Roach consider it to be a better river than the Crouch. Its several changes of direction offer a wider variety of sailing and its upper reaches have remained quite unspoilt. Another advantage is that Havengore is nearby to provide us with a back door to the Thames and Medway or even across the estuary to the (North) Foreland.

From its junction with the River Crouch, about three miles inside Shore Ends, the Roach winds for some six miles in a mainly south-westerly direction up to its tidal limit at Stambridge Mill. Apart from the lower reaches below Paglesham, the Roach is very narrow at low water and not many craft use the river above Barling Ness.

What does make the Roach interesting to many yachtsmen is the network of subsidiary creeks which link the river with the sea over the Maplin Sands. The best-known and most important of these small channels is Havengore Creek which, passing Rushley and Havengore Islands, leads through a lifting bridge at its eastern end to the Thames Estuary. By using this creek after crossing the Maplins near HW, it is possible for small and shallow craft to reach the Roach without having to sail down the W Swin and up the Whitaker Channel.

At its mouth at HW the Roach is more than a quarter of a mile wide, but mud extends from both banks to reduce the LW channel to half that width. The mud extending from Wallasea Ness is marked by the Branklet Spit buoy (Sph Y). On the eastern side of the entrance a substantial amount of mud extends from Nase Point and many boats have been tripped up here. The best water is to be found close to the Branklet spit itself.

QUAY REACH

There is not much less than 6m at LW in the middle of the river right along Quay Reach. The direction of this lowest reach of the Roach is roughly N–S, and because of this it often provides a more comfortable berth than any anchorage in the Crouch below Creeksea. Not only is there good protection from westerly and easterly winds, but there is also plenty of room and good holding ground in stiff mud towards either shore.

On the E shore there are some very weedy and slippery landing steps built into a small promontory in the Foulness seawall. It is possible, but not easy, to land here and walk to Church End for a drink at the weather-boarded George and Dragon pub. The walk takes 30 to 40 minutes, but remember that Foulness is MOD property, so you must keep to the track. You may also visit St Mary's Church, the spire of which, along with those of nearby Little and Great Wakering and Barling churches, served as a useful landmark for sailors along this low lying and otherwise featureless coast. Indeed when St Mary's was re-built in the 1850s, Trinity House made a large donation on condition that it had a spire.

From the entrance up to Horseshoe Corner at the southern end of Quay Reach is just over a mile; then the river turns through more than a right angle to continue westerly into Devil's Reach. The deep water round this bend, known as Whitehouse Hole, is marked by a yellow racing buoy – Roach – in about 6m at LW. The many, named, yellow buoys in the lower reaches of the Crouch and Roach from March to December are used by the Burnham yacht clubs' racing fleets.

The next racing buoy is Wade (formerly Whitehouse) located further up-river, after which the channel divides just below Potton buoy. The principal arm continues westerly along the northern side of Potton Island, leading to Paglesham Reach, while the other branch turns S, along the eastern side of Potton, into the Yokesfleet.

Potton Creek looking north from Great Wakering. Above the boatyard and moorings is the swing bridge connecting Potton Island and, left to right at the top, the River Roach

Just upstream of the second set of cable markers, and between Potton and Wade racing buoys in Devil's Reach, there are oyster crates at LWS. These extend for about 300 yards and are marked by three small green buoys, the end ones having triangular topmarks.

A little further up river, just before the main channel turns southwest along the Potton shore, there are more oyster beds, marked by a pink mooring buoy and withies.

PAGLESHAM REACH

Just before the moorings in Paglesham Reach the main channel turns to the SW abreast the entrance to Paglesham Pool (or Creek). This narrow creek carries such a small amount of water at low tide as to be of little interest for navigation.

Just above the junction of Paglesham Pool with the Roach are the first of the Paglesham moorings, which extend both below and above

PAGLESHAM PORT GUIDE	
Water	At Essex Boatyards
Transport	Buses from East End to Rochford, whence trains to London
Telephone	Near Plough and Sail at top of lane
Food and Drink	Plough and Sail, East End Paglesham, half a mile up lane Tel 01702 258242

Shuttlewood's old black shed. In the late 1800s there was a flourishing fleet of oyster smacks on the river, many of which, along with barges, were built in this very shed.

Moorings are laid on both sides of the channel, and the Crouch Harbour Board's port and starboard-hand buoys mark the extent of a fairway within which anchoring is prohibited. Visiting yachtsmen can anchor just below the moorings off Paglesham Pool. The Crouch Harbour Authority has laid a small landing place inside the Pool, about 100 yards from the concrete pill box on the west shore seawall. This allows (almost) clean landing from a dinghy whence you can walk north to the Punchbowl at Church End or west along the seawall, through the boatyard and up the lane to the Plough and Sail at East End. Craft with little draught or those that can take the ground can anchor in the Pool (the mouth dries at LWS), or might sometimes be able to find an anchorage just outside the northern limit of the fairway. A riding light is essential when anchored in the Roach overnight – the river is regularly used by fishing vessels and at high water by small freighters bound for Stambridge either day or night.

The boatyard moorings in Paglesham Reach have not been maintained in recent years so it is not advisable to use these. However, there are two rows of regularly maintained private moorings immediately downstream of the pontoon and slipway. Labelled RS1 – 13, these moorings are run by members of the Roach Sailing Association, who will allow visitors to use vacant buoys. Please take heed of the tonnage details on each mooring.

'Off Paglesham itself the trees in the background, contrasting with the flat land all around, make it a pleasant place at which to lie at anchor, the more so as Mr Shuttlewood has lately made an excellent hard upon which (one) can land cleanly.'

Since Archie White wrote that about the Roach in 1948, the hard has been widened to a slipway and, alongside it, an all-tide pontoon was nearing completion at the end of 2003. Clean landing is possible at most stages of the tide and you can tie a dinghy to it. However, at the time of writing it was not advisable to bring a yacht alongside this pontoon, the end of which is marked by two fixed green lights. Essex Boatyards Ltd sells motorboats from here and there are no longer any facilities for visiting yachtsmen except for fresh water.

The hamlet of East End, which yachtsmen usually think of as Paglesham, is about half a mile up the lane from the landing. Food and drink are available at the Plough and Sail, at East End, or, further inland, at the Punchbowl, Church End – both traditional, weatherboarded Essex inns.

Above the Paglesham moorings the river forks again at Barling Ness, the main stream continuing westerly towards Rochford and the other arm turning S between Barling Marsh and Potton Island. The continuation of the main channel west of Barling Ness is sometimes referred to as the Broomhill river. There is 1 to 1.5m of water at LWS up as far as the disused Barling Quay on the S bank, after which the channel narrows rapidly into a gutway that can be navigated only towards HW, and then only with much sounding or local knowledge. At HW boats drawing 1 to 1.5m can continue as far up river as the mill at Stambridge – a mile short of the town of Rochford. On the whole, best water will be found roughly midway between the banks in these upper reaches, but the broad entrance to Bartonhall Creek must be avoided on the N bank. A power cable crosses the river hereabouts and is marked by a green conical and a red can buoy.

STAMBRIDGE

Just below Stambridge Mill the river divides for the last time, the southern arm becoming Fleethall Creek where there is a wharf used by small freighters and a slipway at Carters Yard capable of handling craft up to 60 tons and 70ft LOA. A few smaller boats are catered for and some lay up here. The Wakering YC has its clubhouse at this yard and a pontoon that extends downriver, but this is only suitable for shoal draught craft as there is very little water even at springs. The club, which has a bar, is open at weekends and serves Sunday lunch.

Ships bringing grain to Stambridge Mill berth on the N side of the river just below the sluice gates, but yachts are not permitted to use the quay.

YOKESFLEET CREEK

Returning now to the S bank of the river, the branch of the Roach, which turns S at Potton

It is possible to walk to the boatyard at Paglesham Waterside along the seawall from the landing place near Paglesham Pool

Chapter 13

Point, is variously know as Yokesfleet Creek and the Gore Channel. The entrance to this creek requires care as a spit of mud stretches out from Potton Point and there is also an extensive mud flat off the opposite point. Best water will be found close under the Potton or western shore for the first few cables inside. There are depths of about two metres at LW for the first quarter of a mile or so inside the creek, and the spot provides a quiet and comfortable anchorage during either W or E winds.

About a mile within Yokesfleet Creek two lesser creeks branch out on the eastern side. The first is Shelford Creek, which once reached the sea along the S side of Foulness Island; and the second, New England Creek, has been dammed just within its entrance. This barrier across New England Creek provides a useful reference point as it is at the next division of the main channel that Narrow Cuts leads off south-easterly towards Havengore Bridge.

Shelford Creek is blocked by a fixed road bridge towards its seaward end and is therefore of little use to yachtsmen, but there is enough water for most small boats to lie afloat in Yokesfleet Creek or the Middleway, which it becomes above the junction of Shelford and New England creeks. About half a mile along the Middleway the channel again divides, this time around Rushley Island. Narrow Cuts, the more easterly arm, is used by craft passing to and from Havengore Bridge. Although it all but dries out at LW, there is enough water in the gutway through Narrow Cuts to allow boats drawing up to 1.5m to get through towards HW. But the narrow channel is tortuous and must be followed, even at HW, to avoid grounding. After leaving Yokesfleet Creek at the junction of the Middleway, keep close to the port hand sea wall up to a sluice, then begin to alter course towards the starboard bank, using the low roof of a distant barn as a mark. There may be a stake marking a hump on the starboard hand, followed by an even more important red topped stake to be left to port, after which there may be no more marks. On sighting the bridge from Narrow Cuts, do not be tempted to take a short cut at HW, but remain close to the starboard bank. It is certainly preferable for a stranger – if he can – to make his first acquaintance with Narrow Cuts early

on a tide, while the mud is still largely uncovered.

Just before reaching the bridge the channel emerging from Narrow Cuts is joined by Havengore Creek, which winds round the western side of Rushley Island to merge with the Middleway. When bound inwards, there is little point in taking the longer route to the Crouch via Havengore Creek.

The saltings at the southernmost tip of Potton Island extend about 100 metres from the seawall and are covered at high water springs. The best water runs round this point, about 30 metres from the edge of the saltings; the channel begins to fill at about half tide. When leaving the yard at Wakering, bound for the Roach or Crouch via the Yokesfleet, careful sounding will be necessary as the edge of the saltings is unmarked and the leading marks on Rushley Island have gone.

When bound seaward through Havengore Bridge, keep close to the Rushley Island side for about half a mile because the best water will not be found on the outside of the bend, as might be expected. In recent years a mud bank has extended off Mill Bay at the junction of Potton and Havengore Creeks, so deeper draught boats bound for the Havengore Bridge from Potton Creek may need to use the Narrow Cuts route.

POTTON CREEK

Potton Creek joins the Roach between Potton Island and Barling Ness and runs in a southerly direction to join up with Havengore Creek.

A very long spit extends NE'ly from Barling Ness and it is safest to hold the E shore when entering Barlinghall Creek from the Roach. The first reach in the creek, known locally as The Violet, is largely occupied these days by local fishing boats and so it may be difficult to find a space in which to use an anchor.

Barlinghall Creek, leading to Little Wakering Creek, leaves Potton Creek about half a mile south of Barling Ness and winds up to the villages of Barling and Little Wakering. Although barges once visited the quays dotted about the upper reaches of these creeks, the landings are mostly disused and, of course, no water remains at low tide.

About a quarter of a mile above the junction of Barlinghall Creek, beware of a concrete ford between Potton Island and the mainland. It is not safe to try to pass this way before half-flood. From here, the bridge over Potton Creek will be seen about half a mile ahead. This swing-bridge, which is used only by the Ministry of Defence, will be opened on request – VHF Ch 16, 72; Tel 01702

POTTON BRIDGE

Opens on request, daylight hours two hours either side of HW. VHF Ch 16, 72; Tel 01702 219491

219491; or three toots on a horn, Dutch fashion – at any time during daylight hours two hours either side of HW. Keep well over to the E side of the creek when approaching the bridge.

A boatyard with a slipway is situated just S of the bridge.

THE HAVENGORE ROUTE

This passage northwards to the River Roach across the Maplin Sands and via the Havengore bridge, Narrow Cuts, Middleway and Yokesfleet Creeks should only be made during spring tides, and then only by craft drawing no more than 1.5m.

The approach to Havengore Creek over the Maplins crosses the Shoeburyness Gunnery Range and, as firing is more or less continuous on weekdays, it is as well for yachtsmen to understand their rights and responsibilities when intending to use the Havengore route. The complete bye-laws governing firing practice over the Maplin and Foulness sands are to be found in Statutory Rules and Orders No 714 of 1936, obtainable from HMSO. But the section of these bye-laws which is of greatest importance to yachtsmen reads: 'Any vessel wishing to enter Havengore Creek during such time or times as the whole of the target area is not closed in accordance with Bye-law No 3 must enter the

target area not later than half an hour before high water and proceed by the shortest possible course to the Creek.'

Red flags are hoisted from a number of points along the sea wall; among them at Wakering Stairs and at Havengore Bridge, an hour before firing commences and throughout the period of firing. In fact these flags are often left up all the time. It is, in any case, difficult if not impossible to see these signals before setting course across the Maplins from the West Swin.

As firings are almost continuous in daylight hours on weekdays, it is dangerous to make the passage without first obtaining permission. Yachtsmen should telephone the Range Planning Officer at Shoeburyness when, if possible, the bridge will be lifted and firing suspended. Every consideration is given to yachtsmen in this respect.

Night firing is normally confined to periods when the Maplins are uncovered, and in any case, as the swing bridge is no longer manned between sunset and sunrise, the passage cannot be made after dark.

The Maplin sands should not be crossed from the Swin much earlier than three-quarters flood, and it is impossible for any other than light draught boats to get over the Broomway much before high water. The Broomway was originally a causeway built along the Maplin Sands to connect Foulness Island, Havengore and New England Islands with the mainland at Wakering, before any bridge was constructed.

The Broomway stands proud

Traffic signals are shown from the south bascule of Havengore Bridge, which is only manned during daylight hours

of the mud and sand and there is probably about 1.5 to 2.0m of water over it at HWS, but often 0.5m or less at HW neaps.

Havengore Creek cannot be distinguished from the West Swin, as any marks off the entrance are too small to be seen over the 2½ miles.

The survey platform that used to be near the E Shoebury beacon has been dismantled, but a course of 345°M from the beacon will lead towards the entrance to Havengore Creek. There have been attempts in recent years to establish marks that would assist yachtsmen using the Havengore route, but it is extremely difficult to erect structures strong enough to withstand wind and tide for more than a year or so. Two stayed, metal posts were established in 1995: one 200 yards to seaward of the Broomway and one on of the Broomway itself. Just west of the first post is a wreck marked with two round markers. The best water is close to these two posts, but although they can be seen easily from the mouth of Havengore Creek they are difficult to make out from seaward against the coastline. There are many other posts and range markers on the sands.

The gutway leading into the creek is marked with withies (2003), red to port and green to starboard. These sometimes have traffic cones on them which can be confusing. Once between the sea walls the deepest water will be found towards the N bank up to the bridge.

It must be realized that depths over the Maplins and the Broomway will vary considerably with the direction and strength of wind as well as with barometric pressure. Northerly winds will raise and southerly winds will lower the tidal levels, while a decrease or increase in barometric pressure equivalent to 25 millibars (one inch) of mercury will respectively raise or lower the depth of water by 0.3 metres (one foot). Therefore, the more settled the weather, the more likely is the pressure to be high and the tides lower than predicted.

HAVENGORE BRIDGE

The bridge over Havengore Creek has a lifting bascule which allows unrestricted passage for any yacht. The bridge will be opened as required for two hours each side of HW during daylight hours – provided the firing range is not being used. Fortunately, firing seldom takes place at

Looking north west from above Havengore Creek. Inside the bridge the creek divides around Rushley Island, left towards Potton Creek and right into Narrow Cuts

Looking inland from the Havengore Bridge at near LW, Narrow Cut creek curving away to the right

weekends, but anyone planning to use the Havengore route is advised to check beforehand by either telephoning the Range Operations Officer on Southend 01702 383211 or by VHF using the callsign *SHOE BASE*. The bridge keeper can be contacted during HW periods on VHF *SHOE BRIDGE* or by phone on 01702 383436 – the bridge-keeper listens on Ch 16 and works on Ch 72. In addition *SHOE RADAR* can be contacted on 01702 383260 Monday to Friday.

The tidal streams hereabouts are somewhat complicated – largely because of the barrier formed by the Broomway. The flood tide from the Roach and the flood over the Maplins meet and cover the Maplins about two hours before HW, after which the tide runs back into Havengore Creek until HW. Then with virtually no period of slack, the ebb runs out of the creek with great strength until the Broomway is again uncovered. These facts should be remembered when using the Havengore route since, when coming from the Swin, it is important to reach the bridge before the ebb commences; and when bound out of the creek it is equally desirable to be at the bridge before the last hour or so of the flood which runs N into Narrow Cuts.

When bound through the bridge and out of the creek it helps the bridge-keeper if some kind of signal can be made to indicate that the bridge should be raised. Traffic signals will signify when it is safe to proceed. The port

and starboard withies marking the channel upstream from seaward of the bridge continue towards Potton on the landward side, so if you are approaching the bridge from the inside, the marks must be followed in a downstream sequence.

In Conrad's novel *Chance*, the character Powell was in the habit of disappearing mysteriously from the Thames Estuary in his small cutter, but was eventually followed (probably into Havengore) by Marlow, who describes the chase:

'One afternoon, I made Powell's boat out, heading into the shore. By the time I got close to the mud flats his craft had disappeared inland. But I could see the mouth of the creek by then. The tide being on the turn I took the risk of getting stuck in the mud suddenly and headed in. Before I had gone half a mile, I was up with a building I had seen from the river... it looked like a small barn.'

There would have been no bridge over the creek when Conrad wrote *Chance*, but the barn may still exist, for a similar building (at Oxenham Farm) can still be seen over the sea walls in the Havengore area.

Havengore Bridge

Range Operations Officer
Tel 01702 383211; VHF callsign *SHOE BASE*
Bridge keeper during HW periods Tel 01702 383436; VHF callsign *SHOE BRIDGE*
SHOE RADAR Tel 01702 383260 Monday to Friday

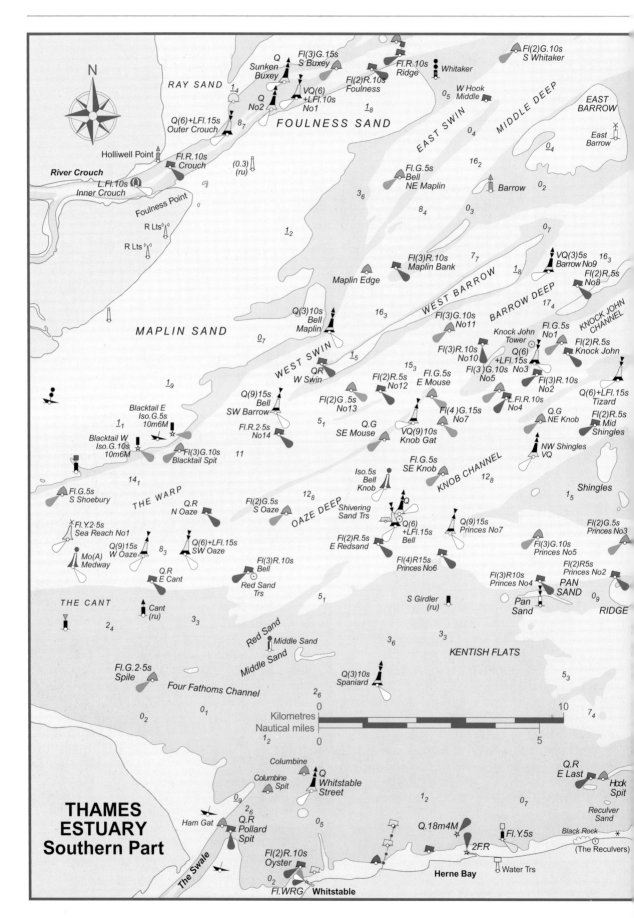

THAMES ESTUARY
Southern Part

THE RIVER THAMES

Tides (Southend Pier)	HW Dover +1.20 Range: Springs 5.2m Neaps 3.4m (HW Tower Bridge approx 1.20 after HW Southend)
Charts	Admiralty SC1185 (Sea Reach), SC2484 (Holehaven to London Bridge), Stanford No 8, Imray C2
Waypoints	NE Maplin Buoy 51°37′.46N 01°04′.79E Maplin Buoy 51°34′.03N 01°02′.29E
	Blacktail Spit Buoy 51°31′.48N 00°56′.75E Southend Pierhead 51°30′.87N 00°43′.41E
	Sea Reach No 1 Buoy 51°29′.45N 00°52′.57E
Hazards	Large ships (steer clear of dredged channel); Floating debris in upper reaches

John Evelyn, whose diary is not so often quoted as that of Samuel Pepys, reported on a day on the Thames he had with Charles II in 1661: 'I sailed this morning with His Majesty in one of his pleasure-boats, vessels not known among us till the Dutch East India Company presented

that curious piece to the King; being very excellent sailing vessels. It was a wager between his other new pleasure-boat frigate-like, and one of the Duke of York's – the wager 100-1: the race from Greenwich to Gravesend and back. The King lost in going, the wind being contrary, but saved stakes in returning.'

Since then there has never been a time when yachtsmen have not sailed on the Thames – some

of them, such as the marine artist Wyllie in his book London to the Nore, have tried to capture the spirit of the London River in, as he put it, '... all of its grime and much of its wonder'.

An increasing number of people are visiting London in their boats now that the river is clean and, in the upper reaches, relatively free from commercial traffic. Unfortunately there are still very few comfortable or attractive anchorages

Chapter 14

The Thames sailing barge, May, *turns down river after leaving the lock at St Katharine Haven*

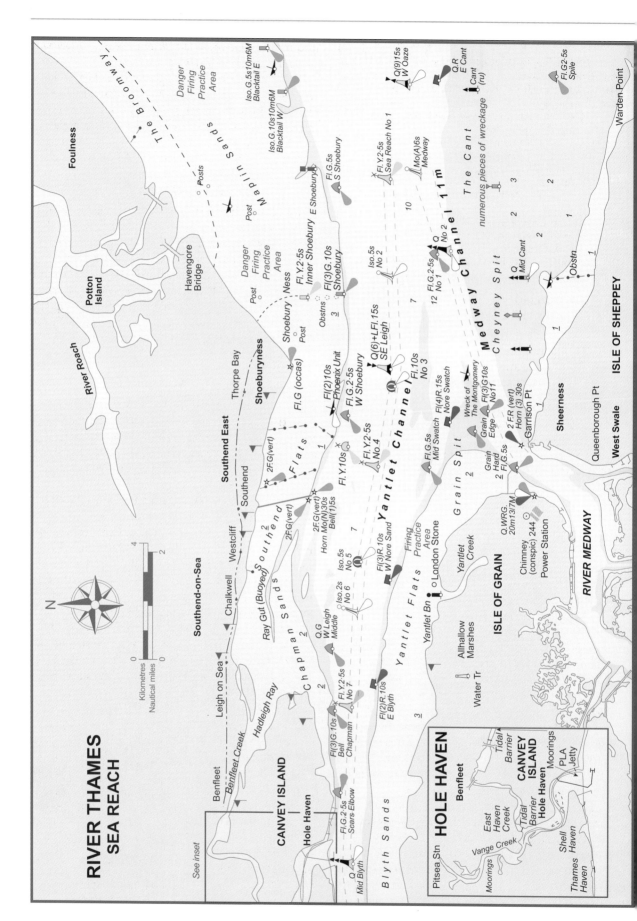

RIVER THAMES
SEA REACH

N

Kilometres
Nautical miles

Foulness

The Broomway

Danger Firing Practice Area

Potton Island

River Roach

Havengore Bridge

Posts

Post

Maplin Sands

Iso.G.5s10m6M Blacktail E

Iso.G.10s10m6M Blacktail W

Danger Firing Practice Area

Post

Q(9)15s W Oaze

Q.R E Cant

E Cant (ru)

Fl.G.2·5s Spile

Warden Point

Fl.G.5s S Shoebury

Fl.Y.2·5s Sea Reach No 1

Mo(A)6s Medway

Shoebury Ness

Fl.Y.2·5s Inner Shoebury E Shoebury

Fl(3)G.10s Shoebury

Iso.5s No 2

10

The Cant

numerous pieces of wreckage

Thorpe Bay

Southend East

Shoeburyness

Post

Obstns 3

Fl(2)10s Phoenix Unit

Q(6)+LFl.15s SE Leigh

Fl.G.5s W Shoebury

Fl.10s No 3

7

12 Fl.G.2·5s No 1

Q No 2

Fl.G.2·5s No 1

Q Mid Cant

Obstn

3

2

1

Mid Cant

2

1

ISLE OF SHEPPEY

Fl.G

(occas)

Fl(2)G.10s

Fl.Y.2·5s No 4

Fl.Y.10s

Fl.Y.2·5s Mid Swatch

Fl(4)R.15s Nore Swatch

Fl(3)G10s No11

Cheyney Spit

Medway Channel 11m

Yantlet Channel

Southend

2·F.G(vert)

2F.G(vert)

Flats

Southend

Flats

1

Horn Mo(N)30s Bell(1)5s

Fl.Y.2·5s No 4

Fl.G.5s Mid Swatch

Wreck of The Montgomery

2·F.R (vert) Horn (3) 30s

1

Sheerness

Southend-on-Sea

Chalkwell

Westcliff

Southend

2F.G(vert)

2F.G(vert)

Fl(3)R.10s No 5

Fl(3)R.10s W Nore Sand

Firing Practice Area

Grain Edge

Fl.G.5s

Garrison Pt

Queenborough Pt

WEST SWALE

Leigh on Sea

Ray Gut (Buoyed)

Iso.5s No 5

Iso.2s No 6

London Stone

Yantlet Flats

Grain Hard 2

Fl.G.5s

RIVER MEDWAY

Hadleigh Ray

Q.G W Leigh Middle

Yantlet Bn

Grain Spit

Q.WRG. 20m13/7M

Chimney (conspic) 244

Power Station

2

Chapman Sands

Fl.Y.2·5s No 7

Fl(2)R.10s E Blyth

Yantlet Creek

Allhallow Marshes

Water Tr

ISLE OF GRAIN

3

CANVEY ISLAND

Hole Haven

Fl(3)G.10s Bell Chapman

2

Blyth Sands

Benfleet

Benfleet Creek

Fl.G.2·5s Scars Elbow

Q Mid Blyth

See inset

HOLE HAVEN

Pitsea Stn

Benfleet

Tidal Barrier

CANVEY ISLAND

Hole Haven

Moorings

PLA Jetty

East Haven Creek

Tidal Barrier

Vange Creek

Moorings

Shell Haven

Thames Haven

THE THAMES Useful Information

Port Control London

VHF: **Ch 12** for The Estuary below Sea Reach No 4 buoy

Ch 68 for the river above Sea Reach No 4 buoy to Crayfordness

Ch 14 above Crayfordness

The half-hourly VHF broadcasts are sometimes of interest to yachts, for example, the tidal information

Port Control London

Seaward to Crayfordness Tel 01474 560311 (Gravesend)

Up river of Crayfordness, Thames Barrier Navigation Centre Tel 0208 855 0315

Thames River Police

Wapping Tel 0207 488 5291; VHF Ch 14 above Crayfordness, callsign *Thames Police Wapping* 24 hours

PLA Patrol Launches

VHF callsign *Thames Patrol* on Ch 12, 68 or 14 according to location

Emergencies

Call Thames Patrol as above

Port of London Authority

Devon House, 58–60 St Katharine's Way, London E1 9LB

Tel 0207 265 2656; Fax 0207 265 2699

---

between Leigh and any of the five marinas in or near London, so that a journey up or down the river is best done on one tide when possible.

Before embarking for the first time on a voyage up the London River to Tower Bridge, there are several things to be considered:

1. By using the tide wisely, the distance (some 40 miles) can usually be covered in seven hours, arriving in London just before high water.

2. Do not expect to find any easy or undisturbed anchorages en route and be aware that casual mooring is not usually possible.

3. In the upper reaches, keep a particularly keen look-out for floating rafts of debris. Besides drums, crates and bottles these will often include large, half-submerged baulks of timber which can stall an engine, damage a prop or bend a shaft. A particular danger nowadays are near invisible plastic sheets.

4. Stow all loose gear. With a fresh wind some reaches of the Thames can be remarkably rough and the wash from fast moving tugs can sometimes come as a surprise.

5. Make sure you understand the procedure for passing through the Thames Barrier in Woolwich Reach.

When sailing in the Thames Estuary or further up-river, it should always be remembered that the dredged channel for shipping is not wide enough to allow a deep-draught vessel to alter course,

and in any case there is plenty of water either side of the channel for yachts.

Port Control London has patrol launches as do the Thames River Police, who are an invaluable source of information regarding moorings, safe anchorages, fuel etc. A useful information leaflet for yachtsmen using the tidal Thames is available from the Port of London Authority (PLA) on request.

APPROACHES

Coming into the Thames from the Channel or the North Sea, it is convenient to consider Sea Reach No 1 buoy as marking the seaward limit of the river. At this point the estuary, to the north of which are Shoeburyness and the Maplin Sands and to the south, Warden Point and the Isle of Sheppey, is about eight miles wide. The edge of the Maplins is steep-to, but the water shoals more gradually to the south, over an area known as the Cant.

SEA REACH

From Sea Reach No 1 Buoy to Lower Hope Point, some 15 miles up-river, the general direction of the channel is westerly. As there is no high ground offering shelter on the Kent shore west of the Medway, a fresh southwesterly wind blowing against the flood tide will kick up a short steep sea.

Shipping bound up the Thames follows the well marked Yantlet dredged channel, which has a least depth of 10m and a width of about two cables up as far as Shell Haven. This channel is marked by a series of seven special buoys, either pillar or spherical, and coloured either yellow or with red and white vertical stripes. However, small craft should steer clear of the main channel, and fortunately there is plenty of water on both sides.

When following an inward course to the north of the dredged channel, a watch must be kept for an obstruction to navigation extending offshore to a point about one mile SE of Shoeburyness. This obstruction – part of a wartime barrier/boom – has a light (Fl Y 2.5s), but does not stretch as far as the drying edge of Maplin Sands, although another post (Fl (3) G 10s) does mark the point

Sea Reach No 1 buoy is considered to mark the seaward limit of the London River

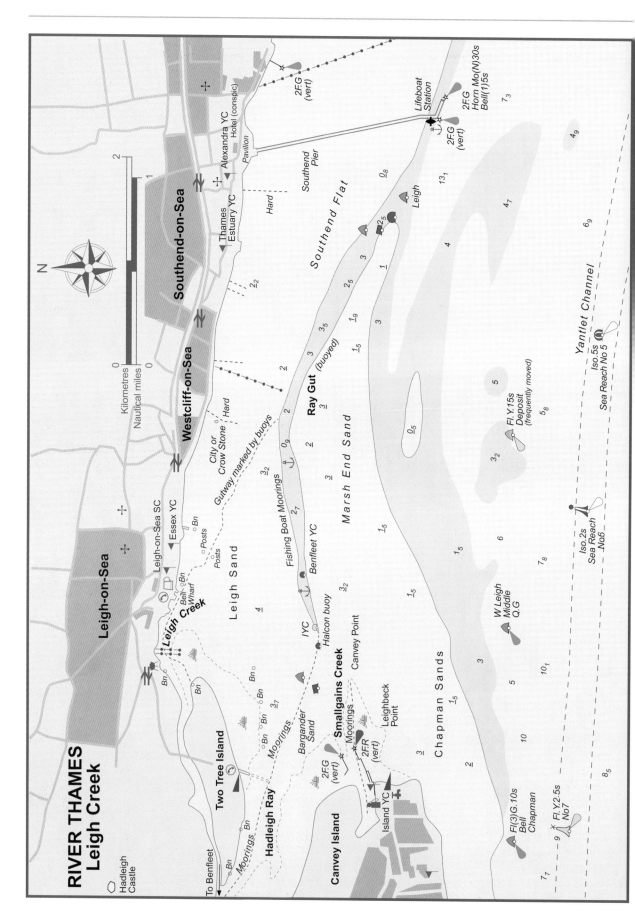

RIVER THAMES
Leigh Creek

Hadleigh Castle

0 Kilometres 1 2

0 Nautical miles 1

N

Leigh-on-Sea

Southend-on-Sea

Westcliff-on-Sea

Alexandra YC

Hotel (conspic)

Pavilion

Thames Estuary YC

Hard

2F.G (vert)

Lifeboat Station

2F.G (vert)

2F.G Horn Mo(N)30s Bell(1)5s

7₃

4₉

Southend Pier

Southend Flat

0₈

Leigh

13₁

4₇

2₅

3

1

4

Yantlet Channel

6₉

2₂

2₅

1₉

3

3

City or Crow Stone

Hard

Gutway marked by buoys

2

3₅

1₉

1₅

2

5

Iso.5s Sea Reach No 5

Leigh-on-Sea SC

Essex YC

Bn

Posts

Posts

Bn

3₂

0₉

2

Ray Gut
(buoyed)

3

Marsh End Sand

0₅

3₂

Fl.Y.15s Deposit
(frequently moved)

5₈

Bell Wharf

Leigh Creek

Fishing Boat Moorings

2₇

Benfleet YC

1₅

6

Iso.2s Sea Reach No6

Leigh Sand

4

IYC

Halcon buoy

Canvey Point

3₂

1₅

1₅

7₈

10₁

Two Tree Island

Bn

Bn

Bn

3₇

Bn

Bn

Bn

Bargander Sand

Moorings

Smallgains Creek

Moorings

Leighbeck Point

W Leigh Middle Q.G

5

Chapman Sands

1₅

10

Hadleigh Ray

Moorings

Bn

2F.G (vert)

2F.R (vert)

Island YC

3

2

10

Canvey Island

To Benfleet

Fl(3)G.10s Bell Chapman

Fl.Y.2.5s No7

Fl.Y.2.5s No7

9

8₅

7₇

where the barrier once reached deep water.

If visibility is reasonable, Southend Pier can be seen from abreast the Shoeburyness obstruction, although a direct course between the two is not advisable between half-ebb and half-flood because it leads over the edge of drying flats. Instead, the West Shoeburyness (Con G Fl G 2.5s) should be left to starboard or close to port.

There is a Coastguard and radio direction finding station at Shoeburyness.

SOUTHEND PIER

This mile-long pier dates from 1829 and seems never to be out of trouble for very long. A fire at the pierhead in 1976 destroyed the Coastguard and Lloyd's stations, a freighter cut clean through the structure and wrecked the RNLI station in 1986, and in 1995 the bowling alley at the landward end was destroyed by fire. Much of the damage has been repaired and the pier is up and running again. It is even possible for a yacht to tie up alongside for a while to take on water or collect stores from the town. The local RNLI lifeboat house and crew

quarters are at the head of the pier.

For a mile or more on both sides of the pier are some 3,000 small boat moorings – all of them drying out on to a more or less muddy bottom. The Halfway YC, near the conspicuous Halfway House pub on Eastern Esplanade, about a mile to the east of the pier, has one visitor's drying mooring for up to 26ft.

There is plenty of water off the end of the pier (5m or 6m) and an anchorage can usually be found on the edge of the flats on either side. There is little protection except from the north.

During the sailing season spherical red racing buoys area laid on the N side of the Sea Reach Channel off Southend.

From the end of Southend Pier, a course due west (M) will lead to the West Leigh Middle buoy (Con G Q G). Leigh Middle is a shoal area that almost dries out along the S edge of the drying sands extending eastward from Canvey Point.

In order to avoid the busy tanker berthing areas at Canvey and Coryton refineries, inward-bound craft from the north are advised by the PLA to cross to the south side of the Yantlet channel at

Leigh-on-Sea – diagonally from the bottom right can be seen Theobalds Wharf alongside the Strand, the cockle sheds alongside the railway, and then the boatyard near the station, with the saltings of Two Tree Island on the left

West Leigh Middle, making sure that the fairway is clear, heading for the E Blyth buoy before turning onto the inward track. Remember that outward-bound ships will pass close to the port-hand fairway buoys. The Mid Blyth, W Blyth and Lower Hope buoys can then be safely passed to the south. Once in Lower Hope Reach, you should cross back to the correct side as soon as it is safe to do so.

Outward-bound to the north yachts should reverse the above route, but cross back to the north between Sea Reach Nos 4 and 5 buoys.

If you are coming in from the south, keep clear to the south of Sea Reach fairway and cross to the north side in Lower Hope as previously described.

A spoil ground buoy is usually located somewhere to the E of W Leigh Middle buoy and is often in little more than 2m at LWS. A green conical bell buoy (Fl (3) G 10s) – Chapman – is established close to the old lighthouse position, about a quarter of a mile south of the drying edge of the Chapman Sands half a mile off the Canvey Island shore. The edge of the sand near here is steep-to, there being depths of 20m within half a cable of the buoy.

About a mile west of Scars Elbow green conical buoy (Fl G 2.5s) is the entrance to Holehaven Creek – a favourite anchorage with earlier

generations of Thames yachtsmen, but becoming less attractive as each year passes and our appetite for oil increases. At one time there was a half-mile gap between the tanker jetties, making the position of Holehaven obvious, but another jetty has been erected directly opposite Hole Haven Bay so that the opening is less easy to distinguish.

After Scars Elbow, there are no further marks on the north side of Sea Reach, but there is deep water right up to the numerous jetties, dolphins and mooring buoys that serve the oil refineries and storage depots. All the jetties and dolphins show two vertical fixed green lights at night.

Powerful traffic lights are shown up and down the river from Holehaven Point and Scars Elbow when tankers are berthing or unberthing.

LEIGH-ON-SEA

Almost the whole of the foreshore of the adjoining towns of Leigh, Westcliff and Southend dries out soon after half-ebb, so yachts drawing more than 1m should not expect to cross Canvey Point Shoals or Marsh End sands at less than three hours before or after high water.

Leigh Creek, however, does enable craft of moderate draught to reach the quays at Old Leigh, where there are a couple of boatyards and several pubs including the Crooked Billet, The Smack and The Peterboat. At the quaint collection of weather-boarded shellfish sheds alongside the railway line you can buy Leigh cockles, brought back by a motorized and much reduced version of the bawley fleet that used to fish under sail for shrimps and whitebait as well as the cockles – a famous local speciality much loved by day trippers.

Except at or near to HW, an approach to Leigh should be made from a position close to the Leigh buoy – Low-Way (Con G) – located about half a mile W of Southend Pier. Although the Leigh buoy is conical and green it must be considered a port-hand mark when entering the Ray Gut. A survey carried out by members of the Leigh SC showed that there is practically no water to the W of it at LWS. The Gut is just over a cable wide between its steep-to banks, and it carries some three metres at LW for a distance of nearly a mile in a generally north-westerly direction. A little way in from the entrance, deep water in the Ray is indicated by permanent moorings and fishing craft.

The channel leading to Leigh Creek and the Creek itself have been re-marked recently as the result of co-operation between Southend Council and local fishermen. But unless a craft is able to take the ground without much inconvenience, it

LEIGH-ON-SEA AND SOUTHEND PORT GUIDE	
Southend Pier	Tel 01702 215620
Water	From Pier, Bell Wharf Leigh, boatyards or yacht clubs
Stores	From shops in Leigh. EC Wed
Chandlery	Small at Mike's Boatyard
Repairs	Lower Thames Marine (previously Johnson & Jago) Tel 01702 479009 (near Leigh station beyond the cockle sheds) slip, hoist and crane; Mike's Boatyard Tel 01702 713151 (on the wharf in Leigh Old Town) cranage, wharfage
Fuel	Diesel and gas from Mike's Boatyard
Transport	Good train service Leigh to London (Fenchurch Street)
Telephone	Outside The Smack
Clubs	Leigh-on-Sea Sailing Club Tel 476788 bar; Essex Yacht Club Tel 01702 478404; Alexandra Yacht Club (Southend) Tel 01702 340363 bar; Thames Estuary Yacht Club (Westcliff) Tel 01702 345967; Halfway YC (Thorpe Bay) Tel 01702 582025; Thorpe Bay Yacht Club Tel 01702 587563, slip, bar, restaurant

Benfleet Yacht Club has its clubhouse on the Canvey shore just below the bridge at the navigable head of Benfleet Creek

will be preferable to bring up in Hadleigh Ray, where several of the local bawleys are usually moored. There is enough water to stay afloat in Hadleigh Ray almost as far west as Canvey Point, but there is little protection except from the north.

At or near HW, a cross-sand route may be taken direct from West Leigh Middle Buoy to Bell Wharf on a bearing of 005°M.

It is sometimes possible for a deeper draught boat to find a berth alongside Bell Wharf, where Leigh Creek closely approaches the old town of Leigh. There is a landing place – a narrow strip of beach – just west of Bell Wharf, and it is also

possible towards HW to land on the groynes further E, close to the clubship Bembridge belonging to the Essex YC.

From Leigh it is approximately two miles to Hadleigh Castle from where there are striking views of the estuary – just as there were in Constable's day.

HADLEIGH RAY AND BENFLEET CREEK

The deep water moorings in Ray Gut extend westward almost to Canvey Point, but thereafter only the shallowest of craft can remain afloat throughout even a neap tide. However, there are hundreds of small craft moored between Canvey Point and the causeway at Two-Tree Island and in Smallgains Creek.

At the western end of Ray Gut, near the Leigh Sands beacon, Island YC and Benfleet YC have established a couple of mooring buoys which can be used when waiting for the tide.

The landing and launching place on Two-Tree Island is approached via the Hadleigh Ray over a shoal patch, which may easily stop a yacht around low water. The outer end of Hadleigh Ray

BENFLEET PORT GUIDE	
Water	From yacht club or yard
Chandlery	Daytime hours at club
Stores	Shops in Benfleet
Repairs	Shipwright near bridge; slipway
Fuel	Diesel at club – daytime hours
Transport	Trains to London (Fenchurch Street)
Club	Benfleet Yacht Club (Tel 01268 792278) Showers

is marked by a pair of port and starboard hand buoys situated just north of the Halcon 'mooring-type' buoy that indicates the entrance to Smallgains creek. Otherwise, a course through Hadleigh Ray from one moored yacht to the next, following the larger craft, will lead to the causeway, which extends to the low water mark.

There is a car park and a road to Leigh Station. A hard-master is present during the day and water is available while he is there, together with an emergency telephone.

Benfleet Bridge and tidal barrier are about two miles upstream of the causeway at Two-Tree Island. The channel of Benfleet creek, which dries out two hours either side of LW, is best learned by sailing up early on the tide. The gutway is marked by a series of numbered red port-hand buoys and two or three green starboard-hand marks. There is a beacon with a conical topmark on the north shore near No 5 buoy, and at this point course must be changed to bring a pair of leading marks in line on the opposite (S) bank. The front one of these two beacons has a triangle topmark and the other a diamond shaped topmark. Moorings are then continuous up to the tidal barrier and road bridge just above the YC, and help to indicate the channel.

Benfleet YC produces a chart of Benfleet Creek, copies of which can be obtained by visiting yachtsmen. Visitors are welcome at the fine clubhouse, situated alongside one of the best slipways in the Thames Estuary. This spotless slip is flushed each tide with an automatic pump which continues for hours and may keep you awake. Some visitor's moorings are available for yachts up to 45ft.

SMALLGAINS CREEK

This little creek off the eastern tip of Canvey Island is hardly more than a mile long, but is packed with drying moorings and stagings on both sides for most of its length. Fishing vessels regularly use it by night and day.

From the Halcon buoy at the entrance, the creek is identified by port-hand buoys up to the Island YC's outer mooring jetties, which are marked on either hand by 2FG and 2FR lights. Approaching the Island YC, the channel turns to port and best water is indicated by sets of leading marks on the north bank and on the IYC staging on the S shore.

Island YC is on the Canvey shore about half a mile inside the creek. Visiting yachtsmen can be accommodated on request and food is available from the modern clubhouse at weekends.

Moorings and stagings at the lower end of the creek belong to the club, which also has a wide concrete slipway.

Further upstream is Halcon Marine, with moorings on both sides of the creek, slipway, fuel and water pontoon, drydock and lifting facilities.

The Halcon fuel pontoon can be reached by craft with a metre draught approximately one hour before HW neaps.

THE KENT SHORE

If the course in from the Estuary has been along the Kent coast, S of the dredged channel and N of the Medway channel, then a course keeping about half a mile S of the Yantlet dredged channel will serve as far as the East Blyth buoy, some five miles away.

The Nore Sand (the first shoal ever to be marked with a light in the Thames Estuary in 1732) used to dry out, but now has nowhere less than two metres over it.

When passing south of the Nore Sand, as from the Medway, an entrance to the Nore swatchway should be shaped from a position close to the Nore Swatch buoy (Can R Fl(4)R 15s). From this mark, a course approximately 300°M will lead close to the Mid Swatch buoy (Con G Fl G 5s) guarding the south side of the shoal. Close south of the Mid Swatch buoy there is eight to nine metres, but there is little more than two cables between the buoy and the very steep edge of Grain sands to the S. The same course (300°M) continued from the Mid Swatch buoy will lead out of the swatchway and up to the W Nore Sand (Can R Fl(3)R 10s).

YANTLET CREEK

There are not many landmarks along the south shore of Sea Reach, but the Yantlet Beacon (black with ball topmark), marking the west side of the entrance to Yantlet Creek, is visible from the W Nore Sand buoy. Small craft can reach this creek via a gutway running roughly north-easterly through the Yantlet Flats, and there is a pool carrying about a metre of water approximately a cable SW of the beacon.

The place is still used by yachtsmen in search of a remote and secluded anchorage, although the whole area is close to the remains of the great oil refinery located just to the south on the Isle of Grain. However, a useful temporary anchorage can be found along the edge of Yantlet Flats in about 4m.

The next light buoy is the E Blyth (Can R Fl(2)R 10s), located about a quarter of a mile off the edge of the flats, which at this point extend for almost a mile from the Kent shore. The drying edge is particularly steep-to abreast the E Blyth buoy, but shelves more gradually further west and changes from sand to sand and mud and then mud alone at the western end of the Sea Reach. The next buoy is the Mid Blyth.

The PLA recommends that yachts should stay south of a line from East Blyth through Mid Blyth to W Blyth to keep clear of the busy tanker berths at Canvey, Shellhaven and Coryton refineries. You should then cross to the correct side in Lower Hope Reach as rapidly as possible when it is safe to do so.

HOLEHAVEN

Owing to the surrounding refinery oil tanks and tanker jetties, Holehaven is not the useful anchorage it once was, but if it blows hard from the east, it provides a useful bolt hole.

Holehaven beacon is not easy to distinguish on the east side of the entrance to the creek, but it bears approximately 50°M from the Mid Blyth buoy and is about half a mile distant. At HW the entrance to Holehaven appears easy because of its apparent width, but in fact the only deep water runs about half a cable from the Canvey or the east side of the inlet. Drying mud with a steep-to edge stretches for nearly half a mile from Shellhaven Point. After entering, a useful leading line is usually provided by the many fishing craft already moored in the creek, all of which should be left close to port.

There is only about 1.5m of water in the entrance abreast the beacon at LWS, but once over this bar depths increase to more than 2m, and about a quarter of a mile inside, soundings deepen to more than 5m in a hole (pool), which no doubt gave the creek its name.

There is no longer a PLA office at Holehaven and the long PLA pier is disused, but there is a wooden causeway just to the south of the pier

PLA Harbour Master	Tel 01474 562462 (weekdays)
Water	From yard of Lobster Smack (by request)
Stores, fuel etc	From Canvey village (one mile). EC Thurs
Transport	Buses from Canvey village to South Benfleet. Trains from S Benfleet to London

where it is possible to land. Once over the sea wall, the Lobster Smack will be there waiting for you as it has for generations of sailing men before. Consult the PLA harbour master by phone concerning moorings in Holehaven. The PLA advise that a temporary semi-sheltered anchorage can be found in the lee of Chain Rock Jetty, above the entrance to the creek.

About half a mile within the entrance an overhead pipe line crosses the creek from the new jetty to Canvey Island. This structure gives a clearance of 30ft (9.2m) at HWS so some boats can pass under and proceed with the tide towards Pitsea up Vange Creek. A couple of miles upstream on the eastern bank is East Haven Creek, which runs behind Canvey Island up to Benfleet. This is closed to navigation, except possibly to very small craft, by a tidal barrier at its mouth.

VANGE CREEK

There are many small boat moorings in this creek, which leads up to the Watt Tyler Country Park, renamed Pitsea Hall, home of the National Motorboat Museum. A slipway, a workshop and telephone are all situated nearby. Pitsea station is about a mile away.

THE LONDON RIVER

Lower Hope
Above Thames Haven, the river turns south round Lower Hope Point into Lower Hope Reach, the width of which diminishes quite quickly from about two miles down to less than a mile off Coalhouse Point. There is room to anchor on Mucking Flats well out of the channel and inside a line of large mooring buoys near to Mucking No 5 buoy (Con G Gp Fl(3)G 10s). This can be a useful place to be in a strong SW'ly. The Tilbury buoy (S Car YB QkFl(6) LFl 15s) off Coalhouse Point is the last of the channel buoys and, for the rest of the way up-river, shore marks are used to navigate from reach to reach.

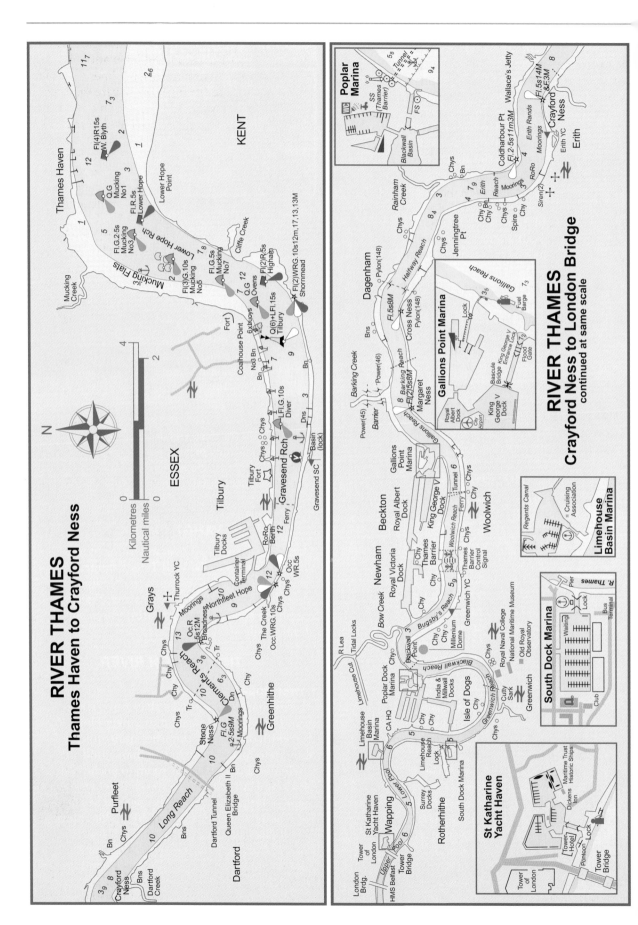

RIVER THAMES
Thames Haven to Crayford Ness

N

Kilometres
Nautical miles

ESSEX

KENT

RIVER THAMES
Crayford Ness to London Bridge
continued at same scale

Poplar Marina

Gallions Point Marina

Limehouse Basin Marina

South Dock Marina

St Katharine Yacht Haven

GRAVESEND

'Gravesend is a wonderful sight ...alive with craft of every type and tonnage ...a strong smell of shrimps impregnates the air,' wrote Francis B Cooke in *Coastwise Cruising from Erith to Lowestoft* (1929). Alas, although fleets of tugs and pilot boats still operate from here, the bawley boats are long gone and the '..tea and shrimps, oilskins, sea-boots and bloaters' with them.

Gravesend Reach runs for about four miles in an E–W direction, with Tilbury Docks to the north and Gravesend to the south of the river. To help scour the Diver shoal, the PLA has built six groynes on the north side of the reach, marked by lit (Fl G) beacons, which are difficult to see coming up river by day and no better at night when the shore lights mask the beacon lights. There are five unlit yellow buoys just downstream of the first groyne off Coalhouse Point and there is no passage inshore of these or the beacons. The best course is from north of the Ovens buoy to Tilbury S Cardinal, and then to leave Diver buoy close to starboard; bear in mind that inbound ships pass close to the Tilbury buoy, so a good lookout astern is recommended.

On the north shore, the Gravesend ferry and cruise liners use the Tilbury landing stage, at the upper end of which there is a RO-RO berth for very large car transporters.

At night piers and stagings of the north bank are marked by two fixed green lights (vert) and those on the south side by vertical pairs of red lights.

The Gravesend Canal Basin bears a large sign – Gravesham Marina. Entry and departure through the lock gates are controlled by traffic lights. The lock-keeper (Tel 01474 352392) is normally on duty around the time of HW and the gates can be opened from 1½hrs before until just after HW.

A temporary mooring can sometimes be found off the Gravesend Sailing Club, where there are two visitors' buoys, one of which can dry out at LWS, but the other, at the east end of the club moorings and marked 'Visitors', gives a clear depth of 2m at all times. There are steps for landing at the lockside near high water, but at other times use the PLA slipway opposite the rowing club at the W end of the Promenade, where it is possible to anchor.

Assistance is always available from members of the Gravesend SC at weekends. The club has scrubbing posts near the river wall and masts can be stepped or unstepped by prior arrangement. Craft should not be left unattended in the Gravesend anchorage, but arrangements can usually be made with the Lock Master to leave a boat in the Canal Basin.

The PLA patrol launch, *Canvey*, previously based at Holehaven, is now based at Gravesend.

Chapter 14

GRAVESEND CANAL BASIN PORT GUIDE	
Lock-keeper	Tel 01474 352392
Water	From standpipe near entrance to lock
Stores	From shops in town
Chandler	Nearby
Fuel	Diesel and petrol from garage in town, half a mile
Crane	Inside the basin, can be used with permission from Gravesend SC:
Gravesend SC	Promenade East, Gravesend, Kent DA12 2RN
Telephone	01474 533974
Facilities	Showers and usual services available at weekends during season

Passing the Ovens buoy looking upriver towards Gravesend Reach, with Tilbury power station chimneys prominent on the Essex shore

Yacht on a mooring in Gravesend Reach just off the entrance to Gravesend Canal Basin. Near HW it is possible to land at the lockside steps

THURROCK YACHT CLUB

Kilverts Wharf, Argent Street, Grays, Essex	
Telephone	01375 373720
	email thurrockyachtclub@btopen world.com
OpeningTimes	Sat and Sun all day; Weekdays 1000 to 1500; Thursday eves 2000 to 2300
Fuel	Diesel during opening hours; petrol two miles away
Visitor's Mooring	By arrangement
Facilities	Showers, toilets, telephone, cooking facilities during opening hrs

GRAYS THURROCK

Northfleet Hope adjoins Gravesend Reach and runs SE–NW for just over a mile to Broadness on the south bank and Grays Thurrock on the north bank.

Moorings belonging to members of the Thurrock YC, on the north shore upstream of the Port of Tilbury Grain Terminal, are located just below the town causeway and abreast the wreck of the old lightship that once served as the club's headquarters. The club now has a new building on Kilverts Wharf, where visiting yachtsmen are welcomed and sometimes a mooring can be arranged. All kinds of supplies can be had from the town nearby.

GREENHITHE

There are some small boat moorings and a useful causeway on the pleasantly rural, wooded foreshore at Greenhithe, opposite Stone Ness (Fl 2.5s), at the southern end of St Clement's Reach.

Close to the shore here is a modern building that housed a merchant navy training college until its closure in 1986. This replaced the earlier training ships, such as the *Worcester* and the *Warspite*, that used to lie off Greenhithe. In 1905 Wyllie recorded that the National Refuge for Homeless and Destitute Children, whose school ship was the old, 50-gun frigate *Arethusa*, had been the means of rescuing some 17,000 lads whose '...only recommendation was that they be good, fatherless and poor.' In the 19th Century there were ex-men of war moored up and down the river, used variously as hospitals, reformatories, nautical colleges, powder stores or convict hulks.

QUEEN ELIZABETH II BRIDGE

This impressive bridge between Dartford in Kent and Thurrock in Essex, with its 54 metres vertical clearance, presents no problem to the yachtsman who passes way below the six lanes of traffic thundering on its way around the M25 overhead.

There are Ro-Ro berths on both banks in Long Reach, up and downstream of the bridge. Legend has it that nearby, where the Mardyke flows into the Thames at Purfleet, is the spot where the first Queen Elizabeth stood to view her fleet at anchor.

ERITH RANDS

This short reach between Crayford Ness and the town of Erith runs for about a mile in an E–W direction.

The Erith YC (Tel 01322 332943) has its headquarters in the old Norwegian car ferry *Folgefonn* on the S shore in Anchor Bay. The club has moorings abreast the clubship and a buoy can usually be found for a visitor. It is possible to land at the club causeway, where there is a standpipe. Frank Cowper in his *Sailing Tours* (1892) declared Erith to be '...a capital place to lie off, as it is well sheltered and we can lie out of the way of the traffic; but it is very crowded in the season.'

Much of the London River traffic these days comprises a vast fleet of sewage ships constantly on the move to and from the estuary and tugs taking endless tows of rubbish barges to disgorge their contents onto a monstrous infill site on the Rainham shore.

In Halfway Reach on the N bank is Ford's Dagenham factory, while opposite is a new and strikingly modern sewage processing plant. This

The Queen Elizabeth II bridge spans the Thames between Dartford in Kent and Thurrock in Essex

building is reminiscent of an ocean-going liner or perhaps a whale, as it stands out against the tower blocks of Plumstead and the high ground at Greenwich in the distance.

GALLIONS REACH

Gallions Point Marina, entered via a lock (five hours either side of HW) at the old entrance to the Royal Albert Basin on the north bank, and with over 100 berths, provides a useful stop-over down river of the Thames Barrier. Diesel and gas are available from the fuel barge *Leonard* (open weekdays) moored off Gallions Pier outside the lock entrance.

WOOLWICH REACH

When passing through Woolwich Reach, there are two hazards to contend with – the ferries which ply between north and south Woolwich, and the Thames Barrier about halfway along the reach. The pair of Woolwich Free Ferries change places across the tideway every few minutes, laden with lorries on each trip.

GALLIONS POINT PORT GUIDE

Gate 14, Royal Albert Basin, Woolwich Manor Way, North Woolwich, London E16 2PU	
Marina	Tel 0207 476 7054; VHF Ch 13 Five hours either side of HW
Facilities	Toilets and showers, pump out ashore
Fuel	Diesel and gas from fuel barge *Leonard* outside entrance. Tel 0207 4748714; VHF Ch 14; open 0900 to 1600 weekdays; Out of hours contact Tel/Fax 0207 5117750
Stores	Locally or in Woolwich on S bank, 15 mins walk to Woolwich Ferry and foot tunnel
Transport	Docklands Light Railway from N Woolwich to central London. London City Airport nearby

One of the hazards in Woolwich Reach can be the Woolwich Free Ferries which cross the tideway every few minutes

Chapter 14

THE THAMES BARRIER

At the tidal-surge barrier across the Thames in Woolwich Reach a system of extremely powerful light signals is used by day and night to indicate which spans are to be used and which are barred to traffic. Two green arrows (lit) pointing inwards will be displayed from each side of a span that is open to oncoming traffic, while red St Andrew's crosses (lit) shown from each side of a span will mean that no traffic must pass through the span in that direction. Anchoring is prohibited in the vicinity of the barrier.

Large illuminated notice-boards are in position on both banks upstream near Blackwall Point and Blackwall Stairs; and downstream near Thamesmead and Barking Power Station. Amber lights shown at these boards warn ships to proceed with caution while red lights require them to stop. Audible warnings can also be issued from these stations.

Whenever possible vessels should take in their sails and use motor power to navigate through the Barrier. Port Control London advises yachtsmen to talk to traffic control on VHF Channel 14, callsign *Woolwich Radio*; or on 0208 855 0315.

BARRIER CLOSURES

From time to time the Barrier is closed for testing purposes, usually only one gate at any one time but occasionally all gates at the same time. Information regarding the dates and times of closures are given by Woolwich Radio on Ch 14 and in PCL's Notice to Mariners.

BUGSBY'S REACH

The Greenwich YC is situated on the south side of the river in the bight between Woolwich and Bugsby's reaches. Part of the Tideway Sailing Centre, the club has extensive new premises comprising a clubhouse on a pier with fine views of the city and the river. Facilities incorporate a slipway, boatlift and many new moorings, including one swinging mooring for visiting

GREENWICH YACHT CLUB

Peartree Wharf, Peartree Way, London SE10 0BW

Telephone	0208 8587339; VHF Ch M (opening hours)
Visitors' moorings	By prior arrangement
Water	At clubhouse
Facilities	Repairs, showers and usual club house facilities Tues and Fri evenings and weekends

In Bugsby's Reach passing the Millennium Dome – the Canary Wharf Tower can be seen over the top of the dome

The entrance to the India and Millwall Docks, Blackwall Basin and the British Waterways Poplar Dock Marina

GREENWICH REACH

This short E-W reach links Blackwall and Limehouse Reaches, round the Isle of Dogs.

Here on the south bank is the Royal Naval College '...standing like a thing of dignity amid the grime of commerce' – as J Wentworth Day described it in *Coastal Adventure* (1949). Nearby is the National Maritime Museum, the *Cutty Sark* and *Gipsy Moth IV*, while not far away at Deptford, the *Mary Rose* was built in the first year of the reign of Henry VIII.

The Meridian is crossed three times on the upstream approach to Greenwich.

It is possible for small craft to anchor just below and in line with Greenwich Pier, which is much used by water buses and pleasure steamers.

yachts up to 30ft, by prior arrangement (vacant members' moorings can also be made available). Anchoring is not allowed because of the considerable commercial traffic in the vicinity, particularly barge trains moored nearby which swing with the tide.

BLACKWALL AND POPLAR DOCK MARINA

Blackwall Point, on the south bank, is (or was) easily identified by the conspicuous Millennium Dome. Opposite, on the north bank is the entrance to Bow Creek and the River Lea, followed by the India and Millwall Docks just east of Canary Wharf Tower. Through the entrance lock of these docks and immediately to starboard in Blackwall Basin is the Poplar Dock Marina.

Visitors' berths are available at this British Waterways-owned facility, but it is essential to book at least 24 hours in advance. The lock opens from 0600 to 2200 at one hour either side of HW; a bridge at the lock, plus two other bridges open in unison.

SOUTH DOCK MARINA

The South Dock Marina is in part of the old Surrey Dock complex on the S bank of the river. The locked entrance, from the southern end of Limehouse Reach, is about two and a half miles down river from Tower Bridge. The conspicuous Baltic Quay building with its five arched rooftops is situated at the SW end of the marina. The lock will open for yachts of approximately 1m draught for about three hours either side of HW; about one hour either side of HW for a 2m draught. There is a waiting pontoon at Greenland Pier just upstream of the lock entrance.

POPLAR DOCK MARINA

Marine Office, West India Pierhead, 420 Manchester Road, London E14 9ST	
Telephone	0207 515 1046; Fax 538 5537 (weekdays); VHF Ch 13 weekends
Entrance lock	One hour either side of HW
Berths	90; visitors should book in advance
Facilities	Water, stores, slip, bar, restaurant, launderette
Transport	Docklands Light Railway: nearest station Blackwall; Canary Wharf Tube (Jubilee Line)

SOUTH DOCK MARINA

Lock Office, Rope Street, Plough Way, London SE16 1TX	
Telephone	0207 252 2244; Fax 0207 237 3806; 24 hour watch on VHF Ch 80
Entrance Lock	3 hrs either side of HW (1m draught); 1 hr either side of HW (2m draught)
Berths	350
Fuel	Diesel and petrol locally (ask at Lock office)
Security	24-hour CCTV
Facilities	Showers, water, telephone on site. Chandlery, provisions, laundry and repairs (crane up to 20 tonnes) – ask at lock office
Transport	Surrey Quays tube

Chapter 14

The entrance to the Limehouse Basin Marina. The lifting bridge operates in conjunction with the lock gates beyond

LIMEHOUSE REACH

The river takes a turn to the north into Limehouse Reach, where to starboard the Canary Wharf Tower and its surrounding buildings on the Isle of Dogs seem to dwarf all else along the river banks. Here and there are glimpses of old London waterfront left behind, but most of the banksides from Woolwich to Tower Bridge have been extensively developed in the past 10 years or so.

LIMEHOUSE BASIN MARINA

On the N bank, just before the river begins its turn to the SW into the Lower Pool, the former Regents Canal Dock (built in 1820) now contains the 90-berth Limehouse Basin Marina and still provides access to the inland waterways network. The swing bridge and lock entrance operate all week, 0800–1800 April 1 to October 31 and 0800–1600 November 1 to March 31 (other times with 24-hour prior notice). There is one metre over the sill at LW Neaps and access is possible for about four hours either side of HW. Since the marina was opened, a towering apartment block has been built on the E side of the entrance making it difficult to identify the swing bridge and lock gates as you approach from downstream. The Barley Mow pub on the waterfront to the west of the bridge has a distinctive white flag pole in front of it. The black swing bridge has Limehouse Marina unmistakably painted in white across its span and this can be picked out when you are abeam of the entrance, where there is a waiting pontoon accessible about one and a half hours either side of LW.

Once through the lock, the pontoon berths are to port; the showers, toilets and laundry facilities are beneath the Lock Keeper's office, an octagonal building on the port-hand lock corner. There are waste disposal and pump out facilities, but no fuelling. The Basin also houses the headquarters of the Cruising Association (CA), managing agents of the marina on behalf of British Waterways.

If you have not been allocated a berth, moor on the walkway to starboard and enquire at the office on the first floor of CA House (entry phone in lobby). The CA bar and restaurant are open on a temporary membership basis to all visiting

LIMEHOUSE BASIN MARINA

British Waterways Lock Office
Tel 0207 308 9930
(24-hour answer phone); VHF Ch 80

Entrance swing bridge/lock
Four hours either side of HW

Cruising Association
1 Northey Street, Limehouse Basin, London E14 8BT

To book berth
Tel 0207 537 2828;
Fax 0207 537 2266
Berths 90

Security Swipe card for access to pontoon and facilities

Water On pontoons

Electricity By arrangement

Showers, toilets, laundry
Beneath Lock Keeper's building

Fuel Petrol and diesel at Esso garage Commercial Road (take own cans)

Gas Docklands Garden Centre near Limehouse Station

Chandlery Pumpkin Marine Tel 0207 480 6630 nearby

Stores Limited from small shop in Narrow Street; more small shops in Salmon Lane (round low level walkway and across Commercial Road); supermarkets on Isle of Dogs

Banks and cashpoints
Banks on South Quay on DLR; cashpoint at Texaco garage near Pumpkin Marine

Transport Docklands Light Railway from Limehouse to Bank or Tower Gateway; British Rail from Limehouse to Fenchurch Street or Southend; No 15 bus from Commercial Road to West End

Canary Wharf Tower on the Isle of Dogs is particularly eyecatching when the sun is on it

yachtsmen; food is served every day, with a carvery or barbecue on Sundays in summer.

At Limehouse Basin, where the Regents Canal meets the Thames, east of the London bridges, there is access to 2,000 miles of inland waterways so, not surprisingly, a number of narrowboats and river cruisers are moored in the marina, which is also a regular venue for waterways rallies.

ST KATHARINE YACHT HAVEN

St Katharine Yacht Haven is close to the Tower of London and immediately below Tower Bridge on the north bank of the river. This busy marina, with berthing facilities for more than 100 craft, must surely be one of the most superbly sited yacht harbours in the world.

Entry to the harbour is by way of a tidal lock (30ft x 100ft), which can be accessed for about two hours either side of HW, between 0600 and 2030 in summer and between 0800 and 1800 in winter. The lock leads into the Central Basin with further access via small lifting bridges to the West or East

ST KATHARINE YACHT HAVEN

50 St Katharine's Way, London, E1 9LB
Harbour Master Tel 0207 482 8350 (24-hour answer phone); 0207 264 5314; Fax 0207 702 2252; email: haven.reception@tayprop.co.uk
VHF Ch 80 during locking times, callsign *St Katharine's*
Customs/Immigration Can be arranged through Haven office
Berths 150 including visitors
Water and Electricity On pontoons
Facilities Toilets, showers and laundry in East and West docks, toilets and showers in Haven office block
Fuel Diesel and gas from barge Burgan outside downstream of lock entrance. Tel 0207 481 1774; VHF Ch 14 callsign *Burgan*
Stores Safeway nearby
Food and Drink Haven Yacht Club has bar and restaurant and temporary membership for visitors. Safeway does take-aways
Transport Tube and buses from Tower Hill to West End and City. Taxis at Tower Thistle Hotel nearby

Docks on either hand. Visiting yachts are usually berthed in the Central Basin or East Dock and a week's notice is required during the summer. There is a permanent harbour master, telephone 0171 481 8350; VHF Ch 80.

Diesel fuel is available from the barge Burgan, moored 400m downstream of the lock entrance.

The inside of St Katharine pier can be used by shoal draught yachts while awaiting entry to the marina (the outside of this pier is heavily used by ferries and trip boats). There are also moorings laid between the lock entrance and HMS *President* pier.

Left: The lifting bridge is raised while yachts enter the lock into St Katharine Yacht Haven
Above: Yachts and a sailing barge locking out of the St Katharine Yacht Haven

THE MEDWAY

Tides (Queenborough)	HW Dover +1.35 Range: Springs 5.1m Neaps 3.3m
Charts	Admiralty SC 2482 River Medway and The Swale, 1834 (Grain Pt to Folly Pt),
	1835 (Folly Pt to Rochester), Stanford No 5, Imray Y18, OS 178
Waypoints	Medway Lt Buoy 51°28'.83N 00°52'.81E, S Montgomery Buoy 51°27'.87N 00°47'.08E
	Grain Hard Buoy 51°26'.98N 00°44'.16E, Queenborough Spit Buoy 51°25'.82N 00°43'.93E
Hazards	Wreck of the *Richard Montgomery*. Overfalls near Sheerness Fort on ebb
Medway Ports	VHF Ch 74 and 16 (24 hour) Callsign *Medway Radio*
Harbour Master	Tel 01795 561234

For centuries the Medway was the Navy's river, with dockyard bases at Sheerness and Chatham, and the even older forts at Folly Point and Darnet Ness. The first warship built at Chatham was launched in 1586, and at Chatham's World Naval Base, formerly the Historic Dockyard and Museum, you can see the most complete Georgian/early Victorian dockyard in the world.

For the yachtsman, the Medway offers very good sailing in the lower reaches, where on the south side there are some quiet anchorages in settings that can have changed little since the Romans established their potteries and even less since the prison-hulks were moored in the area during the Revolutionary and Napoleonic wars. Those who are not afraid of mud can still find relics of both these periods, even though they were separated by thousands of years. By

Approaching the entrance to the Medway, the 800ft power station chimney on the Isle of Grain is a prominent landmark

contrast, the north shore of the river as far west as Long Reach is now almost entirely given over to a power station, a container terminal and what has become a disused oil refinery.

The river is navigable by quite large vessels for some 13 miles from its mouth at Sheerness to Rochester, where the headroom under the bridge is 30ft at LWS. The tide flows for a further 12 miles to Allington Lock, one mile above the lower arched bridge at Aylsford. Then, for a further 17 miles, the river winds through pleasant country to Maidstone and Tonbridge, with eleven locks. Craft drawing 2m can get as far as Maidstone, while those drawing 1.2m can reach Tonbridge. Maximum length 18m, beam 4.5m.

The Port of Sheerness is responsible for the ports at Sheerness, Isle of Grain, Faversham and Rochester. There is considerable commercial traffic in both the Medway and the Swale, and Sheerness itself is solely a commercial harbour.

LANDMARKS

From the Thames Estuary the tree-covered cliffs of Warden Point on the Isle of Sheppey, some six miles east of the Medway entrance, are conspicuous. On the west side is the 800ft chimney of the Grain Power Station, the most prominent daylight mark in the whole of the Thames Estuary, sometimes visible from as far north as the Wallet. The chimney displays four sets of four vertical red lights, the top ones of which are flashing.

On the east side of the entrance is Sheerness Port and the fort at Garrison Point, from which a powerful flashing light is shown by day or night when large ships are under way.

APPROACHES

There are three main approaches to the Medway (see River Thames Sea Reach chart on page 106):

(i) The main deep water route. From the Medway Pillar Lt Buoy (RWVS Mo(A)6s Sph topmark) some three-quarters of a mile south of Sea Reach No 1 Buoy, the channel runs in a W by S'ly direction between Sheerness Middle Sand and Grain Spit to the west, and the flats of the Cant to the east. It is wide and well lit, with all the starboard hand buoys having white or green lights and the port having red. The stranded wreck of the ammunition ship *Richard Montgomery* lies on Sheerness Middle Sand, very near No 7 and No 9 buoys. It is dangerous but clearly marked by special buoys (yellow) on all sides.

The tidal stream off the approach sets W by N and E by S at a maximum rate of $2\frac{1}{2}$ and 3 knots respectively, slightly across the channel, but as Garrison Point is neared they run fairly up and down the channel.

(ii) The Nore Swatch, formerly known as the Jenkin Swatch, is not quite so important now that the Nore Sand has 2m or more over it at LWS. From the west the Swatch can be located by the West Nore Sand Lt Buoy (Can R Fl(3) R 10s), which lies on the south side of Sea Reach almost opposite Southend Pier. A course of 120°M leads to pass the Mid Swatch light buoy (Con G Fl G 5s) close to port and, continued, reaches the Nore Swatch light buoy (Can R Fl(4)R 15s). From here a S'ly course leaving Grain Edge Buoy (Con G) to starboard leads into the main channel.

(iii) Across the Cant. Vessels making from the eastward via the Four Fathom Channel or out of the West Swale can carry about 3m least water on a course 300°M from the Spile Buoy (Con G Fl G 2.5s), keeping about two miles from the Sheppey shore. Several unlit beacons and Cheney Spit, a shingle bank with about 1m least water, extend eastwards from Garrison Point. These hazards make it inadvisable to get much closer than a mile offshore. Cheney Rocks, an unmarked drying patch of stones, lies half a mile off the eastern end of Sheerness town. A N cardinal buoy (VQ) marks the seaward end of the Jacob's Bank obstruction extending from the shore just east of Garrison Point. Tides over the Cant are slacker than those in the channels. The Medway may also be entered through the Swale (see Chapter 16).

ENTRANCE

The entrance to the Medway is between Garrison Point to port and Grain Hard buoy (Con G Fl G 5s) to starboard.

Massive landmarks have been created on the west side of the entrance in the form of Grain Power Station with its enormous buildings and 800ft chimney, the latter showing four vertical red lights at night.

Garrison Point is steep-to, and on the first of the ebb during spring tides there are considerable overfalls on the east side of the entrance near the Garrison shore.

A powerful white light (Fl 7s) shown from Garrison Point means that a large ship is under way and small craft must keep clear.

On the Grain shore the flats run out for half a mile almost to the Grain Hard buoy. No attempt should be made to pass to the west of this buoy

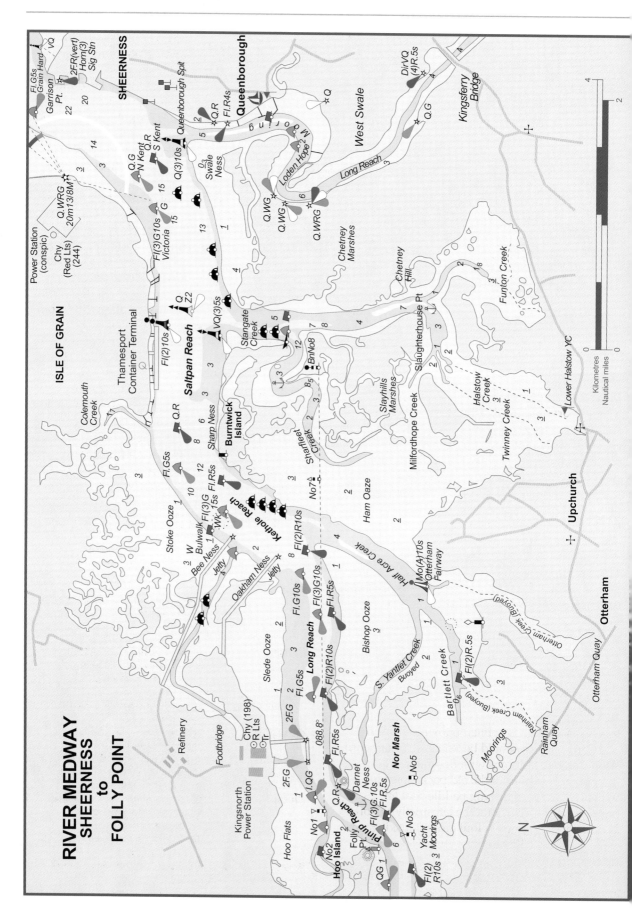

RIVER MEDWAY
SHEERNESS
to
FOLLY POINT

ISLE OF GRAIN

SHEERNESS

Queenborough

Power Station (conspic)

Chy (Red Lts) (244)

Q.WRG 20m13/8M

Thamesport Container Terminal

Colemouth Creek

Saltpan Reach

Burntwick Island

Stangate Creek

Chetney Marshes

West Swale

Long Reach

Swale Ness

Loden Hope

Kingsferry Bridge

Chetney Hill

Slaughterhouse Pt

Funton Creek

Stoke Ooze

Bee Ness

Bulwalk

Kethole Reach

Oakham Ness

Sharp Ness

Sharfleet Creek

Slayhills Marshes

Milfordhope Creek

Halstow Creek

Twinney Creek

Lower Halstow YC

Upchurch

Refinery

Footbridge

Kingsnorth Power Station

Slede Ooze

Jetty

Jetty

Long Reach

088.8°

Bishop Ooze

Ham Ooze

Half Acre Creek

S. Yantlet Creek

Otterham Fairway

Bartlett Creek

Rainham Creek (Buoyed)

Otterham Creek (Buoyed)

Rainham Quay

Otterham Quay

Otterham

Pinup Reach

Darnet Ness

Nor Marsh

Hoo Flats

Hoo Island

Folly Pt.

Yacht Moorings

Moorings

Garrison Pt.

Grain Hard

Queenborough Spit

N Kent

S Kent

Victoria

BnNo8

No7

No5

No3

No1

No2

Kilometres

Nautical miles

Large commercial ships come through the moorings at Queenborough on their way to and from the West Swale

side before the all-tide landing pontoon, which is also owned by the local council. The T-head floating pontoon, marked by 2 FR vertical lights, is just down-river from the original hard. Go ashore here for stores and water, but remember that to get back onto the pontoon via the gate, you need to purchase a token from the Queenborough Yacht Club, the chandlers, the pub or any town trader. A stay alongside is limited to 15 minutes, unless prior arrangement can be made with the harbour master.

Two large grey (2003) buoys near the hard are intended for rafting by visitors, up to four boats on each. A ferry operates at weekends, which can be contacted on VHF – see Trot Boat details below. It should be noted that the hard extends a long way and care must be taken to avoid its submerged end.

There is a concrete barge used for mooring on the west side of the river, opposite the hard. The east side of the channel is marked by a red can

as there are the remains of an obstruction running out from the Martello Tower.

Once inside, the river broadens out and the busy commercial harbour of Sheerness will be seen to port. The flood runs at 2.5 knots at springs, setting sharply on to Garrison Point and causing a pronounced north-going eddy along the Sheppey shore.

The ebb runs hard, 3 knots or more at springs, on the Sheerness side, causing overfalls. However, it is much weaker on the Grain side of the river, so a yacht entering against the stream should seek this shore, remembering that the edge of the mud is quite steep.

Anchoring is prohibited on the NW side of the river because of the commercial traffic. On the east shore the Lappel, once an anchorage, is now infilled and used as a container/car park which is often brilliantly illuminated at night.

QUEENBOROUGH

A sheltered mooring will be found at Queenborough, a mile and a half further south and just inside the West Swale. The entrance is narrow and is marked by Queenborough Spit Pillar buoy (E Car BYB VQ(6) 10s), which should be left close to starboard. After this, two dolphins with flashing red lights, marking the remains of the old packet pier, in regular use by the Flushing paddle boat ferries a hundred years ago, should be left strictly to port because of the extremely foul ground inside them.

For the next mile or so the river is lined on both sides by more than a hundred moorings that are controlled by the Swale Borough Council. There are several visitors' moorings (yellow) on the east

QUEENBOROUGH PORT GUIDE	
Supervisor Harbour Master	
	On Town Quay. (Tel 01795 662051) VHF Channel 8 Callsign *SHEPPEY ONE*
Water	On all-tide landing or tap near top of causeway
Stores	Shops including Co-op in town. EC Wed
Repairs	Jim Brett Marine Tel 01795 668263. Yard with slip in Queenborough Creek
Fuel	Garage in town
Chandler	Bosuns Stores near top of hard Tel 01795 662674
Transport	Train service to London via Sittingbourne, station 0.5 mile
Trot Boat	VHF Ch 8 callsign *Sheppey One*. Daytime hours weekends only (due to staff shortages)
Clubs	Queenborough YC (bar meals, water and showers) open Fri eves and weekends Tel 01795 663955; Sheppey YC (Cruiser Section)
Food and Drink	Several pubs and restaurants in town

(Fl R 3s). Anchorage is forbidden in the fairway because of the large coasters that come by; a series of lit beacons on the mainland shore are used by the commercial shipping navigating Loden Hope and around Long Point into the West Swale.

Keep clear of the entrance to Queenborough Creek, a narrow gut that leads in behind the town, the course of which is marked by half a dozen red can and green conical buoys. Queenborough Quay, where there is a boatyard, can be reached via the creek around HW.

The tide runs south past Queenborough for the first hour after HW.

SHEERNESS TO ROCHESTER

Standing on up the Medway through Saltpan Reach the river widens and tidal streams are less strong. Almost the whole of the north shore is occupied by tanker and container ship berths and these are marked by vertical pairs of fixed green lights. At the western end of all these jetties is Colemouth Creek, which formerly joined the Yantlet Creek in the Thames to form the Isle of Grain. This carries 2m at low water for half a mile, but is of little interest because of its environment.

Very few yachtsmen sailing past the power station and container port on the Isle of Grain will know that, in 1897, the Royal Corinthian Yacht Club made a deal with the South Eastern Railway Company to move its headquarters from Erith to Port Victoria. A splendid clubhouse was erected and members came down from London by train to join their yachts on moorings opposite Stangate Creek.

A line of large, unlit buoys extends along the south side of Saltpan Reach about a half mile east of the entrance to Stangate Creek. Three other mooring buoys (Nos 2, 3 and 4) are located in mid-channel, the first and last of which are lit (Q R).

STANGATE CREEK

This creek, running south of Saltpan Reach, provides perhaps the most useful anchorage in the Medway. A spit extends from the western side of Stangate Creek and this is marked by an E Cardinal pillar buoy (BYB VQ (3) 5s). The eastern side of the entrance is fairly steep-to.

Half a mile into the creek, wreckage on the starboard hand is marked by a green conical buoy and just beyond, opposite a red can buoy, is the entrance to Sharfleet Creek.

The creeks hereabouts have a remote and ghostly feel to them. Perhaps this is not surprising as at low tide Roman pottery can sometimes be found, although there are no longer coffins in the saltings as described in the Wyllies' book London to the Nore (1905). 'Doubtless the poor fellows died on the hulks that during the wars of a hundred years ago were here moored as prison-ships.'

For a further mile to the south, the depths in Stangate Creek decrease gradually from some 10m to about 4m LWS at Slaughterhouse Point, where the creek divides. Funton Creek to port holds water for only a little way, but can provide a quiet berth. To starboard, the main channel carries 2m for a quarter of a mile or so and then divides again into Halstow, Twinney and Milford Hope Creeks, all of which dry out. At tide time it is possible for shoal draught craft to reach the wharf at the head of Halstow Creek, where there is a Saxon church, an inn and the Lower Halstow SC. If staying, one must take the ground.

SHARFLEET CREEK

There is a sheltered anchorage in relatively deep pools within Sharfleet Creek, but at weekends there is often not very much room! From about four hours flood it is possible to wriggle right through the creek and out into Half Acre, passing just south of Beacon No 7 (BW triangle topmark). The whole area is a maze of creeks and saltings and for the first time passages over drying areas should only be attempted on a flood with frequent soundings.

MIDDLE REACHES

Leaving Stangate for the main river it is desirable to stand well out before turning west in order to pass round the pillar buoy marking the spit at the entrance. Once clear of this all is plain sailing until the river takes its SW'ly turn at Sharp Ness.

The passage is well marked with fairway buoys, which are all lit, but a good look-out must be kept, especially at night, for any unlit mooring buoys on the east side of the channel opposite Bee Ness Jetty.

There are two conspicuous jetties in Kethole Reach, the dilapidated Bee Ness and Oakham Ness, used for unloading oil from tankers. Close to the west of the first one – Bee Ness Jetty – is East Hoo Creek which, although uniformly narrow, carries a useful depth of water for about half a mile within its entrance and therefore offers a quiet anchorage except in E'ly or SE'ly winds. No more than two cables north-east of the end of this jetty lies the wreck of Bulwark, marked with one green conical buoy (Fl(3) 15s) and one unlit red can.

Towards the south end of the Kethole Reach, opposite Oakham Ness Jetty, is the entrance to Half Acre Creek. This broad creek carries four to six metres at low water for about a mile where it then splits into Otterham, Rainham and South Yantlet Creeks, the junction being marked by a red and white Otterham Fairway light buoy flashing the Morse 'A' 10 sec. Otterham and Rainham creeks both lead south towards the shore before drying out, but South Yantlet Creek, marked by four unlit spherical buoys (RWVS), joins the main river just south of Darnet Fort, where it dries 0.7m at LWS, although at half tide there will be some 2m over the bar. The best water can be found on a W'ly (°M) course from No 4 buoy (RWVS) with a spherical topmark.

OTTERHAM CREEK

The five port and two starboard hand buoys marking the gutway into Otterham Creek are unlit because this narrow channel is little frequented by commercial traffic nowadays. The quay at the head of the creek was once used by sailing barges to load cement. Now there is a yard and two small shops nearby.

RAINHAM CREEK

Small freighters occasionally use Rainham Creek at HW to reach Bloors Wharf. There is also a little quay near the ruins of Goldsmith's old cement works, the mud for which was dug from the neighbouring marshes and brought to the dock in spritsailed 'muddies'.

The entrance to the creek is marked by a red can light buoy (Fl R (2) 5s), while a couple of unlit red nun buoys (see introduction chapter for explanation) mark the gutway further in.

The main river from the entrance to Half Acre Creek bends westward along Long Reach, where the deep water is hardly more than a quarter of a mile wide. Long Reach is dominated by the buildings and chimneys of Kingsnorth Power Station on the north shore. Three port hand buoys (Nos 18, 20 & 22) mark the south side of the channel along this reach.

HOO MARSH PASSAGE

Middle Creek, which near its entrance provides a useful anchorage, leads through Hoo Flats towards the old wharves near the village of Hoo. The creek is tortuous, but quite well buoyed.

The entrance to the creek is marked with a conical green buoy to be left close to starboard, after which a red can must be left to port. Then, turning SW with Gillingham gas holder ahead, another conical green buoy is left to starboard. Having turned sharply to the north with Hoo Church ahead, the fourth mark, a yellow and black South Cardinal buoy, is passed on its S side, after which the remaining buoy, a red can, is left to port before reaching either the quays or the marina at Hoo.

This passage should only be attempted on the last hour or so of the flood, until it is known, as the gutways are narrow and very tortuous.

MIDDLE CREEK TO GILLINGHAM

At the western end of Long Reach, opposite the entrance to Middle Creek, the main river bends to the south to round Darnet Ness into Pinup Reach. Darnet Ness, on which stands a fort, is marked by a red beacon (QR) and is steep on its northern face, but should not be approached too closely on its western side because of a causeway projecting from it. South of this causeway there is anchorage with shelter from easterly winds, near the entrance to South Yantlet Creek.

In Pinup Reach the flood sets sharply towards

Darnet Ness, with its fort, is marked by a porthand beacon, and here the river swings to the south into Pinup Reach

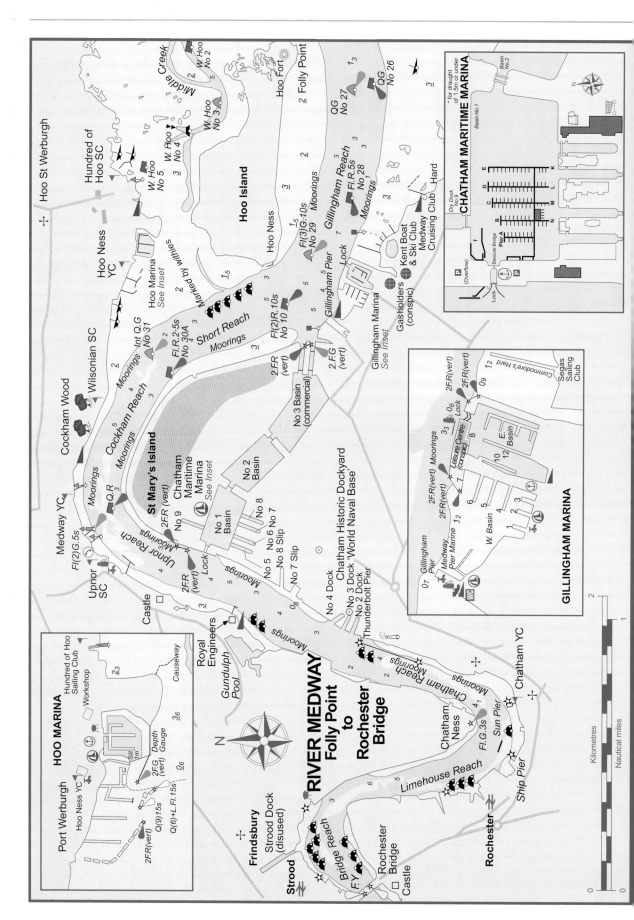

CHATHAM MARITIME MARINA

* for draught of 1.5m or under

Basin No.1
Basin No.2
Dry Dock No.2
Bascule Bridge
Pier A
Lock
P (Overflow)
P
f

E
D
C
B
A
K
L
M
N

GILLINGHAM MARINA

Commodore's Hard
Segas Sailing Club
2.F.R (vert) 0.9 1.2
2.F.R (vert) 0.6 Lock
Moorings 3.3
E. Basin 8
Leisure Centre (conspic) 10 12
2.F.R (vert) 6 7
W. Basin 5
2.F.R (vert) 1 2 3
Gillingham Pier 0.7
Medway Pier Marine 12

HOO MARINA

Port Werburgh
Hundred of Hoo Sailing Club
Workshop
2.3
Hoo Ness YC
Sill 1m
Depth Gauge 3.6
2.F.G (vert) 0.6
Q(9)15s
Q(6)+L.Fl.15s
2.F.R(vert)

RIVER MEDWAY Folly Point to Rochester Bridge

Hoo St Werburgh
Middle Creek
W. Hoo No 2
W. Hoo No 3
5
Hundred of Hoo SC
W. Hoo No 4 3
W. Hoo No 5 3
Marked by withies
Hoo Fort
Folly Point 2
Hoo Island
QG No 27 1.3 QG No 26 3
Gillingham Reach 3
Fl.R.5s No 28 3
Moorings No 1 3
Moorings 7
Hoo Ness 3
Hoo Ness YC
1.5
Fl(3)G.10s No 29 1.5
Gillingham Pier 5 4
Lock 5
Gillingham Marina See Inset
Gasholders (conspic)
Kent Boat & Ski Club
Medway Cruising Club
Hard 3
Short Reach 3
Moorings
Int Q.G No 31
Fl.R.2.5s No 30A 2
3
Fl(2)R.10s No 10
2.F.R (vert)
2.F.G (vert)
No 3 Basin (commercial)
Wilsonian SC
2
Cockham Wood
Moorings
Cockham Reach 4 5
Moorings 3
St Mary's Island
Chatham Maritime Marina See Inset
No 2 Basin
Q.R No 9 3
2.F.R (vert)
Medway YC
Fl(2)G.5s 3
Moorings Upnor Reach
Upnor SC
2.F.R (vert) 4 Lock
No 1 Basin
No 8
No 6 No 7
No 5 No 8 Slip
No 7 Slip
Chatham Historic Dockyard 'World Naval Base'
No 4 Dock
No 3 Dock
No 2 Dock
Thunderbolt Pier
Moorings
Castle
Royal Engineers
Gundulph Pool
Frindsbury
Strood Dock (disused)
Strood
Bridge Reach
F.Y.
Rochester Bridge
Castle
Rochester
Chatham Reach Moorings
Chatham Ness
Fl.G.3s
Sun Pier
Ship Pier
Chatham YC
Limehouse Reach 6
Segas Sailing Club
N
Kilometres 1 2
Nautical miles 1 2
0

In Pinup Reach approaching Gillingham Reach. The conspicuous building beyond the green buoy is the leisure centre adjacent to Gillingham Marina

A prominent waterside leisure centre building is located on the upstream side of the Gillingham Marina lock entrance. The fuel pontoon is on the extreme right of the picture

Folly Point on the starboard hand, on which stands another fort. A rocky spit projecting some 200m from this point is marked by Folly Beacon (BW Con topmark) and no attempt should be made to pass between it and the shore – in fact this corner should be given a wide berth because a spit of mud seems to be extending ever further from it.

Rounding Folly Point into Gillingham Reach, the mud stretches some 300 yards from the north shore and the course should be set for the left hand side of the large gas holder at Gillingham until out in mid-stream.

The south side of this reach is lined with the moorings of the Medway Cruising Club, which stands on Gillingham Strand, just east of the gasworks. Landing is possible at the causeway at all states of the tide. Once abeam of the gas holders, the entrance to Gillingham Marina becomes apparent. A conspicuous waterside leisure centre building is immediately upstream of the lock gates.

GILLINGHAM MARINA

The locked basin section of Gillingham Marina can accommodate 250 craft and is accessible through a lock for about four hours each side of HW during daylight hours. Bear in mind that tides run hard across the entrance. Yachts in the tidal basin section of the marina, upstream of the lock entrance, can arrive or leave for about two hours before or after each high tide. There are deep water moorings in the river for arrival or departure at other times. Fuel can be obtained from the upstream side of the lead-in pontoon (angled across the run of the tide to deflect the stream) on the west side of the lock entrance. Visiting yachts can usually be accommodated in the locked basin but it is preferable to book at least 24 hours in advance. Hoists and extensive repair facilities are available at the marina, and a well stocked chandlery is a short walk away

on Pier Road with a general store next door.

A small marina (Medway Pier Marine Tel 01634 851113) is situated off the end of Gillingham Pier with pontoon berths for about 35 boats.

At the western end of Gillingham Reach is the locked entrance to the commercial quays of Chatham Docks in Basin 3, while Basin 2 contains the Arethusa watersports centre.

The river now turns NW round Hoo Ness into Short Reach, with the high wooded bank of Cockham Reach ahead and the prominent housing development on St Mary's Island lining the riverside to port from Finborough Ness to Upper Reach.

Hoo Ness, with a small jetty (two pairs vertical fixed green lights), is steep-to, but to the NW of it a large expanse of mud, covered at half-tide, must be crossed to reach the marina at Hoo.

GILLINGHAM PORT GUIDE	
Telephone	01634 280022; Fax 280164
VHF	Ch 80 Callsign *Gillingham Marina Lock*
Lock Access	Four hours either side of HW daylight hours
Water and Shorepower	All berths
Fuel	Diesel, petrol and gas from lead-in pontoon upstream side of lock entrance
Showers	Two unmetered shower blocks and launderette
Stores and Off Licence	Pier Road
Chandlery	Pier Road Tel 01634 283008
Repairs	Autoyachts Tel 01634 281333; slipway, 20 ton straddle lift
Security	24-hour
Leisure Centre	On site
Food and Drink	Bar and club temporary membership available
Transport	Gillingham main line station three mins taxi ride. Helicopter landing pad on site

HOO

Hoo Marina, constructed adjacent to the old harbour, was the first marina to be established on the East Coast. Its new basin is protected by a sill so that there is a depth of about 1.5m of water inside. Usual services are supplied to the finger berths, with toilets and showers ashore.

The marina can be approached across the mud flats near HW, but is accessible three hours either side of high water (5ft draught) via a creek or gully known locally as the Orinoco. Entrance to this gully is almost a mile from the yacht harbour and about half a mile NW of Hoo Ness. The creek mouth is usually marked by a West Cardinal pillar buoy to starboard, to be found just inside a line of large Medway Port Authority mooring buoys and about five orange buoys which are connected to assist fore and aft mooring. The latter can be used while waiting for the tide to make.

The Orinoco is identified by posts to be left to port. But the final mark, a small yellow buoy, must be left close to starboard immediately before crossing the sill.

The Hoo Ness YC is nicely situated on the shore overlooking the old harbour, slipway and mud berths. It has a bar and restaurant and visitors are welcome. A walk through the chalet park to the nearby village of Hoo St Werburgh will bring you to the churchyard where it is thought that Dickens based the meeting of Pip with the escaped convict in *Great Expectations* – the prison hulks used to lie in the river nearby.

There is a pleasant walk from Hoo Marina to Upnor along part of the Saxon Shore Way that runs below Cockham Woods – to remain dry shod it is best undertaken before or after HW.

HOO PORT GUIDE

Hoo Marina	Tel 01634 250311; Fax 251761 VHF Ch 80
Water	At marina and Hundred of Hoo SC
Stores	Well-stocked general store in adjacent chalet park. Shops at Hoo village. EC Tues
Fuel	Diesel (own cans) and gas from marina
Repairs	Chandlery and 20 ton crane at marina. Slip and crane in W Hoo Creek
Transport	Buses to Rochester
Telephone	At chalet park
Clubs	Hoo Ness YC, has bar and restaurant; Hundred of Hoo YC Tel 01634 250102 (mooring sometimes available for visitors)

UPNOR PORT GUIDE

Medway YC	Tel 01634 718399
Water	From clubhouse or Cabin Yacht Stores
Stores	Shop in village nearby (open Sundays)
Fuel	From club
Chandler	Nearby
Transport	Buses to Rochester and Chatham
Clubs	Upnor SC Tel 01634 718043. Medway YC, Wilsonian SC

COCKHAM REACH & UPNOR

The Medway YC at Lower Upnor is situated in Cockham Reach, the prettiest reach on the tidal Medway. The river here is thick with yacht moorings (many fore-and-aft) on both sides, three lines on the north shore and a single trot round the bend on the south side. If a mooring cannot be found, a brief stay (10 mins) can be made at the pontoon off the Medway YC.

Upnor SC is on the waterfront at Upnor between The Pier Inn, which usually has a barge or two moored nearby, and The Ship.

Above the clubs is Upnor Castle, which once guarded the river against the marauding Dutch fleet, and a little further up river on the west bank is the Royal Engineers (RE) base and YC. From time to time the Royal School of Military Engineering carries out high speed boat operations in Chatham Reach – at speeds well in excess of the normal permitted limit.

CHATHAM

Chatham Maritime Marina is located on the east side of the river in Chatham Dockyard No 1 Basin. The entrance is about halfway between Upnor Castle and the RE base on the west shore. Just beyond the entrance is the conspicuous No 5 Pumphouse building, below which is a long line of moorings in the river.

There is 24-hour lock access with 1.5m over the sill at MLWS. A waiting pontoon is situated

The very pretty Cockham Reach – the Wilsonian SC can be seen nestling between the trees on the wooded foreshore

The sailing barge Xylonite *and a Twister under power in Upnor Reach. Upnor Castle can be seen in the trees on the left*

outside immediately downstream of the lock gates. Opened in 2001, the marina has 300 berths, excellent toilet, shower and laundry facilities, fuel pontoon, boat lifting and hard standing. The Ship and Trades pub is a short walk away, with a convenience store next door. Other than fast food in the nearby factory outlet shopping centre, the only alternative source of supplies is in Rochester High Street some two and a half miles away.

The marina is ideally placed (a 10 minute walk) for visiting the award-winning, 80-acre living museum at the Historic Dockyard Chatham, open daily during the summer. You really should not leave the Medway without experiencing this sizeable slice of maritime history. Allow a whole

day as there is so much to discover including the destroyer HMS *Cavalier*, lying in No 2 Dry Dock where Nelson's *Victory* was built, the submarine *Ocelot*, the Victorian naval sloop HMS *Gannet*, and the covered slips, not to mention The Ropery, with its quarter-mile-long rope walk dating back to 1618, where rope is still made commercially.

The history of the River Medway can also be recalled by visiting St Mary's Church to see the Medway Heritage Centre.

Continuing upriver beyond the Maritime Marina, Chatham Reach is dominated by the

Chapter 15

CHATHAM PORT GUIDE

Chatham Maritime Marina	
	Tel 01634 899200; Fax 899201
	email: chatham@mdlmarinas.co.uk
VHF	Ch 80
Lock Access	24 hour (draught 1.5m or less)
Water & Electric	On pontoons
Fuel	Diesel and petrol
Facilities	Toilets, showers, laundry
Repairs	20 ton crane
Stores	Shop nearby
Food and Drink	Pub nearby, restaurants in Rochester
Historic Dockyard	
	Tel 01634 823807; www.chdt.org.uk

The enormous covered slips at the Historic Naval Dockyard dominate Chatham Reach

The entrance to Chatham Maritime Marina lock with the road bridge raised. A waiting pontoon is to the left in the picture

enormous structures of the covered slips on the Dockyard side. Some of these date back to 1838 when the original 17th Century slipways were covered. After the drydocks and Thunderbolt Pier, where there are some Victory Marine pontoon berths downstream, the impressive Anchor Wharf storehouses come into view on the waterfront at the southern end of the Dockyard complex.

On the opposite, west side of Chatham Reach, towards Chatham Ness, are industrial quays where aggregate dredgers operate by day and night.

ROCHESTER

Once past the church and the Command House nestling in the trees, the river starts to swing around Chatham Ness in a northwesterly direction into Limehouse Reach, Rochester.

It is no longer possible to land at Sun Pier, however, you could get ashore at the nearby port authority floating pier to the the W of Chatham YC, leaving dinghies clear of the pontoon front.

Both sides of Limehouse Reach are lined with commercial wharfs and there is regular coastal freighter traffic right up to Rochester Bridge. Bridge Reach is busy with barges, tugs, cranes and sundry craft, including (2003) the old Radio Caroline ship and a derelict Russian submarine.

The clearance under Rochester road and rail bridge is approximately 20ft (6m) at HWS. There is not much depth of water at LWS, but the best arch to use is on the starboard side going up river.

In the upper Medway, with shallow draught and lowered mast, it is possible to reach Maidstone and Tonbridge via eight locks, the first of which is Allington.

Bridge Reach Rochester with the old Radio Caroline *ship on the right and the road and rail bridge beyond*

THE SWALE

Tides (Harty Ferry)   HW Dover +1.25 Range: Springs 5.3m Neaps 3.2m

Charts   Admiralty 2571 (East Swale), 2752 (The Swale Windmill Creek to Queenborough),
Stanford No 5, Imray Y 14, OS 178

Waypoints   Whitstable Street Buoy 51°23'.86N 01°01'.60E, Pollard Spit Buoy 51°22'.98N 00°58'.56E

Many editions ago it was pointed out that the Swale is not a river and could more correctly be described as a ria – meaning a submerged valley. Whatever we call it, it divides the Isle of Sheppey from the mainland of Kent, is seventeen miles in length and follows a tortuous course in a general east-west direction.

In ancient days it was the usual route for craft bound for London from the Channel, and it still provides an inside passage between the Medway and the North Kent shore off Whitstable.

The opposing tidal streams meet somewhere near the mouth of Milton Creek. A good time to start through the Swale from W to E is an hour or so after low water at Sheerness.

The West Swale is entered from the Medway between the vast container/car park south of Sheerness, once an area of mudflats known as the Lappel, and the extensive Queenborough Spit, the end of which is marked by an E Cardinal Pillar buoy (BYB VQ(6) 10s).

The facilities at Queenborough have already been described in the chapter on the Medway, since this anchorage is often thought of as being part of that river rather than the Swale.

LODEN HOPE

Above Queenborough the river turns SW through Loden Hope. Drying mud flats fill the whole of the SE bight from Queenborough hard to the jetty

Looking down Faversham Creek from near Iron Wharf at the top of a very high spring tide

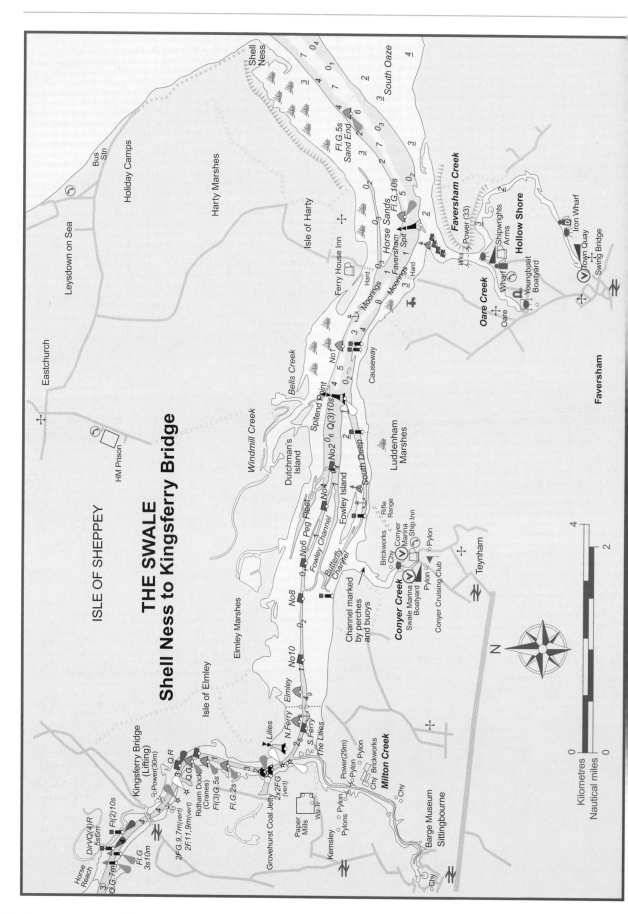

THE SWALE
Shell Ness to Kingsferry Bridge

ISLE OF SHEPPEY

Shell Ness

South Oaze

Faversham Creek

Horse Sands

Hollow Shore

Oare Creek

Faversham

Leysdown on Sea

Eastchurch

Harty Marshes

Isle of Harty

Ferry House Inn

HM Prison

Windmill Creek

Dutchman's Island

Spitend Point

Luddenham Marshes

Elmley Marshes

Fowley Channel

Fowley Island

Butterfly Channel

South Deep

Rifle Range

Conyer Creek

Teynham

Isle of Elmley

Milton Creek

Sittingbourne

Barge Museum

Kingsferry Bridge (Lifting)

Ridham Dock (Cranes)

Grovehurst Coal Jetty

Kemsley

Paper Mills

Horse Reach

N. Ferry
S. Ferry
The Lilies
Lilies

Elmley

on the NE face of Long Point. A drying horse (shoal) in mid-stream almost opposite the jetty is marked by a green conical buoy but, if the north side is taken, Long Point should be rounded in mid-channel with due regard to mud flats off the north shore. A series of three lit beacons (first two QWG and third QRGW) on the mainland shore are used by large coastal freighters to navigate this narrow channel around Long Point.

As the river turns south along Long Reach the best water is towards the west side of mid-channel.

About a mile after Long Point (in Horse Reach) two prominent cable notice-boards will be seen on NE bank. Abreast of these there is a small horse (shoal) practically in mid-channel. This is marked by two red can buoys and should be passed on its SW side about one-third of the river width off the Kent shore.

There are two sets of leading marks, with lights to assist vessels through Horse Reach. The first pair of marks and lights (flashing green) are on the south bank and provide a leading line of 120°M while the second pair, bearing 105°M, are located on the west bank and flash red.

From Horse Reach, Kingsferry Bridge is seen spanning the river ahead. Although here the river is narrow and carries quite large ships, small craft can usually find temporary anchorage on the SW shore just by the bridge. This is also the best spot for landing from a dinghy as the surface is hard.

Kingsferry Bridge will open to allow vessels with fixed masts to pass on request, provided always that railway traffic permits. If a train is on the line between Sittingbourne and Sheerness, the bridge may not be opened and do not be surprised if this sometimes results in a wait of half an hour or so.

Sets of six 'traffic lights' are displayed on the south buttress of the bridge, near the bridge-keeper's cabin. The lights are grouped in two vertical lines of three, the top pair white, middle pair orange and lowest pair green. The bridge keeper can be contacted on VHF Ch 10.

The traditional signals for a yacht to give when wishing to pass through the bridge is to hoist a bucket in the rigging or make one long and four short sound signals.

When both green and red lights are flashing, the bridge is about to be lifted. When fixed green lights are shown it has been fully raised. Flashing red lights signify that the span is being lowered, while a flashing orange light indicates that the bridge is not working and craft should keep clear. If no lights at all are shown, then nothing will happen because the bridge is shut down.

The height clearance with the span raised is 27m at LWS. The width between the bascules is also 27m. Tidal streams run strongly: from three to four knots on the first of the flood and the first of ebb. Construction work on a second Swale crossing is due to start in the year 2004.

Two more sets of lights, on the W bank near Ridham Dock, are there to lead ships through the bridge, the front being 2 FG and the rear 2 FW on a line of 155°M.

Just beyond the bridge on the SW shore is Ridham Dock which, purely commercial, serves the large paper mills nearby. It is usually occupied by sizeable freighters for which look-out should be kept around high water when they may leave via the bridge.

Two port- and two starboard-hand light buoys have been established in Ferry and Clay Reaches between Ridham Dock and Grovehurst Coal Jetty, where the channel is no more than half a cable wide at LW.

A little over half a mile further east is the nominal point at which the two tidal streams meet (see later). The river then turns to the east past the entrance to Milton Creek, which may be considered the end of the western half of the Swale.

MILTON CREEK

This area is likely to be of greatest interest to industrial archaeologists who may wish to visit the Dolphin Yard Barge Museum at Sittingbourne; but even they may be well advised to get there by road rather than via the creek. The museum is usually open on Sundays and Bank Holidays from Easter to mid October.

EAST SWALE

The approach from seaward commences at the Columbine buoy (Con G) about 2½ miles north of Whitstable town, but from this distance the precise entrance to the Swale is not easily recognised. A course of 235°M passing along the SE edge of the Columbine Shoal, leaving the Columbine Spit buoy (Con G) to starboard, will lead to the next visible marks in about a mile. The Pollard Spit light buoy (Can R QR) should be left to port and the Ham Gat buoy (Con G) to starboard. The Pollard Spit extends north from Whitstable Flats, an area of sand and mud to the east of Whitstable.

From a point midway between Ham Gat and Pollard Spit buoys a course of 220°M leads into the river, passing Shell Ness to starboard about a

There are good services at Iron Wharf near the top of Faversham Creek on the south shore just outside the town

quarter of a mile off. Cottages and coastguard buildings are conspicuous above its light-coloured shell shingle beach and, in conditions of poor visibility, Shell Ness is a useful check on distance from the next mark – the Sand End buoy (Con G FlG 5s) about a mile away on the same course.

Whitstable Flats and the Swale entrance are an oyster fishery area and care should be taken not to anchor or ground on the oyster beds.

Once inside the river entrance the tides set fairly, but at the entrance they are affected to some extent by the main Thames Estuary streams. Hence there is a tendency for vessels entering on the flood to be set over towards the Columbine, while leaving on the ebb the set is towards Pollard Spit.

Throughout this long entrance the width of the channel is between two and three cables up to the Sand End buoy, after which the channel narrows.

Next there is a pair of unlit buoys off the entrance to Faversham Creek. The one to starboard marks the south side of the Horse Shoal, while the other (N Card BY) is on the end of the spit extending from the north bank of the creek.

HARTY FERRY

Immediately to the west is Harty Ferry, the most popular anchorage in the Swale. A hard on the north shore provides access to the Ferry House Inn (Tel 01795 510214), where food is served all day at weekends, making it a favourite destination for local yachtsmen.

It is said that the inn may have begun as a trading post servicing a Roman garrison on Sheppey, with supplies from Faversham on the mainland. About a mile away from the pub, which only recently was put on mains electricity, is the 900 year old church of St Thomas the Apostle, still lit by oil lamps and candles in this remote corner of Sheppey known as the Isle of Harty.

The last ferry service here closed in 1941, but the remains of the winding mechanism from a cable-drawn ferry dating from 1657 can still be seen.

A favoured berth (except during strong easterlies) is under the north shore near the hard, but beware the fierce current on the early ebb, particularly at night. This can be a dangerous anchorage with strong winds from the east.

There are few facilities available to the boats moored at Harty Ferry, although there is an emergency telephone near the top of the ferry hard on the south bank. Nearby is the Oare Marshes Nature Reserve run by Kent Wildlife Trust. For other services and stores the nearest places are Oare (1 mile) or Faversham (2 miles).

West from Harty, a green conical buoy half a mile ahead should not be approached too closely, as in SW winds it wanders over the mud.

From here the channel shoals and becomes narrower. Ahead to port will be seen the higher parts of Fowley Island, a long shoal parallel to the Kent shore, marked by an E Cardinal buoy, behind which lies South Deep.

The Shipwrights Arms at Hollowshore

Even at high water springs, as in this picture, there is very little water at the head of Faversham Creek near the town jetty

Lilies buoy (black and yellow S Cardinal with black topmark).

Past Milton Creek, the banks of the river are closer together, and the good water now occupies about a third of the available river width. Although there are few marks to assist, it is fairly easy to negotiate this part of the river as there is appreciably greater depth than in the eastern end.

Remember that the direction of buoyage and marking changes at Milton Creek.

The E Cardinal Fowley Spit buoy is not too easy to pick out, but the spit is extensive and shoals steeply to the south, so a careful watch must be kept on the depth.

The main channel, which soon narrows to little more than half a cable, leaves Fowley to port and lies approximately midway between the north edge of Fowley and the Sheppey shore. Passing Fowley Island the only guides are five port-hand buoys, and then, further west, two green conicals, Elmley and N Ferry, which indicate the best water. The channel is, however, so narrow that a fair wind is essential anywhere near low water.

Further west, two posts mark the hards of Elmley Ferry where James II boarded a boat in 1688 and fled the country. The hards extend well offshore beyond the posts and that off the south shore has some stakes embedded in it. The best water lies a trifle to north of a line midway between the posts. The ferry no longer functions, but the remains of the Ferry House can be seen on the south bank.

ANCHORAGE

Just west of Elmley Ferry, on the mainland side, there is space to anchor, out of the fairway, in about three metres of water.

From here, the river swings round towards the north between the green conical N Ferry and the red can S Ferry buoys, passing a patch of saltings that largely masks the entrance to Milton Creek. The best water will be found more or less in a direct line towards Grovehurst coal jetty, which shows two FG lights at night. The entrance to Milton Creek is opposite the

THE EAST SWALE CREEKS

FAVERSHAM CREEK

Faversham Creek branches off to the south of the Swale just east of Harty Ferry and is marked at its entrance with a N Cardinal (BY) buoy, to be left to starboard when entering. Sometimes there is also a port hand buoy or beacon at the entrance to keep boats off the mud on the east side of the channel.

The creek itself pursues a winding course for about three and a half miles up to the town of Faversham. For the first half mile up to the junction with Oare Creek (to starboard) the channel is fairly wide and well marked with port and starboard buoys.

In behind the seawall at Hollow Shore is the Shipwright's Arms, an ancient pub with character, much frequented by those connected with barges, smacks and wooden craft. The pub is famous for its real ales, all from Kentish breweries, and holds an annual beer festival, usually on the late spring bank holiday weekend. The yard nearby is always interesting because of the old gaffers that congregate there. The services at the yard are those that relate to repairs and maintenance: a slip, a crane and a dock.

Landing is possible near the inn from about four hours before to four hours after HW. Shallow draught boats can lie afloat throughout a neap tide off the inn.

Above the junction, Faversham Creek narrows and dries right out. Shoal-draught craft with

Chapter 16

power can make the trip up to Faversham, starting at about four hours flood. Local advice is to follow the curve of the creek between buoys rather than head from buoy to buoy. The creek is occasionally used by barges up to the town, but there is no longer any commercial traffic.

Faversham Creek is well marked with buoys and beacons up to the last port-hand buoy, just before the Southern Water depot on the south side. The channel is then in the centre of the creek up to the Iron Wharf Boatyard on the south shore, where the best water is about six feet out from their dry dock. There are good services at this yard, largely aimed at DIY enthusiasts, including the dry dock which is capable of accommodating a Thames Barge. The yard will provide a tug or a pilot if required. Certainly if you plan to go up to the town, you will need local knowledge. Nearby is the Iron Wharf YC, a small but comfortable club with an outdoor barbecue which visiting yachtsmen are welcome to use. Traditional boat builder, Alan Staley, has a shed and slipway on the site.

A little further upstream on the south shore is Standard Quay, on the outskirts of Faversham, where moorings are for traditional boats, most of which are barges. Here, just as at Hollow Shore, there are interesting craft to be seen alongside or in the lighter/dry docks. On the quayside, The Monks' Granary, currently housing a garden centre, is one of the oldest surviving warehouses in Britain. On the opposite shore is a recently completed (2003) waterside housing development.

About half a mile from Iron Wharf the rather tortuous channel leads up into Faversham, a fine market town boasting 500 listed buildings presided over by the unusual 'crown' spire of the

FAVERSHAM CREEK PORT GUIDE

Pilot and/or Tug	Ironwharf Boatyard Tel 01795 536296
Moorings	Drying
Water	At yard
Fuel	Diesel from Ironwharf Boatyard
Gas	From garden centre at Standard Quay
Repairs	15 ton crane, shipwrights and engineers (sailmaker and electrician if required)
Chandlery	Small one at Iron Wharf
Facilities	Toilets, showers and launderette at Iron Wharf
Stores	Two supermarkets, other shops and banks in Faversham; market Tues, Fri and Sat; EC Thurs
Food and Drink	Iron Wharf YC, Tel 01795 530352, has outdoor barbecue; Anchor pub at Standard Quay, The Albion, Upper Brents; pubs and restaurants in Faversham

parish church. Once the centre of the nation's explosives industry, Faversham is home to Britain's oldest brewery, Shepherd and Neame. The Albion, on the northern bank just below the little swing bridge, and The Anchor, near Standard Quay, are handy places for yachtsmen to sample the Kentish ale, or try one of the many other pubs and restaurants in the town.

Access to berths on the small town jetty is restricted and even at HWS there is very little water, so the best way to visit the town is to walk in from Iron Wharf via Standard Quay (about 10 minutes).

OARE CREEK

From Hollowshore it is about a mile to the village of Oare, which can be reached around HW by boats requiring up to 2m of water via a creek marked by withies. There are stages with boats moored to them practically all the way along the SE bank of Oare Creek, while at the head of the creek drying pontoons have been constructed to form a small marina within a few yards of the road to Faversham. As well as repair and haul-out facilities for craft up to 30ft, Youngboats has a well stocked chandlery and provides diesel and gas. Access is around one and a half hours either side HW.

Alternatively, it is a pleasant half hour walk from the landing at Hollow Shore along the creekside up to Oare village, with its two pubs, The Castle and the Three Mariners.

OARE AND HOLLOW SHORE PORT GUIDE

Hollowshore Services Tel 01795 532317
Youngboats (Oare) Tel 01795 536176;
www.youngboats.co.uk

Water	From yards at Oare and Hollow Shore
Stores	From shop at Oare
Chandler	Youngboats Tel 536176
Fuel	Diesel from both yards, gas from Youngboats
Repairs	Yards at Oare and Hollow Shore. Slipways. Crane up to 5 tons at Hollowshore and 8 tons at Oare
Transport	Bus from Oare to Faversham
Club	Hollow Shore Cruising Club Tel 01795 533254; Bar
Food and Drink	Shipwright's Arms, Hollow Shore Tel 01795 590088. Ferry House Inn, Harty, Tel 01795 510214

Looking down Conyer Creek from the redeveloped Swale Marina pontoons. Conyer Creek Marina is located further downstream beyond the quayside housing

There are two marinas at Conyer, both of which offer berths alongside drying pontoons, so are only suitable for shoal draught craft.

Conyer Creek Marina is the first to be reached, on the port-hand side just beyond a group of houseboats. The drying pontoons are situated alongside houses which are part of a new (2003) waterside development on the quay, where Conyer Marine boatyard was previously located. Ted Spears welcomes visiting yachtsmen and groups from clubs – in summer, barbecue facilities are available – and he will advise on access up the creek.

Further up the creek, past the Ship Inn and the houseboats in The Dock, are the pontoon mud berths of Swale Marina, formerly Jarman's Boatyard. This is at the head of the creek, which

CONYER CREEK

There are two ways into Conyer Creek from the South Deep inside Fowley Island. Swale Marina produces a useful laminated entrance guide and can advise on the latest state of the marks.

Coming from the east (Harty Ferry), the East Cardinal buoy at the end of Fowley Spit is left to starboard, before following the lines of moorings past a green nun buoy with topmark and then a red nun buoy, up to a pair of withies signifying the entrance to Conyer Creek. Leave the one with a triangle topmark close to starboard and then follow the sequence of starboard-hand marks that lead close to the sea wall near the old Butterfly Wharf. Note that a little upstream of this wharf the hulks of two barges have collapsed down the side of the creek bank, with some wreckage protruding. Thereafter, pairs of withies with triangular or disc topmarks will lead you, if there is enough water, round the outside of the bends and up to Conyer village.

The second way into Conyer Creek is via a gulley known as the Butterfly channel. Shoal draught craft approaching from the west (Queenborough) can, starting from No 8 buoy in the main channel, turn SE and sound across the spit off the western end of Fowley Island into the deeper water of South Deep. A pair of perches (withies) indicates the entrance to the Butterfly channel, which at first leads close under the sea wall on the western side of the entrance, but then turns abruptly to the east before reaching Conyer Creek itself at a junction marked with a perch bearing a double triangle topmark.

CONYER PORT GUIDE	
Conyer Creek Marina	Tel 01795 521711; Mobile 07971641129
Swale Marina	Tel: 01795 521562; Fax 520788; email: swale.marina@virgin.net; www.swalemarina.co.uk
Water and electricity	Both marinas
Facilities	Toilets, showers at both marinas
Stores	Teynham, 1½ miles
Repairs	Swale Marina: travel hoist, 30 ton crane, slipway up to 30 tons, scrubbing posts by arrangement
Sailmaker	Wilkinson Sails at Swale Marina; Tel 01795 521503
Chandlery	Basic fittings at Swale Marina
Transport	Bus service to Teynham and Sittingbourne. Trains to London, Dover and Ramsgate from Teynham or Sittingbourne
Club	Conyer Cruising Club at Swale Marina: conyercc@tesco.net
Food and Drink	Barbecue facilities by prior arrangement at both marinas; Ship Inn, Conyer, sometimes serves food; Tel 01795 520778

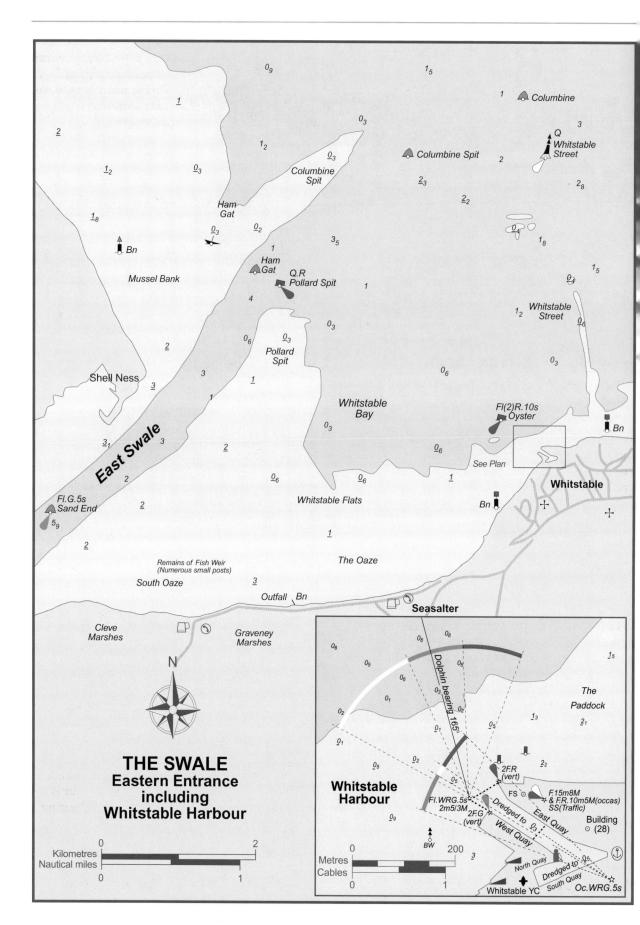

0₉

1₅

Columbine

1

Columbine Spit

Q
Whitstable
Street

3

2

2₈

2₃

2₂

0₃

0₃

Columbine
Spit

1₂

2

1₂

0₃

Bn

0₃

Ham
Gat

0₂

0₄

1₈

1₈

Mussel Bank

Ham
Gat

1

3₅

0₄

1₅

Q.R
Pollard Spit

1

Whitstable
Street

4

0₃

1₂

0₆

2

0₃

0₆

Pollard
Spit

0₃

1

3

3

Shell Ness

3

1

Whitstable
Bay

Fl(2)R.10s
Oyster

Bn

East Swale

3₁

3

2

0₃

0₆

See Plan

Whitstable

2

0₆

0₆

1

Fl.G.5s
Sand End

2

Whitstable Flats

Bn

5₉

2

1

The Oaze

Remains of Fish Weir
(Numerous small posts)

South Oaze

3

N

Outfall   Bn

Seasalter

Cleve
Marshes

Graveney
Marshes

THE SWALE
Eastern Entrance
including
Whitstable Harbour

0₆

0₈

0₈

1₅

0₅

0₅

The
Paddock

0₆

0₃

0₁

1₃

2₁

0₂

0₁

0₅

**Whitstable
Harbour**

0₁

2₂

0₅

2.F.R
(vert)

0₅

FS

F15m8M
& F.R.10m5M(occas)
SS(Traffic)

Fl.WRG.5s
2m5/3M

Dredged to 0₃

East Quay

2.F.G
(vert)

Building
(28)

West Quay

0₉

BW

Dredged to 0₅

North Quay

3

Whitstable YC

South Quay

Oc.WRG.5s

Kilometres		
Nautical miles		

0   2

0   1

Metres		
Cables		

0   200

0   1

The local fishing fleet operates out of Whitstable Harbour where there is a busy quayside fish market situated left of the white van shown in this picture

dries out completely, but the serviced pontoons can be accessed by most boats for about one hour either side of HW. Visitors' berths are available and club groups can be accommodated by arrangement. Facilities on the redeveloped (2003) site include hoist, crane, slipway, repair workshop, spray centre and sail loft, and a barbecue is available for parties. The Conyer CC has its clubhouse near the marina office.

WINDMILL CREEK

Runs off to the north about one mile west of Harty Ferry. The spit off its western side is marked with a post. It formerly cut some miles inland, but it has now been blocked and is of little interest except to wildfowlers.

WHITSTABLE HARBOUR

This small harbour lies two or three miles east of the entrance to the East Swale. It is controlled by Canterbury Council and is used regularly by small freighters working from commercial aggregate and timber quays. The local fishing fleet also operates out of the harbour, where there is a flourishing quayside fish market.

Whitstable offers emergency shelter to yachtsmen who are prevented from making the Thames or Medway during a westerly or south-westerly blow. However, berthing for yachts is temporary and at the discretion of the harbour

master. Moreover, the harbour is busy, dirty and drying, and therefore would only be recommended as a last resort.

The narrow entrance to Whitstable can be reached only over the shoal water that extends for more than a mile offshore. The best approach, not before half flood, is from a position about a mile W of the Whitstable Street buoy (N Card Q) on a course of 170°M. This is held until within half a mile of the harbour entrance by which time, if it is dark, the Whitstable Oyster buoy (Can R Fl(2)R 10s) will be seen on the starboard bow, while continuing on the same course brings you to within the green sector of a flashing light on the W Quay dolphin just off the harbour entrance.

This dolphin and a conspicuous tall granary building provide useful daylight marks. The light on the dolphin has WR and G sectors and flashes every five seconds. The white sector serves shoal draught boats approaching from the west, while the red sector is to keep craft off the shoal called Whitstable Street. At the head of the harbour is a leading light OcWRG5s, the white sector bearing 127°M into the entrance. The traffic signals on the north east arm of West Quay show fixed white for harbour open and fixed red for harbour closed.

Whitstable is famous for shellfish, particularly oysters, and hence incorporates plenty of seafood restaurants. Whitstable YC occupies a prime

Chapter 16

position on the seafront and, like many sailing clubs along the N Kent shore, caters mainly for catamaran and dinghy sailors. There are, however, some drying moorings along the shore used by shoal draught cruising yachts.

SWALE TIDES

Tidal streams in the Swale are peculiar because of the two outlets to the sea. At LW Sheerness, it is slack water almost throughout the Swale. As the flood commences, it naturally enters from both ends, the streams meeting at about Fowley, or even as far west as Elmley on very high tides. At HW Sheerness, it is slack throughout the Swale, and for the first hour after HW the whole body of water moves eastward when, at about Long Point, the westerly stream reverses direction and ebbs back into the Medway. Meanwhile the remainder of the water carries on moving to the east. As the ebb continues, the point of separation of the stream also moves eastwards, until ultimately the separation occurs near Fowley.

As a result of this there is an east-going stream for about nine hours every tide at Elmley, while at Kingsferry Bridge the tide sets to the east for eight hours. By the time Harty is reached, the duration of east and west-going streams is about six hours

each, but it is sometimes useful to know that on the north side of the West Swale there is a west-going eddy for as much as an hour before the ebb stops flowing eastward on the south side of the river.

The early ebb is strong, until the banks are uncovered, approaching 3 or 4 knots at Kingsferry.

In the East Swale, tides are considerably affected by prevailing winds, with easterlies causing the higher levels.

WHITSTABLE PORT GUIDE	
Harbour Master	Tel 01227 274086; Fax 265442; email:harbour@whitstable.telme.com
VHF	Channels 16,12 or 9 Callsign *Whitstable Harbour Radio*; from 0830 to1700 (Mon–Fri) or any day from 3 hrs before and 2 hrs after HW (tidal information available)
Water	Alongside at harbour, and YC
Stores	Shops in town. EC Wed
Chandler	Whitstable Marine, The Seawall Tel 01227 262525
Fuel	Garages nearby
Transport	Train service to London (Victoria)
Customs Office	Tel 01304 224151 (24hr)
Club	Whitstable YC (Tel 272942) can sometimes offer a mooring
Food and Drink	Restaurant and bar at YC; pubs and restaurants in town

In a prime position on the seafront, Whitstable YC caters mainly for catamaran and dinghy sailors

CROSS ESTUARY ROUTES

There is a story by Archie White in which an old West Mersea barge skipper tells a young fellow with his first command how he can sneak through the Rays'n, past the Ridge Buoy (or rather where it used to be) over the top of the Whitaker Spit and out into the Swin off Shoebury; thereby reaching the London River well ahead of all the other barges that had been storm-bound with him in the Blackwater.

It is a good story and probably true, because it certainly is possible to cut many corners by using the swatchways in the Thames Estuary.

PRECAUTIONS

Before any yachtsman sets out to cross the shoal-infested mouth of the Thames, he must give careful consideration to a number of things that may not have seemed important to him during short distance cruising between adjacent rivers within sight of land. They are:

1. Corrected Compass. If visibility should close in when half way across, a reliable compass will be essential.
2. Corrected Charts. A copy of this book, even if it is the latest edition, is not adequate for crossing the Thames Estuary. Admiralty chart No 1183 will be necessary and must be corrected up to date. Even then it should always be remembered that during the several years that often elapse between surveys of a particular area carried out by the PLA Hydrographic Department, significant changes often take place, particularly in the very swatchways that are of special interest to yachtsmen. For this reason a reliable echo-sounder will be indispensable.

3. Tidal information. Work out and understand what the tide will be doing at all important points along the route – not only at the time you hope to be there, but also for later times in case you are delayed. For this purpose the tidal diagrams included will be useful, although the larger scale Tidal Stream Atlas (No 249) published by the Admiralty will be even better. Remember that depths will vary according to direction and strength of wind and barometric pressure – tidal predictions are just that.
4. Waypoints. Prepare a list of all waypoints that might prove useful. These may be, for convenience, taken from the list published in *Reeds Nautical Almanac*, section 9.4.4, East Anglian Waypoints. They should also be plotted on the chart to ensure that they constitute a safe route and have been correctly entered into the GPS or other navigation software.

WEATHER FORECAST

The latest possible weather forecast for the area must be obtained for a period at least twice as long as the time the passage is expected to take.

Some useful numbers are:

Marinecall 09066 526 239 (The Wash to North Foreland area forecast)

Marinecall 09068 226 455 (Walton-on-the-Naze, Weybourne, Sheerness coastal reports) or VHF Ch 02.

EMERGENCY EQUIPMENT

Ensure the adequacy of emergency equipment, including: VHF, flares/smoke signals, life-jackets, liferaft/dinghy.

CONDITIONS IN THE ESTUARY

Since the southbound passage across the estuary will generally be made during the SW-going flood tide, it must be realized that when the wind is from the SW, as it so often is, then a short and very steep sea gets

Chapter 17

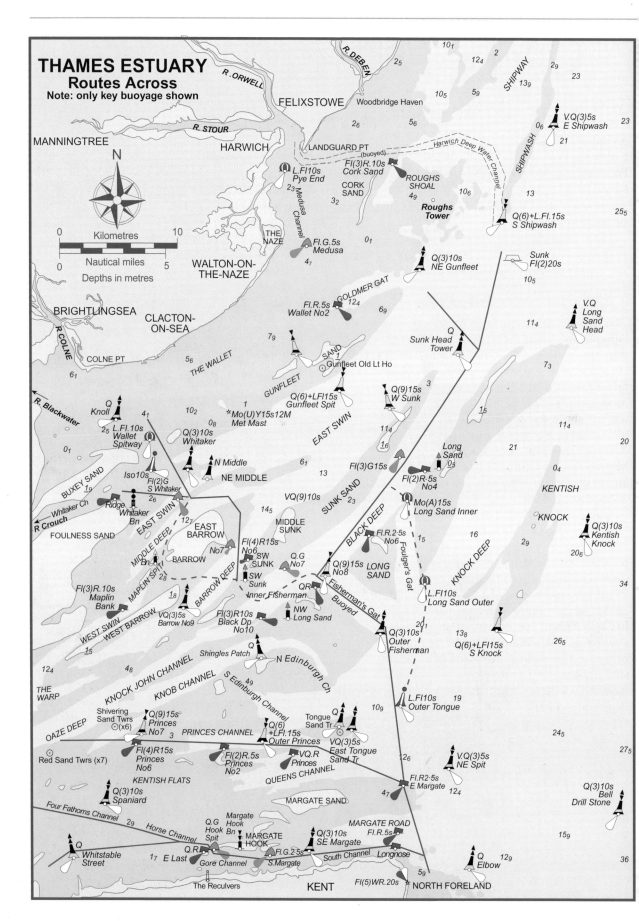

THAMES ESTUARY
Routes Across
Note: only key buoyage shown

MANNINGTREE

R. ORWELL

R. DEBEN

R. STOUR

FELIXSTOWE
Woodbridge Haven

HARWICH
LANDGUARD PT
(buoyed)

L.Fl10s
Pye End

Medusa
Channel

23

FI(3)R.10s
Cork Sand

CORK
SAND

CORK
SAND

ROUGHS
SHOAL

Roughs
Tower

Harwich Deep Water Channel

SHIPWAY

SHIPWASH

V.Q(3)5s
E Shipwash

Q(6)+L.Fl.15s
S Shipwash

THE
NAZE

Fl.G.5s
Medusa

WALTON-ON-
THE-NAZE

Q(3)10s
NE Gunfleet

Sunk
Fl(2)20s

BRIGHTLINGSEA

CLACTON-
ON-SEA

COLNE PT

R COLNE

Fl.R.5s
Wallet No2

GOLDMER GAT

THE WALLET

GUNFLEET

SAND

Gunfleet Old Lt Ho

Sunk Head
Tower

V.Q
Long
Sand
Head

R. Blackwater

Q
Knoll

L.Fl.10s
Wallet
Spitway

Q(3)10s
Whitaker

*Mo(U)Y15s12M
Met Mast

Q(6)+LFl15s
Gunfleet Spit

EAST SWIN

Q(9)15s
W Sunk

V.Q

Iso10s

Fl(2)G
S Whitaker

N Middle

NE MIDDLE

Fl(3)G15s

Long
Sand

KENTISH

KNOCK

Q(3)10s
Kentish
Knock

BUXEY SAND

Ridge

Whitaker
Bn

EAST SWIN

MIDDLE DEEP

EAST
BARROW

Whitaker Ch

R Crouch

FOULNESS SAND

MIDDLE
SUNK

VQ(9)10s

SUNK SAND

Fl(2)R.5s
No4

Mo(A)15s
Long Sand Inner

KNOCK DEEP

Bn

BARROW

No7

Fl(4)R15s
No6

SW
SUNK

Q.G
No7

Q(9)15s
No8

Fl.R.2·5s
No6

BLACK DEEP

LONG
SAND

Foulger's Gat

Maplin
Bn

MAPLIN SPIT

BARROW DEEP

SW
Sunk

Inner Fisherman

QR

Fisherman's
Buoyed

Gat

L.Fl10s
Long Sand Outer

Q(3)10s
Kentish
Knock

Fl(3)R.10s
Maplin
Bank

WEST BARROW

VQ(3)5s
Barrow No9

Fl(3)R10s
Black Dp
No10

NW
Long Sand

Q(3)10s
Outer
Fisherman

Q(6)+LFl15s
S Knock

WEST SWIN

WEST BARROW

Shingles Patch

N Edinburgh Ch

KNOCK JOHN CHANNEL

KNOB CHANNEL

S Edinburgh Channel

L.Fl10s
Outer Tongue

THE
WARP

OAZE DEEP

Shivering
Sand Twrs
(x6)

Q(9)15s
Princes
No7

PRINCES CHANNEL

Q(6)
+LFl.15s
Outer Princes

Tongue
Sand Tr

Q

East Tongue
Sand Tr

VQ(3)5s

V.Q(3)5s
NE Spit

Red Sand Twrs (x7)

Fl(4)R15s
Princes
No6

Fl(2)R.5s
Princes
No2

VQ.R
Princes

QUEENS CHANNEL

KENTISH FLATS

Q(3)10s
Spaniard

MARGATE SAND

E Margate

Q(3)10s
Bell
Drill Stone

Four Fathoms Channel

Horse Channel

Q.G
Hook Spit

Margate
Hook Bn

MARGATE
HOOK

MARGATE ROAD

Fl.R.5s

Longnose

Q
Elbow

Whitstable
Street

Q

E Last

Q.R

Gore Channel

S.Margate

Fl.G.2·5s

Q(3)10s
SE Margate

South Channel

The Reculvers

KENT

Fl(5)WR.20s

NORTH FORELAND

up in anything more than a moderate breeze.

For many of us, the first time we find ourselves in command of a yacht out of sight of land is when we set out from one or other of the Essex or Suffolk rivers and proceed seaward beyond the Spitway and the Whitaker Bell buoy or round the NE Gunfleet. The distance across the Thames Estuary between say, Clacton and the North Foreland, is about 25 miles, so we should not be surprised that it feels different out there amidst the shoals, especially when the buoys don't come up as soon as we would like!

SWIN SPITWAY OR WHITAKER BUOY TO NORTH FORELAND

There was a time when almost anyone crossing the Estuary passed from the East Swin into the Barrow Deep through a swatchway opposite Barrow No 9 buoy; but No 9 buoy has been moved a mile or so SW and no longer marks the entrance to the swatch. This route can still be taken provided it is realized that there is very little water just north of the Barrow Beacon. A narrow shoal extends for about two miles in a SW'ly direction from the W side of the East Barrow Sand and the way through from the Middle Deep passes close north of the beacon and over a ridge with less than 1m at LWS.

Another possible route passes north of the E Barrow Sand and into the Barrow Deep that way. From close north of the Ridge (Can R) or the S Whitaker (Con G) buoy, shape an E'ly (°M) course to pass about a mile south of the N Middle (N Cardinal) buoy until Barrow No 7 buoy (Con G FlG 2.5s) bears S (°M). Then, with the sounder going, skirt round the NE edge of the East Barrow Sand to leave Barrow No 7 close to starboard. Another mile on a S'ly course will bring the SW Sunk Beacon in view, and this should be passed close to on a course of 135°M with the NW Long Sand Beacon ahead about three miles away, until deep water is found in the Black Deep. When safely through the swatch, change course towards Black Deep No 10 buoy (Can R Fl(2)R 5s). It is not safe to pass on a direct line between No 6 buoy in the Barrow Deep and No 7 buoy in the Black Deep.

From Black Deep No 10 a NE'ly course up the Black Deep for about two and a half miles will take you to the Inner Fisherman (Can R Fl(3)R 10s) and beyond it the Black Deep No 8 (W Card Q 9 15s) marking the entrance to the Fisherman's Gat. The North Edinburgh Channel has silted and is no longer buoyed.

The Fisherman's Gat, marked on both sides with buoys, is now the designated commercial channel and is used regularly by large ships. Foulger's Gat, further north near Black Deep No 6 (Can R Fl R 2.5s), is indicated at both ends by SWMs and offers an alternative route across the Long Sand for leisure craft.

After emerging from the Fisherman's Gat, the Outer Fisherman (E Card Q (3) 10s) will provide a useful mark from which to shape a S'ly (°M) course passing the Outer Tongue (SWM L Fl 10s Whis) to the East Margate buoy (Can R FlR 2.5s) and then on to the North Foreland.

THE TIDE

Southbound

In order to make the most of the passage on a rising tide it will be necessary to be near the Whitaker Bell buoy just before low water – which is rather convenient for those leaving the Crouch but does mean that those coming through the Spitway will have to be careful.

The aim is to get into the Barrow Deep just as the flood starts running SW'ly and then, by making an average of 4 or 5 knots over the ground, reach the Fisherman's Gat followed by the Foreland before the N going stream starts, about an hour before HW Dover.

Northbound

When crossing the Estuary for the first time from Dover or Ramsgate, it will be best to stem the last of the south going tide up the North Foreland so as to get the benefit of the flood through the Fisherman's Gat and across the Estuary.

Unfortunately this usually means arriving at the entrance to the Crouch or the Spitway at about HW, with the prospect of the whole of the ebb to run out of the Essex rivers. The only way this can be avoided is to take the risks involved in crossing the Estuary on a falling tide – which certainly cannot be recommended for the inexperienced. However, those bound for Harwich or the Suffolk rivers can carry the ebb north.

HARWICH TO NORTH FORELAND

Those wishing to cross the Estuary from the Suffolk rivers need not use the Wallet and the Spitway, but can enter the Black Deep past the ruined Sunk Head Tower, marked by its N Cardinal buoy (N Card Q). Thereafter proceed about 7 miles to the SW, leaving the Black Deep via Foulger's Gat, before heading to the Outer Tongue buoy (L Fl 10s Whis).

Foulger's Gat, which can be used in preference to the busy Fisherman's Gat, is marked at each end by SWMs. These buoys are similar in design to the Woodbridge Haven buoy and it has been reported that they are not easy to identify, particularly if you are going north when they can be confused with bigger buoys in the Black Deep.

The channel is entered via the SWM (Mo A 15s), Long Sand Inner, about one mile to the NE of Black Deep No 6 (Can R Fl R 2.5s). A S'ly (°M) course for about three miles will take you through to the SWM (Fl 10s), Long Sand Outer, at the Knock Deep end of the Gat. From here, shape a slightly more W'ly course for the Outer Tongue, and thence E Margate (Can R Fl R 2.5s) and the Foreland.

THAMES, MEDWAY OR SWALE TO NORTH FORELAND

There are various routes that can be taken in a W–E direction along the north coast of Kent, but in general craft from the Thames or the Medway will tend to use the Princes Channel, about five miles offshore, while those coming from the Swale or Whitstable are more likely to go through the Gore Channel, much closer inshore. The historic 'Overland' route from Thames to North Foreland departs from the Medway Channel, near Nos 4 or 6 buoys, on a course to the Spile buoy (G Con Fl G 2.5s). Whence via the Horse Channel to the East Last and Hook Spit buoys at the entrance to the Gore Channel off Reculver.

PRINCES CHANNEL

Note the buoys marking the Princes Channel were renamed and numbered in 2000. The Princes Channel can be said to commence between the Princes No 6 (Can R Fl(4)R 15s) and the Princes No 7 (W Card Q (9) 15s Bell) buoys and to continue in an easterly direction past the Princes No 5 (Con G Fl(3) G 10s) for about five miles between the South Shingles shoal to the north and the Ridge and the Tongue Sands to the south.

At its narrowest point, abreast the Princes No 2 buoy (Can R Fl (3) R 10s), the deep water is almost a mile wide. From this position, an E'ly (magnetic) course will lead past the Princes No 1 (S Card Q (6) & LFl 15s Bell) and the Princes (Can R Fl (2) R 5s) buoys,

by which time the N and S Cardinal Tongue Sand Tower buoys should be in sight pretty well straight ahead.

When these buoys are close abeam, a course can be laid – about 150°M – to clear the Foreland after leaving the East Margate (Can R Fl (2) R 2.5s) about half a mile to starboard.

GORE CHANNEL

Waypoints

This route is closer inshore and rather more difficult because of the many drying shoals off the Kent coast between Herne Bay and Margate.

Starting from the Whitstable Street buoy (N Card Q), a course of 95°M will lead (after about six miles) to the East Last (Can R QR) and Hook Spit (Can G) buoys, marking the narrow swatch over the western end of the Margate Hook Sand. Because of rocky patches off the Reculvers, do not approach the shore closer than two miles or proceed eastwards until these two buoys have been found. The twin rectangular towers of the Reculvers will help in locating the buoys.

Once through the swatch, shape a course of 110°M to leave the Margate Hook Beacon (S Card Topmark) and the South Margate buoy (Con G FlG 2.5s) at least a quarter of a mile to the North. From the South Margate buoy an E'ly (magnetic) course will lead to the SE Margate buoy (E Card Q(3) 10s) a little more than two miles away.

The passage can then be continued to round the Longnose red can buoy, which is about a mile offshore. There is a lit red can (Fl R 5s) about half a mile N of the unlit Longnose.

TIDAL CONSTANTS

Place		Add (+) to or Subtract (–) from times of HW at:	Height relative to Chart Datum (metres)			
			SPRINGS		NEAPS	
		Dover	MHW	MLW	MHW	MLW
1 Lowestoft		−1.33	2.4	0.5	2.1	1.0
2 Southwold		−1.05	2.4	0.5	2.1	0.9
3 Orford River	Orford Haven (Entrance)	+0.15	3.2	0.4	2.6	1.0
	Orford Quay	+1.00	2.8	0.6	2.3	1.1
4 River Alde	Slaughden Quay (Aldeburgh)	+1.55	2.9	0.6	2.6	1.0
	Snape Bridge	+2.55	2.9	0.8	2.4	0.8
5 River Deben	Woodbridge Haven (Entrance)	+0.25	3.7	0.5	2.9	1.0
	Waldringfield	+1.00	3.6	0.4	3.0	0.9
	Woodbridge	+1.05	4.0	0.4	3.1	0.9
6 Harwich Harbour	Harwich	+0.50	4.0	0.4	3.4	1.1
7 River Orwell	Pin Mill	+1.00	4.1	0.4	3.4	1.1
	Ipswich	+1.15	4.2	0.3	3.4	1.0
8 River Stour	Wrabness	+1.05	4.1	0.4	3.4	1.1
	Mistley	+1.15	4.2	0.3	3.4	1.0
9 Walton Backwaters	Walton-on-the-Naze (Pier)	+0.30	4.2	0.4	3.4	1.1
	Stone Point	+0.40	4.1	0.5	3.3	1.2
10 River Colne	Colne Point	+0.40	5.1	0.4	3.8	1.2
	Brightlingsea	+0.50	5.0	0.4	3.8	1.2
	Wivenhoe	+1.05	4.9	0.3	3.6	–
	Colchester (The Hythe)	+1.15	4.2	–	3.1	–
11 River Blackwater	Bench Head Buoy	+1.20	5.1	0.5	3.8	1.2
	West Mersea (Nass Beacon)	+1.10	5.1	0.5	3.8	1.2
	Tollesbury Mill Creek	+1.20	4.9	–	3.6	–
	Bradwell Quay	+1.10	5.2	0.4	4.2	1.3
	Osea Island	+1.25	5.3	0.4	4.3	1.2
	Heybridge Basin	+1.30	5.0	–	4.1	–
	Maldon	+1.35	2.9	–	2.3	–
12 River Crouch	Whitaker Beacon	+0.50	4.8	0.5	3.9	1.3
	Burnham-on-Crouch	+1.15	5.2	0.2	4.2	1.0
	Fambridge	+1.20	5.3	0.3	4.2	1.1
	Hullbridge	+1.25	5.3	0.3	4.2	1.1
13 River Roach	Paglesham	+1.10	5.2	0.2	4.2	1.0
	Havengore Creek	+1.10	4.2	0.4	3.4	1.1
14 River Thames	Southend Pier	+1.20	5.8	0.5	4.7	1.4
	Holehaven	+1.30	5.9	0.4	4.7	1.4
	Gravesend	+1.45	6.3	0.3	4.7	1.4
	Erith	+2.00	6.6	0.1	4.9	1.2
	Tower Bridge	+2.40	6.8	0.5	5.9	1.3
15 The Medway	Queenborough	+1.35	5.7	0.6	4.8	1.5
	Rochester	+1.50	6.0	0.3	4.9	1.3
16 The Swale	Whitstable	+1.20	5.4	0.5	4.5	1.5
	Harty Ferry	+1.25	5.7	0.6	5.1	1.2
	Milton Creek	+1.35	5.7	0.6	4.8	0.5

GLOSSARY

ENGLISH	DUTCH	FRENCH	GERMAN
Abeam	Dwars	Par le travers	Querab
Ahead	Vooruit	En avant	Voraus
Anchorage	Ankerplaats	Mouillage	Ankerplatz
Astern	Achteruit	En arrière	Ruckwarts, achtern
Athwart	Dwars over	Par le travers	Aufwaschen
Bank	Bank	Banc	Bank
Bar	Drempel	Barre	Drempel
Bay	Baai	Baie	Bucht
Beach	Strand	Plage	Strand
Beacon	Baken	Balise	Bake
Bight	Bocht	Anse	Bay
Binoculars	Kijker	Jumelles	Fernglas
Black	Zwart	Noir	Schwarz
Board	Slag	Bordée	Schlage
Boatyard	Jachtwerf	Chantier	Yachtwerft
Breakwater	Golfbreker	Brise-lames	Wellenbrecher
Bridge	Brug	Pont	Brucke
(fixed)	(Vaste brug)	(Pont fixe)	(Feste brucke)
(lifting)	(Beweegbare brug)	(Pont basculant)	(Hubbrucke)
(swing)	(Draaibare brug)	(Pont tournant)	(Drehbrucke)
Buoy	Ton, boei	Bouée	Tonne, Boje
Cable (distance of approx 183m)	Kabellengte	Encablure	Kebellange
Castle	Kasteel, slot	Château	Schloss
Causeway	Straatweg (door het water)	Chaussée	Damm
Channel	Vaarwater	Chenal	Fahrwasser
Chart	Zeekaart	Carte marine	Seekarte
Chart Datum	Reductievlak: kaartpeil	Zero des cartes	*Karennull
Church	Kerk	Eglise	Kirche
Cliff	Steile rots	Falaise	Felsen am Seeufer
Coastguard	Kustwacht	Garde, Côtière	Kustenwache
Conspicuous	Opvallend	Visible, en evidence	Aufflallig
Course	Koers	Cap, route	Kurs
Creek	Kreek	Crique	Kleine Bucht
Customs	Douane	Douane	Zoll
Degree	Graad	Degre	Grad
Depth	Diepte	Profondeur	Tiefe
Diesel oil	Dieselolie	Gas-oil, mazout	Diesel-Kraftstoff
Dolphin	Dukdarf, meerpaal	Duc d'Albe	Dalben, Dukdalben
Draught	Diepgang	Profondeur	Wassertiefe
Dredged	Gebaggerd vaarwater	Chenal dragué	Gebaggerte fahrrinne
Dries	Droogvalland	Assèche	Trockengallend
East	Oost	Est	Ost
Ebb	Eb	Marée descendante	Ebbe
Echo sounder	Echolood	Echo sondeur	Echolot
Eddy	Draaikolk	Tourbillon	Stromwirbel
Entrance	Ingang, zeegat	Entrée	Einfahrt
Estuary	Mond	Estuair	Flussmundung
Fair tide	Stroom mee	Courant favorable or portant	Mitlaufender Strom
Fairway	Vaargeul	Chenal	Telweg
Ferry	Veer	Bac, ferry	Fahre
Flagstaff	Vlaggestok	Mât	Flaggenmast
Flashing light	Schitterlicht	Feu a éclats	Blinkfeuer
Flood	Vloed	Marée montante	Flut
Ford	Waadbare plaats	Gué	Durchwaten
Foreshore	Droogvallend strand	Côte découvrant à marée basse	Küstenvorland
Foul tide	Tegenstroom	Courant contraire or debout	Gegenstrom
Fuel	Brandstof	Carburant	Kraftstoffe
Green	Groen	Vert	Grun
Groyne	Golfbreker	Brise-lames	Wellenbrecher
Gully	Goot	Goulet	Graben
Gunnery Range	Ballistiek	Artillerie	Artilleriewissenschaft
Gutway	Goot	Goulet	Graben
Handbearing compass	Handpeilkompas	Compas de relevement	Handpeilkompass
Harbour Master	Havenmeester	Chef or Capitaine de port	Hafenkapitan
Hard	Hard	Débarquement	Landung
Headland	Voorgebergte	Promontoire	Vorgebirge
Height, headroom	Doorvaarthoogte	Tirant d'air	Durchfahrtshöhe
High Water	Hoogwater	Pleine mer	Hochwasser
Hill	Heuvel	Colline	Hügel

ENGLISH	DUTCH	FRENCH	GERMAN
Horizontal stripes	Horizontal gestreept	à bandes horizontales	Waagerecht gestreift
Horse	Droogte	Basse	Untief
Island	Eiland	Ile	Insel
Jetty	Pier	Jetée	Anlegesteg
Knot	Knoop	Noeud	Knoten
Landing	Ontscheping	Débarquement	Landung
Launderette	Wasserette	Laverie	Waschsalon
Lead	Lood	Plomb de sonde	Lot
Leading Line	Geleidelijn	Alignement	Leitlinie
Lifeboat	Reddingboot	Bateau de sauvetage	Rettungboots
Light Vessel	Lichtschip	Bateau-phare	Feuerschiff
Lighthouse	Lichttoren, vuurtoren	Phare	Leuchtturm
Lobster	Zeekreeft	Homard	Hummer
Lock	Sluis	Écluse, sas	Schleuse
Low Water	Laagwater	Basse mer	Niedrigwasser
Magnetic	Megnetisch	Magnetique	Mißweisend
Marks	Merkteken	Parcour	Bahnmarke
Marsh	Moeras	Marais	Sumpf
Metes	Geleidelijn	Alignement	Leitlinie
Middleground	Middelgronden	Bancs médians	Scheidingstonnen
Mooring	Meerboei	Bouée de corps-mort	Ankerboje
Mud	Modder	Vase/Boue	Schlick, Schlamm
Narrow	Nauw	Etroit	Eng(e)
Navigable	Bevaarbaar	Navigable	Befahrbare
Neaps	Doodtij	Morte eau	Nippitide
Occulting	Onderbroken	Occultations	Unterbrochenes
Offing	Open zee	Le large	Legerwall
Oil	Olie	Huile	Schimierol
Orange	Oranje	Orange	Orange
Oyster	Oester	Huître	Auster
Paraffin	Petroleum	Pétrole	Petroleum
Petrol	Benzine	Essence	Benzin
Perch	Steekbaken	Perches, pieu	Pricken
Pier	Pier	Jetee	Pier
Piles	Palen remmingwerk	Poteaux	Pfahl
Pilot	Loods	Pilot	Lotsen
Pontoon	Ponton	Ponton	Ponton
Port	Bakboord	Babord	Backbord
Post Office	Postkantoor	La Poste	Postamt
Quay	Kaai	Quai	Kai
Radio Beacon	Radiobaken	Pylone de TSF	Funkmast
Railway	Spoorweg	Chemin de fer	Eisenbahn
Range (of tide)	Verval	Amplitude	Tidenhub
Red	Rood	Rouge	Rot
Repairs	Reparaties	Réparation	Ausbesserung
Riding Light	Ankerlicht	Feu de mouillage	Ankerlampe
Rocks	Rotsen	Rochers	Klippen, Felsen
Sailmaker	Zeilmaker	Voilier	Segelmacherei
Saltings	Zouttuin	Marais	Sumpf
Sand	Zand	Sable	Sand
Shelving	Hellen	Incline	Neigung
Shingle (shingly)	Grind,Keisteen	Galets	Grober Kies
Shoal	Droogte	Haut fond	Untiefe
Shops	Winkels	Magasins	Kaufladen
Showers	Douche	Douche	Dusche
Slipway	Sleephelling	Cale de halage	Slipp, Helling
South	Zuid	Sud	Süd
Spit	Landtong	Pointe de terre	Landzunge
Springs (tides)	Springtij	Vive eau, grande marée	Springtide
Staithe	Kade	Quai	Kai
Starboard	Stuurboord	Tribord	Steuerbord
Steep-to	Steil	Côte accore	Steil
Stores	Voorraad	Provisions	Vorrate
Swatchway	Doorgang	Couloir/passage	Passage
Take the ground	Aan de grond	Echoue	Auf grund sitzen
Tanker	Tanker, Tankschip	Bateau citerne	Tanker, Tankschiff
Topmark	Topteken	Voyant	Toppzeichen
Tortuous	Bochtig	Tortueux	Gewunden
Town	Stad	Ville	Stadt
Vertical stripes	Verticaal gestreept	à bandes verticales	Senkrecht gestreift
Village	Dorp	Village	Dorf
Visitor's berth	Aanlegplaats (Bezockers)	Visiteur	Festmacheplatz
Water	Water	l'eau	Wasser
Weather	Weer	du temps	Wetter
West	West	Ouest	West
Wharf	Aanlegplaats	Debarcadere	Werft
Withy	Buigzaam en sterk	Perches, pieux	Pricken
Wreck	Wrak	Épave	Wrack
Yacht Club	Jacht Club, Zeilvereniging	Yacht Club, Club Nautique	Yacht Klub
Yellow	Geel	Jaune	Gelb

BIBLIOGRAPHY

Several references have been made to books relating to the rivers and creeks of the Thames Estuary and this is a list of some of those and other books that are worth seeking through a public library if they are out of print.

Arnott, WG — **Suffolk Estuary,** published by Norman Adlard (1950)

Alde Estuary, Norman Adlard (1952)

Orwell Estuary, Norman Adlard (1954)

Benham, Hervey — **Last Stronghold of Sail,** George Harrap (1947)

Francis B Cooke — **Coastwise Cruising from Erith to Lowestoft,** Edward Arnold and Co (1929)

Copping, AE — **Gotty and the Guv'nor,** first published by T Nelson & Sons and then by Terence Dalton (1987)

Cowper, Frank — **Sailing Tours Part 1,** first published 1882 and then by Ashford Press in 1985

Durham, Dick — **The Last Sailorman,** Terence Dalton (1989)

Emmett A and M — **Blackwater Men,** Seax Books (1982)

Featherstone, Neville & Lee-Elliott, Edward — **Reeds Eastern Almanac 2004,** Nautical Data (2003)

Frost, Michael — **Boadicea CK213,** Angus & Robertson (1974)

Griffiths, Maurice — **The Magic of the Swatchways,** first published by Edward Arnold (1932) and Adlard Coles (1986)

Ten Small Yachts, Edward Arnold (1933)

Swatchways and Little Ships, George Allen & Unwin (1971) and Adlard Coles (1986)

Innes, Hammond — **East Anglia,** Hodder & Stoughton (1986)

Leather, John — **The Salty Shore,** Terence Dalton (1979)

The Sailor's Coast, Barrie & Jenkins (1979)

Lewis, John — **A Taste for Sailing,** Terence Dalton (1989)

Roberts, Bob — **Coasting Bargemaster,** Edward Arnold (1949) and Terence Dalton (1985)

A Slice of Suffolk, Terence Dalton (1978)

Ransome, Arthur — **We Didn't Mean to go to Sea,** Jonathan Cape (1937) and then by Penguin Books

Secret Water, Jonathan Cape (1939) and then by Penguin Books

Seymour, John — **The Companion Guide to East Anglia,** Collins (1970)

Simper, Robert — **The Deben River,** Creekside Publishing (1992)

Tripp, Alker — **Suffolk Sea Borders,** Bodley Head (1926) and Maritime Press (1972)

Shoalwater and Fairway, Bodley Head (1924) and Maritime Press (1972)

White, Archie — **The Tideways and Byways of Essex and Suffolk,** Edward Arnold (1948)

Wyllie, WL and Mrs — **London to the Nore,** A & C Black (1905)

INDEX